GREAT EXPEDITIONS

Published by Collins

An imprint of HarperCollins Publishers
Westerhill Road
Bishopbriggs
Glasgow G64 2QT

First published 2016
Paperback edition 2019

A catalogue record for this book is available from the British Library

ISBN 978-0-00-834782-6

10 9 8 7 6 5 4 3 2 1

Printed and bound by CPI Group (UK) Ltd, Croydon CR0 4YY

www.harpercollins.co.uk

MIX
Paper from
responsible sources

FSC
www.fsc.org   **FSC™ C007454**

This book is produced from independently certified
FSC™ paper to ensure responsible forest management.

For more information visit: www.harpercollins.co.uk/green

CREATED BY

Mark Steward   Alan Greenwood
Christopher Riches   Richard Happer

CONTENTS

FOREWORD

With the advance of modern technology our world seems smaller. We have apps that can translate a phrase at the touch of a button, travel is more affordable and new places can be discovered by swiping a screen. Yet there is still so much to be discovered. What has not changed since early explorers set out with little more than a map is the spirit required to undertake an expedition; the love of a challenge and the mental and physical toughness a person needs to call on when things may not be going their way. Exploration is about more than putting a flag in a map. It's about the experiences that change us and the people we meet along the way.

I have found over the years that the best way to travel and explore is on foot. There's nothing like treading the paths and tracks to get a real impression of a country, its landscape and its culture. The many explorers who went before me didn't have helicopters on hand or gadgetry to make their lives easier. Whether they were trekking the banks of the Nile or scaling peaks in the Himalayas; breaking new trails in the jungles of Asia or crossing unknown deserts, it was these early pioneers who inspired me.

David Livingstone's journey to find the source of the Nile was a large part of the motivation behind my own nine-month expedition walking the length of the world's longest river. It was reading about these adventures as a young man that set me on my path, starting in the army and eventually undertaking world-first expeditions of my own. Like Livingstone, I was also documenting my journey, keeping scribbles in a notebook rather similar to the one he used. But then again, I was able to use technology such as cameras he could only have dreamt of. We were both creating our own records of a shared experience more than 150 years apart.

As I have learned, modern day expeditions are not immune to danger. Whilst the promise of a helicopter can give the impression of a safety net, there is still a huge risk for anyone undertaking a remote climb or trek. Nature, whether it's driving winds, freezing temperatures or intense heat, poses just as much risk today as it did a hundred years ago. The results can be tragic, as anyone who followed *Walking the Nile* will know. For early explorers such as Amundsen,

Shackleton and Nansen, the Poles proved the ultimate challenge. Things inevitably go wrong but it's at these times that a person can show what they're made of. This book is a celebration of the few brave people who defied terrible odds and conditions to prove something vital to both the world and themselves. For every risk, the rewards are huge.

The stories featured in this book form an extensive list of human achievement that has had a huge impact on the world today. No space mission has quite captured the imagination of the world like the Apollo 11 moon-landing or had such a profound impact on science as Charles Darwin's voyages. Sometimes these stories, such as the Challenger journey to the deepest point on Earth, are so extraordinary they can seem like science fiction. Personally, the expeditions that I love are the long-distance overland journeys, such as those by the intrepid Frenchwoman Alexandra David-Néel who in 1924 crossed the Himalayas in midwinter and entered a forbidden Tibet in native disguise. Perhaps less well known, but an achievement that deserves to be recognised.

There is still much to explore and plenty of experiences to be had, and I am sure that within our lifetime we will see more Great Expeditions that are just as impressive as the ones detailed in this book. I for one hope to keep following in the footsteps of the explorers who have gone before.

LEVISON WOOD

THE GIANT LEAP
APOLLO 11 AND THE MOON LANDINGS

"The 'a' was intended. I thought I said it. I can't hear it when I listen on the radio reception here on Earth, so I'll be happy if you just put it in parenthesis."

Neil Armstrong commenting on his own quote and the most famous space line ever spoken:
'That's one small step for [a] man, one giant leap for mankind'.

The first step on the moon by a man was also the last of an eight-year odyssey by the largest expedition team in human history. On 20 July 1969, Neil Armstrong had travelled 384,000 km (240,000 miles) in four days – the equivalent of nine circumnavigations of the Earth – through the deadly vacuum of space. But the Apollo program that put him there had employed the skills of 400,000 people for nearly a decade. More than 20,000 companies and universities had supplied equipment and brainpower. The project cost $24 billion and was easily the largest and most technologically creative endeavour ever made in peacetime. It was nothing less than the longest, most dangerous and most audaciously conceived expedition the world had ever seen. The catalyst was the singular vision of one man.

On 12 April 1961, the Russian cosmonaut Yuri Gagarin became the first man in space. Just eight days later, US President John F. Kennedy (who had only been in office for three months) wrote this in a memo to his Space Council:

> *Do we have a chance of beating the Soviets by putting a laboratory in space, or by a trip around the moon, or by a rocket to go to the moon and back with a man. Is there any other space program which promises dramatic results in which we could win?... Are we working 24 hours a day on existing programs? If not, why not?*

His choice of words – 'beating' and 'win' – made it very clear that he was intent on winning the Space Race.

At this point, the United States was lagging behind the Soviet Union. One American astronaut, Alan Shepard, had flown into space, but he had not achieved orbit. The first Russian Sputnik craft had orbited the Earth in 1957.

NASA was given the funds to launch a completely new space program – Apollo – dedicated to achieving Kennedy's stated goal 'before this decade is out, of landing a man on the Moon and returning him safely to the Earth'. A new Manned Spacecraft

Center (nicknamed 'Space City') for human spaceflight training, research, and flight control was built in Houston, Texas. A vast launch complex (now known as The Kennedy Space Center) was built near Cape Canaveral in Florida.

Hundreds of the planet's greatest scientific brains would spend the coming years solving seemingly impossible problems at breakneck speed, to create a rocket and spacecraft that could get a crew into orbit, then onwards to the Moon, down to its surface, and then repeat all these steps in reverse.

The program suffered a serious early setback. The Command Module of Apollo 1 caught fire on 27 January 1967, during a pre-launch test, killing astronauts Virgil Grissom, Edward White, and Roger Chaffee. But NASA learned from the disaster and went back to the drawing board to make their craft safer. In December 1968, the second manned Apollo mission, Apollo 8, was successfully launched. It became the first manned spacecraft to leave Earth orbit, reach the Moon, orbit it and return safely to Earth. After two more successful launches, Apollo 11 was cleared for launch on 16 July 1969.

On 16 July, 1969, Neil Armstrong, Edwin 'Buzz' Aldrin and Michael Collins strapped themselves into *Columbia*, the command module of Apollo 11. This tiny conical cabin would carry the three astronauts from launch to lunar orbit and back to an ocean splashdown eight days later. Connected to the bottom of the command module was the cylindrical service module, which would provide propulsion, electrical power and storage during the mission. Below that was *Eagle*, the lunar module that would make the actual descent to the Moon's surface.

Their tiny habitat was bolted on to the top of a colossal Saturn V rocket. At 111 m (363 ft) high, Saturn V stood 18 m (58 ft) taller than the Statue of Liberty. It is still the tallest, heaviest, and most powerful rocket ever built.

❝ But why, some say, the Moon? Why choose this as our goal? And they may well ask, why climb the highest mountain? Why, 35 years ago, fly the Atlantic?

....

We choose to go to the Moon. We choose to go to the Moon in this decade and do the other things, not because they are easy, but because they are hard; because that goal will serve to organize and measure the best of our energies and skills; because that challenge is one that we are willing to accept, one we are unwilling to postpone, and one we intend to win... ❞

President John F. Kennedy

The gargantuan engines roared for eleven minutes, burning 2 million kg (5 million lb) of liquid oxygen and kerosene at over 13 metric tonnes per second to hoist the three astronauts into the heavens.

Two and a half hours after topping 40,000 km/h (25,000 mph) and reaching orbit, another rocket burn set them on course for the Moon. The astronauts spent the next three days coasting through the void. On the fourth day they passed out of sight behind the Moon and fired rockets to ease them into orbit 100 km (62 miles) above the dusty surface.

Armstrong and Aldrin climbed into the *Eagle* and said farewell to Collins. He would remain alone in *Columbia* in orbit while his colleagues walked on the surface. The landing craft separated and for twelve minutes a computer guided Armstrong and Aldrin down. Fear flashed through mission control five minutes into the descent when Aldrin instructed the computer to calculate their altitude and it blinked back an error message. Should they abort? Engineers coolly worked out that it was safe to override the message and go on.

But just a few minutes later there was further cause for alarm. Armstrong saw that the crater the computer was piloting the *Eagle* into was strewn with large boulders. He took manual control and guided the craft further downrange, burning extra fuel. When the *Eagle* finally touched down in the Sea of Tranquility, it had a mere 30 seconds of fuel left.

Touchdown was the softest landing that the pilots had ever experienced. Lunar gravity is one-sixth of that on Earth, and the astronauts felt no bump on landing — they only knew they were definitely down when a contact light came on.
'Houston, Tranquility Base here. The Eagle has landed!' said Armstrong, unquenchable joy surging in his normally cool voice. But rather than step outside straight away, Armstrong and Aldrin spent the next four hours resting in the cockpit. They yearned intensely to get outside but were also full of trepidation. Would their spacesuits protect them from the vacuum? Would they be able to take off again?

The time had come. Neil Armstrong stepped out of the *Eagle*, descended the ladder and walked on the moon, 109 hours and 42 minutes after he had left planet Earth. An estimated 530 million people watched Armstrong's televised image and heard his voice describe the event as he took '...one small step for [a] man, one giant leap for mankind'. After 20 minutes, Aldrin followed him and became the second human being to make footsteps in moondust. The astronauts put the TV camera on a tripod about 9 m (30 ft) from the lander to transmit their actions. Half an hour into their moonwalk, they spoke to President Nixon by telephone. The two astronauts spent the next two and a half hours collecting rock samples, taking photographs and setting up experiments. As well as planting a US flag, they also left a Soviet medal in honour of Yuri Gagarin, who had been killed in a plane crash the year before. Armstrong and Aldrin were on the Moon's surface for 21 hours and 36 minutes. This included seven hours of sleep. The ascent stage engine fired successfully and they lifted off, leaving the descent module behind. Just under four hours later, *Eagle* docked with *Columbia* in lunar orbit, and the three crew were reunited. *Columbia* headed home. Three days later, Armstrong, Aldrin and Collins fell back to Earth as heroes.

This astonishing achievement inspired a whole generation with the technical and creative possibilities of space. The Apollo program brought 382 kg (842 lb) of lunar rocks and soil back to Earth, transforming our understanding of the Moon's geology and history. The program funded the construction of the Johnson Space Center and Kennedy Space Center. Huge advances in avionics, telecommunications, and computers were made as part of the overall Apollo program.

Politically, the Space Race was won – decisively – by America. JFK had been assassinated six years before his dream became reality but the Soviets had been beaten, as he had wanted.

Apollo 11 was the first in a flurry of launches. Apollo 12 became the second successful mission to the Moon just four months later, in November 1969. Apollo 13 famously had a malfunction on the journey out and had to return home without touching down on the Moon. Apollos 14 to 16 all landed safely on the lunar surface. In December 1972, Apollo 17 was the sixth – and final – manned spacecraft to make a Moon landing. In total, twelve Apollo astronauts walked on the Moon. No humans have gone further than Earth orbit in the decades since.

One of the most unexpected glories of the expedition was actually an image of home: the extraordinarily delicate beauty of the blue Earth as seen from our natural satellite. It was a sight that few had imagined but which utterly transfixed all astronauts who witnessed it.

RACE TO THE SOUTH POLE

THE EXPEDITIONS OF ROALD AMUNDSEN AND ROBERT FALCON SCOTT

"I may say that this is the greatest factor – the way in which the expedition is equipped – the way in which every difficulty is foreseen, and precautions taken for meeting or avoiding it. Victory awaits him who has everything in order – luck, people call it. Defeat is certain for him who has neglected to take the necessary precautions in time; this is called bad luck."

From The South Pole, *by Roald Amundsen*

The search party had found the tent. Steeling themselves, the men looked inside. As they expected, the emaciated bodies of Captain Robert Scott and two companions lay frozen solid, shrouded in drifting snow. Scott's sleeping bag was thrown open and his coat was unfastened; he had hastened the end. Somewhere outside, forever lost in the merciless Antarctic, were two other men who had also perished. Such was the price they paid for coming second in the race to the South Pole.

When Robert Falcon Scott left Britain on his 1911 attempt to be first to reach the South Pole, he was already a national hero. He had commanded the Discovery Expedition of 1901–04, which included another great explorer, Ernest Shackleton. Scott and Shackleton had walked further south than anyone else in history: they got to within 850 km (530 miles) of the pole.

While Scott was making his record-breaking South Pole approach, Roald Amundsen was making a pioneering polar trip at the opposite end of the world. Born in 1872 into a Norwegian family of maritime merchants, Amundsen had been forced by his mother to study medicine. When she died he packed up his books and, aged 21, left university for a life of adventure. Amundsen led the 1903–06 expedition that was the first to traverse the Northwest Passage. On this trip he also learned some Inuit skills that would stand him in good stead; how to use sled dogs to transport stores and how much better animal skins were at insulating in the cold and wet than the heavy, woollen parkas typically used by European explorers.

In 1909, Scott heard that his former fellow explorer Shackleton had got to within 180 km (112 miles) of the Pole on his Nimrod Expedition before being forced to turn back. Scott was aware that other polar ventures were being planned and, gripped by 'Pole-mania', he duly announced that he would lead another Antarctic expedition. Hopes were now high that a Briton would be the first to stand on the bottom of the world, and Scott did not want to

A historical Bird's-eye view map of Amundsen's South Pole Expedition. Scott's route can also be seen (with added annotations) as it followed the same route as Shackleton's 1907–09 expedition.

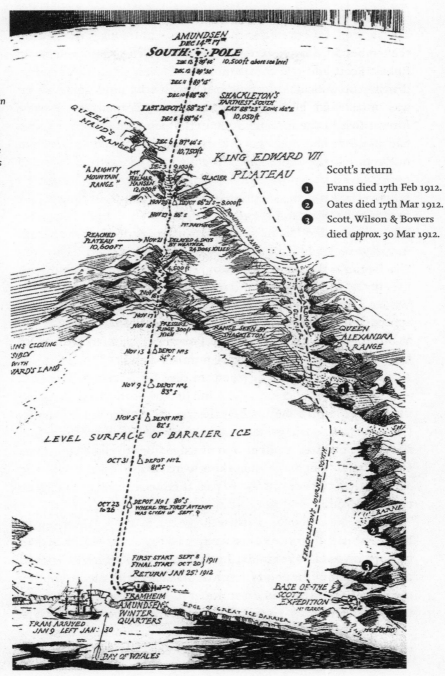

AMUNDSEN
DEC 14TH 17TH
SOUTH POLE
10,500ft above sea level
DEC 13 ½ 89°45'
DEC 12 ½ 89°30'
DEC 11 89°15'
DEC 10 88°56'
LAST DEPOT 88°25' S
DEC 8 ½ 88°16'
DEC 6 ½ 87°40'S
10,750ft
DEC 3 ½ 9,100ft

SHACKLETON'S
FARTHEST SOUTH
LAT 88°23' LONG 162°E
10,050ft

QUEEN MAUD'S RANGE

"A MIGHTY MOUNTAIN RANGE"
MT HELMAR HANSEN 12,000ft

KING EDWARD VII PLATEAU

GLACIER

NOV 29 ∆ DEPOT 85°2'S = 8,000ft

NOV 17 ½ 86°S

MT ANTHONY

DOMINION RANGE

REACHED PLATEAU 10,600ft → NOV 21 ½ DELAYED 4 DAYS BY WEATHER.
24 DOGS KILLED

6,500 ft

NOV 18

NOV 17

NOV 16 ½ PRESSURE RIDGE 300ft HIGH

RANGE SEEN BY SHACKLETON

QUEEN ALEXANDRA RANGE

INS CLOSING
SIBLY
WITH
VARD'S LAND

NOV 13 ∆ DEPOT N°5
84°

NOV 9 ∆ DEPOT N°4
83°S

NOV 5 ∆ DEPOT N°3
82°S

LEVEL SURFACE OF BARRIER ICE

OCT 31 ∆ DEPOT N°2
81°S

OCT 23 to 26 ∆ DEPOT N°1 80°S
WHERE THE FIRST ATTEMPT WAS GIVEN UP SEPT 9

FIRST START SEPT 8 } 1911
FINAL START OCT 20 }
RETURN JAN 25 1912

FRAM ARRIVED JAN 9 LEFT JAN 30

FRAMHEIM AMUNDSEN'S WINTER QUARTERS

EDGE OF GREAT ICE BARRIER

BAY OF WHALES

BASE OF THE SCOTT EXPEDITION
MT TERROR

MT EREBUS

SHACKLETON'S JOURNEY SOUTH

BARNE

Scott's return

1 Evans died 17th Feb 1912.

2 Oates died 17th Mar 1912.

3 Scott, Wilson & Bowers died *approx.* 30 Mar 1912.

disappoint. His expedition sailed from Cardiff in June 1910 on the former whaling ship, *Terra Nova* on a seven-month journey to Antarctica.

While Scott was looking south, Amundsen had his sights set on the North Pole. However, in 1909, he heard that two separate American expeditions, led by Robert Peary and Frederick Cook, had both attained this goal, so he decided instead to head for Antarctica. (Peary and Cook are both now generally considered not to have attained the North Pole.) Amundsen and his crew left Oslo on the *Fram* (the ship previously used by Fridtjof Nansen, see page 188), heading south on 3 June 1910.

When Scott got to Melbourne, Australia, he found a telegram from Amundsen, announcing that he was 'proceeding south'. The *Terra Nova* stopped for supplies in New Zealand and then turned south in late November. Scott now had a run of what he termed 'sheer bad luck'. A heavy storm killed two ponies and a dog, and also caused 10,200 kg (10 tons) of coal and 300 l (65 gallons) of petrol to be lost overboard. The *Terra Nova* then got stuck in the pack ice for twenty days before managing to break clear.

The *Fram's* run south in the meantime, had been relatively smooth.

The Pole attempts had to be made in the Antarctic summer as conditions were too severe during the rest of the year. This period of relatively better weather and constant light only lasted from November to March. The plan was to arrive during one summer, set up camp and see out the winter, then push for the Pole when the next summer's weather window opened.

The *Terra Nova* finally reached Ross Island on 4 January 1911. Scott's team set up their base camp at a cape near where he had camped on his Discovery Expedition nine years before. They had at least nine months before they would make their Pole attempt. In the meantime, Scott was determined to keep busy, and to pursue their scientific goals. He sent a party east to explore King Edward VII Land and Victoria Land. This team was returning westward when it was astonished to see Amundsen's expedition camped in the Bay of Whales, an inlet on the eastern edge of the Ross Ice Shelf. The Norwegians had arrived on 14 January. Amundsen was friendly to the Englishmen, offering them a welcome to camp nearby and care for their dogs. These offers were declined and the party returned to base camp. Scott wrote about the meeting in his journal: 'One thing only fixes itself in my mind. The proper, as well as the wiser, course is for us to proceed exactly as though this had not happened. To go forward and do our best for the honour of our country without fear or panic.'

There were three main stages to be tackled on the 1,450 km (900 mile) trek to the Pole: crossing the Ross Ice Shelf (an area the size of France); ascending a glacier to reach the polar plateau; and then crossing that plateau to the Pole itself. Once at the pole the journey then had to be done in reverse.

The two expeditions planned different strategies for their attempts. Amundsen would use his beloved dogs to pull his team and supplies all the way to the Pole. Scott would use a combination of ponies (which Shackleton had used on his record push), dogs and motor sleds to haul the big loads across the ice shelf. This would allow the men to save their strength for the ascent onto the plateau and the push for the Pole, which they would do pulling their own sleds.

They could not haul all the supplies they would need, so both parties had to lay out caches of food on their routes. This had to be done before winter arrived to allow the expeditions to start in earnest in the following spring.

On 27 January, Scott hurriedly began laying supplies but their ponies were not up to the task and several died. The men were also slowed by a vicious blizzard. These delays made Scott decide to lay their main supply point, One Ton Depot, 56 km (35 miles) north of its planned location. This decision would cost the returning party dearly.

The Norwegian party used skis and dog sleds to lay supply caches at 80°, 81° and 82° south on a route aimed directly at the Pole, without major incident.

Winter descended and both expeditions settled down in their base camps to ride it out.

On 8 September 1911, Amundsen's team set out for the Pole but within days they were beaten back by savage weather. They immediately began preparing for another attempt and, on 19 October, a group using four sledges and fifty-two dogs set off from base camps on a direct line south. They spent nearly four weeks crossing the ice shelf before reaching the base of the Antarctic plateau. Here they discovered a new glacier, which was shorter and steeper than the colossal Beardmore Glacier that Scott was ascending. They shot several of their dogs for food. After a four-day climb up this icy staircase, they reached the plateau on 21 November.

Scott's motor sleds, laden with supplies, departed on 24 October, but only ran for 80 km (50 miles) before breaking down. The drivers had to haul the gear themselves in an exhausting 240 km (150 mile) trek to the rendezvous. Scott's main party left base camp on 1 November 1911 — Amundsen had already been going for twelve days. Scott's teams reached the start of the Beardmore Glacier on 4 December. By now they were more than two weeks behind Amundsen.

They were tent-bound by a blizzard for five days and then took nine days to ascend the gargantuan 200 km (125 miles) long Beardmore Glacier. Scott's team stepped onto the lifeless Antarctic plateau on 20 December. They caught up a little time here and the final team of five men — Scott, Wilson, Oates, Bowers and Evans – set out on foot for the Pole.

Scott's team slogged on across the vast white emptiness, passing Christmas on the ice. On 30 December, their hearts lifted a little as they had caught up with Shackleton's 1908–09 timetable. However, in reality they were all suffering from exhaustion, frostbite and hunger. They passed Shackleton's record mark of (88° 23' S) on 9 January. Despite their pain, they could feel that their prize was within reach. They trudged on.

On 17 January 1912, Scott looked up from the endless snow at his feet to see a black flag fluttering above a small tent. Amundsen had led his five men, sixteen-dog team on a straight run to the Pole. They encountered little difficulty on the plateau and on 14 December 1911 they made the first human footprints at the bottom of the world. They had erected a tent and left a letter detailing their achievement.

Scott had been beaten to this long-sought goal by thirty-four days. 'All the daydreams must go,' wrote the anguished explorer in his diary. 'Great God! This is an awful place.' There was nothing for the distraught men to do but start the 1,300-km (800-mile) return journey. This was a savage undertaking and the exhausted team were pained with frostbite and snow blindness. The first man to die was Edgar Evans. He succumbed on 17 February after falling down a glacier.

The remaining four trekked on but Lawrence Oates' toes had become severely frostbitten and he knew that he was holding back his colleagues. On 16 March, Scott wrote in his diary that Oates stood up, said 'I am just going outside and may be some time,' then walked out of the tent and was never seen again.

> ❢ We knew that Oates was walking to his death...
> it was the act of a brave man and an English gentleman. ❢

The three surviving men camped for the last time on 19 March. A ferocious blizzard kept them in their tent in temperatures of -44°C (-47°F) and sealed their fate. They died of starvation and exposure 10 days later. They were 18 km (11 miles) short of One Ton Depot. Had it been in its planned location, they would have made it. Scott was the last to die.

*‘ Every day we have been ready to start for our depot 11 miles away,
but outside the door of the tent it remains a scene of whirling drift.
I do not think we can hope for any better things now. We shall stick
it out to the end, but we are getting weaker, of course, and the end
cannot be far. It seems a pity, but I do not think I can write more. R.
Scott. Last entry. For God's sake look after our people. ’*

Both quotes from Captain Scott's diary

Amundsen's team arrived back in base camp six weeks after
reaching the Pole, on 25 January 1912. They were in Australia at
the start of March. News of their success was telegraphed to the
world.
Scott was hailed as a tragic hero, brave in the face of certain death.
His legend was held up to inspire generations of Britons. When
Amundsen found out about Scott's death, he said, 'I would gladly
forgo any honour or money if thereby I could have saved Scott his
terrible death.'

The search party which found Scott and his colleagues collapsed
the tent over the bodies then built a cairn of snow above, placing
a cross made from their skis on top. Today, after a century of
snowstorms, the cairn, tent and cross now lie under 23 m (75 ft)
of ice. They have become part of the ice shelf and have already
moved 48 km (30 miles) from where they died. In 300 years or so
the explorers will once again reach the ocean, before taking to the
water and drifting away inside an iceberg.

DARWIN AND THE *BEAGLE*

CHARLES DARWIN'S VOYAGE ON HMS BEAGLE

"When on board HMS Beagle, as naturalist, I was
much struck with certain facts in the distribution of
the inhabitants of South America, and in the geological
relations of the present to the past inhabitants of that
continent. These facts seemed to me to throw some
light on the origin of species..."

Introduction to Darwin's
On the Origin of Species by Means of Natural Selection

Charles Darwin served as the naturalist of the five-year voyage of the surveying ship HMS *Beagle*, during which it circumnavigated the world. His observations of the natural world, particularly in the southern hemisphere, provided the evidence which led him to develop the theory of evolution.

Darwin was born in Shrewsbury in 1809, the son of a prominent local physician and the grandson of two leading lights of the Industrial Revolution, Josiah Wedgwood and Erasmus Darwin. He was educated at Shrewsbury School, and in 1825 he went with his brother to study medicine at Edinburgh University. His dislike of anatomy and surgery quickly drove him away from a career in medicine and he left Edinburgh without a degree in 1827. The following year, he started at Christ's College Cambridge, with the aim of becoming an Anglican clergyman. Most importantly, he became a friend of John Henslow, a botany professor who enthused Darwin with a love of and fascination in nature.

Darwin graduated in 1831 and was then recommended by Henslow as a gentleman collector for what was planned as a two-year trip to South America, commenting that his recommendation was 'not on the supposition of *yr.* being a finished Naturalist, but as amply qualified for collecting, observing, & noting any thing worthy to be noted in Natural History'. After some persuasion, Darwin's father agreed to the trip (important because he had to fund all his son's costs, apart from food, which was provided by the Admiralty).

The trip was to be on HMS *Beagle*, a small survey ship that was 27 m (90 ft) long and weighed in at around 245 tonnes (241 tons). The boat was captained by Robert Fitzroy, a keen amateur naturalist and scientist, and, along with surveying the coast of South America, one of its missions was to trial the new Beaufort wind scale. Darwin shared a cabin with the ship's mate and a midshipman, and it was also his study. And so it was on 27 December 1831, HMS *Beagle* sailed out of Plymouth — a day late, for the crew had celebrated Christmas Day too enthusiastically

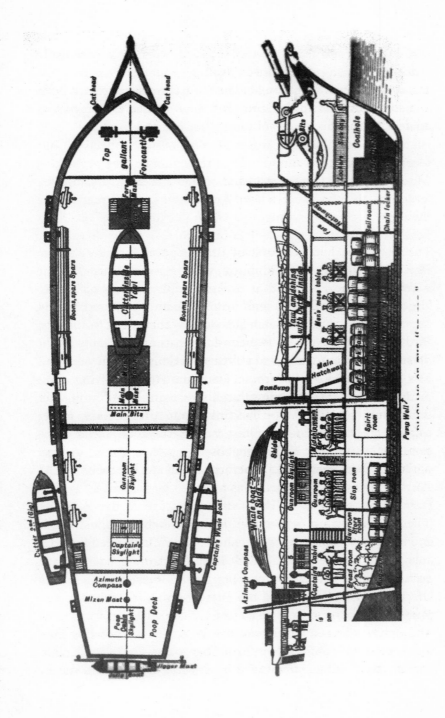

and were unfit to leave the day before. Darwin was soon badly stricken by seasickness, a bad beginning to a long voyage.

It was too rough to land on Madeira and, because there had been a cholera outbreak in England, they were refused permission to land in the Azores. On 16 January, they reached the Cape Verde islands, where Darwin's work of observation, collecting and recording began. His questioning mind could be seen at work — why for example, was there a band of shells 14 m (45 ft) above sea level in a cliff when such a band would have been formed under the sea?

The *Beagle* reached the coast of Brazil by the end of February 1832, and while the ship did much surveying work, Darwin spent much of the next six months on land, exploring and gathering large collections of specimens from the country around Rio de Janeiro, Buenos Aires and Bahia Blanca. By the end of November, Darwin had shipped back two consignments of specimens, from preserved beetles to fossils of animals previously unknown.

The *Beagle* then sailed south, to Tierra del Fuego, arriving there on 17 December: '...we were saluted in a manner becoming the inhabitants of this savage land. A group of Fuegians partly concealed by the entangled forest, were perched on a wild point overhanging the sea; and as we passed by, they sprang up and waving their tattered cloaks sent forth a loud and sonorous shout.'

Darwin was shocked by the primitive nature of the Fuegians (meeting one group he commented 'these were the most abject and miserable creatures I anywhere beheld'). Puzzled by why anyone would live such a tough life in so unforgiving a place he concluded 'Nature by making habit omnipotent, and its effects hereditary, has fitted the Fuegian to the climate and the productions of his miserable country.'

The *Beagle* ventured to Cape Horn: 'we saw on our weather-bow this notorious promontory in its proper form — veiled in a mist, and its dim outline surrounded by a storm of wind and water'.

The weather around Cape Horn was severe and the ship was nearly overwhelmed:

❨ At noon a great sea broke over us . . . The poor Beagle trembled at the shock, and for a few minutes would not obey her helm; but soon, like a good ship that she was, she righted and came up to the wind again. Had another sea followed the first, our fate would have been decided soon, and for ever. ❩

In April 1833, the *Beagle* left Tierra del Fuego for the Falkland Islands, very recently after Britain had reasserted sovereignty, replacing the Argentinians, and then returned to Montevideo. While the *Beagle* continued its survey work, Darwin explored inland around Buenos Aires and Montevideo, rejoining the *Beagle* on 28 November. They returned to Tierra del Fuego and then sailed along the Strait of Magellan: 'The inanimate works of nature – rock, ice, snow, wind, and water – all warring with each other, yet combined against man – here reigned in absolute sovereignty.' Finally, on 10 June 1834 they reached the Pacific, and on 23 July they arrived at the warmth of Valparaiso. From here Darwin went on a six-week expedition into the Andes.

The surveying of southern Chile continued into 1835. Here he saw the effects of a devastating earthquake on the city of Concepción; he noticed that rocks has been forced upwards by the earthquake, evidence of the force of rock movement that was slowly pushing up the Andes. In the months that followed he undertook various inland expeditions until 7 September, when the *Beagle* sailed from Peru for the Galapagos Islands.

The *Beagle* stayed for five weeks and Darwin was an exhaustive collector: 'The natural history of this archipelago is very remarkable: it seems to be a little world within itself; the greater number of its inhabitants, both vegetable and animal, being found nowhere else,' and the evidence amassed provided the spur for Darwin to develop his theory of evolution.

The *Beagle* then set sail across the Pacific, reaching Tahiti in November, northern New Zealand in December, and Sydney on 12 January 1836. The *Beagle* next sailed to Tasmania, then onto the Keeling Islands (now Cocos Islands) in the middle of the Indian Ocean. By June they had reached Cape Town in South Africa, where they stayed for a month, and then it was on to St Helena and Ascension Island.

Finally, after a brief return to Brazil, the *Beagle* docked at Falmouth on 2 October 1836. Fitzroy had completed much valuable surveying work and Darwin had gained the knowledge and enthusiasm to devote his life to natural history, and his greatest achievement, the publication in 1859 of *On the Origin of Species*, which outlined his landmark theory of evolution.

STAR MAN

Yuri Gagarin: The man who fell to Earth

*"Rays were blazing through the atmosphere of the
Earth, the horizon became bright orange, gradually
passing into all the colours of the rainbow: from light
blue to dark blue, to violet and then to black. What
an indescribable gamut of colours!"*

Yuri Gagarin

12 April 1961. A farmer and her daughter are tending to a calf on the vast expanse of the Russian steppe when an otherworldly figure approaches them. The visitor is dressed in a bright orange boiler suit. His face is obscured by a white helmet and he is dragging several metres of rope and cloth in his wake.

The figure speaks: 'Don't be afraid,' he tells them. 'I am a Soviet like you, who has descended from space. I must find a telephone to call Moscow!'

The stranger is the first person to leave our planet. Yuri Gagarin, the 27-year-old son of a carpenter and a milkmaid, had spent the previous 89 minutes circling the Earth in *Vostok 1*, reaching speeds of more than 27,400 km/h (17,000 mph) and a highest point of orbit of 328 km (204 miles). No human had ever travelled further from Earth, or faster.

Just a few minutes before his encounter with the farm workers, Gagarin had been withstanding extreme heat and severe gravitational force as the *Vostok 1* capsule, barely bigger than a saloon car, battered its way through Earth's atmosphere. Now he was calm as he waited with an excited crowd of surprised farm workers for the helicopter which would take him back to the control team. News of the mission was about to become broadcast on Soviet state radio and Gagarin would become the most famous man in the world.

Yuri Gagarin's world-changing mission was first prize in a race between two global super powers; the Union of Socialist Soviet Republics and the United States of America. The 'space race' was a battle between the America's Project Mercury and Russia's Vostok programme for the conquest of space. For the two cold war foes the prestige of being the first nation to send a human being into space compelled them to sink vast resources into their space programmes and by the spring of 1961 both sides were on the brink of manned spaceflight.

The course of history could have been very different. The Americans had planned to launch Freedom 7, a sub-orbital flight piloted by Alan Shepard, on 24 March 1961 but opted to undertake one last, unmanned, test flight instead. By the time Shepard made it to space on 5 May 1961, his place in history had been taken.

In truth, Gagarin's orbit of the Earth was worthy of humankind's first foray into space. Whereas Shepard was thrust briefly into sub-orbit for just a few minutes; Gagarin's journey took him on a lap of the whole planet, encompassing both sunset and sunrise on his 89-minute orbit.

Vostok 1 was the embodiment of mechanical force. Its engines generated 4,800 kN (900,000 lbf) of thrust and Gagarin would be subjected the equivalent of six times the force of gravity on Earth at key points on the mission. This ferocious burst of energy would be needed to propel *Vostok 1* through Earth's atmospheric boundaries and out into the nothingness of space. Once into Earth orbit, *Vostok 1* would continue on a journey eastwards above the Russian steppe and Siberian wilderness before plotting a course over the Pacific Ocean towards the southernmost tip of South America. At this point the craft would head north over the Atlantic and the rainforests and deserts of Africa before descending back to Earth in the Russian motherland.

On the morning of the *Vostok 1* mission, Gagarin was calm as he waited to board the craft at the Baikonur Cosmodrome in the Samara region. He was accompanied by Gherman Titov, the standby pilot. The two would-be cosmonauts had been working together and vying with each other for the berth in *Vostok 1* for more than a year. They had been informed of Gagarin's selection at a meeting on 8 April, just four days before the mission. The two men then took part in a staged re-enactment of the meeting for the benefit of a film crew, with Gagarin delivering a somewhat stilted acceptance speech while Titov watched on.

One factor in Gagarin's selection was his diminutive stature. At just 1.57 m (5 ft 2 in) tall, he required less room and was somewhat lighter than Titov, a point worth consideration on a mission where every inch and ounce was scrupulously measured.

The television cameras which had documented Gagarin's selection were now waiting for him inside *Vostok 1's* cramped interior. They recorded the pilot looking composed as he waited for the ground team to complete their launch protocols.

At 9.07 am local time it was time to go. In a cacophony of flames and fumes the spacecraft powered skywards, urged on by Gagarin's shout of 'Poyekhali!' ('Let's go'). In just 10 minutes the craft had spent all the power from its rockets, which were jettisoned, and the tiny forward capsule emerged into space and set off on a circumnavigation of the globe.

Gagarin gave a regular commentary on his progress, his words are noticeable mainly for their matter-of-factness. In 89 minutes – less time than it takes to play a football match – his orbit was complete and what were potentially the most dangerous moments of Gagarin's mission commenced. As the *Vostok* capsule re-entered Earth's atmosphere, the world's first spaceman was buffeted and boiled. The buffeting was caused by drag, as the fast-falling spacecraft shuddered against the outer layers of Earth's atmosphere. The boiling was caused by aerodynamic heat as friction from re-entry raised temperatures within the craft considerably. As he plummeted towards terra firma, Gagarin experienced an estimated 8G of force on his body amidst temperatures in excess of 38°C (100°F).

At around 7 km (23,000 ft) above ground, *Vostok's* hatch sprang open. Two seconds later Gagarin was ejected, falling to Earth and on to his encounter with the unsuspecting farmhands.

He was the first human ever to leave the planet and, equally importantly, the first to return. He would become a household name around the world and, in a ceremony overseen by President Nikita Khrushchev shortly after the mission, a Hero of the Soviet Union.

The journey into space was only the beginning of Yuri Gagarin's travels. The Soviet Government, keen to capitalise on the prestige of their space programme, arranged a world tour for their first cosmonaut. Gagarin lunched with Queen Elizabeth II in the United Kingdom; he spoke at a rally with Fidel Castro in Cuba; he attended functions in Finland, Iceland, Hungary and Brazil and stopped off in Canada, spending the night on a farm in Pugwash, Nova Scotia.

Further travels to France, Afghanistan, Greece, Egypt and Sri Lanka were to follow before, in 1965, Gagarin returned to his trade as a pilot. He served at the Star City cosmonaut training base and graduated with honours as a cosmonaut engineer. On 27 March 1968 he was piloting a jet on a routine training flight when it crashed near Moscow, killing Yuri Gagarin and the instructor who accompanied him.

Gagarin, who was married with two daughters, received a state funeral and his ashes were interred in the walls of the Kremlin.

His great expedition into the world beyond our world had lasted just 89 minutes but the legacy of his mission would endure forever.

❛ I saw for the first time the Earth's shape. I could easily see the shores of continents, islands, great rivers, folds of the terrain, large bodies of water. The horizon is dark blue, smoothly turning to black. . . the feelings which filled me I can express with one word—joy. ❜

Yuri Gagarin

FINDING NEW LAND
Leif Eriksson's voyage to Vinland

*"So they followed this plan, and it is said that they
loaded up the afterboat with grapes, and the ship itself
with a cargo of timber. When spring came, they
made the ship ready and sailed away. Leif gave this
country a name to suit its resources:
he called it Vinland."*

As recorded in the thirteenth-century Greenlanders' Saga

While there will always be speculation about who was the first European to land on the North American continent (was it St Brendan in the sixth century, for example?), there is clear evidence that Leif Eriksson did reach Newfoundland at the start of the eleventh century, both from accounts in two Icelandic sagas and from the discovery of a Viking settlement at L'Anse aux Meadows in northwestern Newfoundland.

The story starts with Erik the Red, one of the Vikings who had come from Norway to settle Iceland. He did not get on well with the other Vikings, and on a voyage in 982, landed on Greenland. It was summer, and he had found a land of green pastures by the coast, and so gave it the name 'Greenland', then unaware that beyond that southern coastal fringe it was covered in ice all year around. Erik saw great potential here, and his plans to colonize it came to fruition in 986, when he sailed with twenty-five ships and around 700 people from Iceland to Greenland.

One Viking arrived back on Iceland after a trading trip to discover that his father had already sailed to Greenland and he wished to follow as soon as possible, even though it was getting late in the season. So it was that Bjarni Herjolfsson set off from Iceland, but soon the wind dropped and the fog descended so that he could no longer navigate. Once the fog lifted after a few days, he sailed on and then sighted land. The sailors asked Bjarni whether it was Greenland, but he replied that it was not, for when they sailed close by they found that the land was 'not mountainous but covered with small wooded knolls'. They sailed on for another two days and saw more land, but Bjarni declined to land, much to the anger of his crew. After another three days they saw a country with high mountains and glaciers. Bjarni regarded it as pretty worthless, and set sail again, this time reaching Greenland, where he was reunited with his father. He and his crew are the first recorded Europeans to see North America (most likely Labrador and Baffin Island) but Bjarni was much criticized for not landing. Thereafter he stayed with his father and did not go sailing again.

' They saw no grass, the mountain tops were covered with glaciers..... '

The Greenlanders' Saga

Now Leif Eriksson, the son of Erik the Red, heard the tale of Bjarni and thought he would like to visit such lands. He visited Bjarni and purchased his boat and recruited a crew of thirty five. The first land they reached was most likely Baffin Island, an inhospitable place according the Saga's description: 'They saw no grass, the mountain tops were covered with glaciers, and from sea to mountain the country was like one slab of rock. It looked to be a barren, unprofitable country.' He called it Helluland (Land of Flat Stones).

They sailed on and saw more land, most likely Labrador, with gently sloping forested land along its coast. This he called Markland (Forest Land). Then they sailed on again and reached more land, first landing on an island, where the Saga recounts that 'they discovered dew on the grass. It so happened that they picked up some of the dew in their hands and tasted of it, and it seemed to them that they had never tasted anything so sweet.'

They then beached their boat and landed on the mainland. Given the time of year they decided that they would settle here for the winter and return home in the spring. They built turf huts, ate the plentiful salmon from the rivers and lakes, and had a remarkably mild winter ('there was no frost by night, and the grass hardly withered'). Leif sent out groups to explore the area round about, and on one occasion, a German member of the crew called Tyrkir, was separated and returned later than the rest of his party with the news that he had found grapes and vines. Come spring they loaded the boat with wood and grapes and sailed away from the land Leif called Vinland.

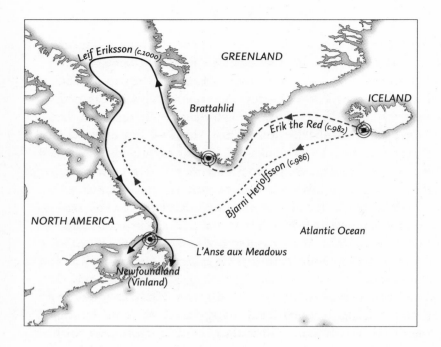

> *There was no lack of salmon in the river or lake, bigger salmon than they had ever seen.*
>
> The Greenlanders' Saga

Leif's brother, Thorvald, then made a trip back to Vinland and settled at the camp Leif had made. For the next two summers they explored the land, only towards the end meeting the native inhabitants. The first they met, they captured and killed and they were then attacked by larger numbers. All survived apart from Thorvald, who died of an arrow wound and was buried in Vinland. The remaining Vikings sailed away the following spring and did not return.

In 1960, at the tip of the Great Northern peninsula in the far northwest of Newfoundland, the remains of a Viking settlement was discovered at L'Anse aux Meadows. From their excavations, archaeologists have been able to recreate the turf huts, of typical Viking design, and to date the active life of the settlement from 990 to 1030, which links well with the account of the trips of Leif and Thorvald, as recorded in the *Greenlanders' Saga*. Combined, there is sufficient evidence to establish that the Vikings were the first Europeans to reach North America.

This discovery punctured the long-held belief that John Cabot was the first European to reach North America. Cabot (Giovanni Caboto) was born in Italy in 1450, probably in or near Genoa. Like his fellow Genoese, Christopher Columbus, Cabot considered that the best way to get to China and the Spice Islands would be by sailing west, and he became interested in a more northerly route than Columbus. Known to be living in Bristol by 1495, he received a Royal charter from Henry VII to claim any land discovered for England, and was commissioned by the merchants of Bristol. He set sail in a small boat, the *Matthew*, from Bristol, along with his crew of eighteen. On 24 June 1497, they made landfall on Newfoundland, probably at Cape Bonavista. He reported that 'the natives of it go about dressed in skins of animals; in their wars they use bows and arrows, lances and darts, and clubs of wood, and slings. This land is very sterile. There are in it many white bears, and very large stags, like horses, and many other animals. And in like manner there are immense quantities of fish — soles, salmon, very large cods, and many other kinds of fish.' He named the land 'New Founde Lands' and by tradition he also named one sheltered harbour St John's, now the provincial capital, because he first landed on Newfoundland on St John's Day.

He returned to Bristol, firmly believing that he had discovered a new route to China, and was enthusiastically welcome back to the Royal Court. He was quickly given permission to make another trip, with five boats. He left in spring 1498, but neither he nor his ships returned.

ADRIFT IN THE PACIFIC
THOR HEYERDAHL: THE *KON-TIKI* MAN

*"One learns more from listening than speaking.
And both the wind and the people who continue
to live close to nature still have much to tell us
which we cannot hear within university walls."*

Thor Heyerdahl

The story of one of modern history's greatest achievements in exploration is rooted in a very personal tragedy. Bjarne Kroepelien, a well-to-do wine merchant from Norway, had a lifelong obsession with the islands of the southern Pacific Ocean. He travelled to the area in his twenties and fell in love with the daughter of a Tahitian tribal leader. The pair were married but their union was to end bitterly when Tuimata, his wife, was one of the victims of a Spanish Flu epidemic on the island in 1918. The heartbroken merchant returned to Oslo and the family business. He never again visited Tahiti but his love for the islands, their culture and their people lived on. Over the years Kroepelien amassed the world's largest collection of Polynesian literature — more than 5,000 books in total.

His collection was to have a remarkable legacy — one that was the change the way anthropologists understood the spread of humankind. Thor Heyerdahl, a zoology student at the University of Oslo, gained access to Kroepelien's archive and pored over the texts within. These studies led Heyerdahl to a radical theory about how the Polynesian islands were settled. The mainstream academic understanding was that the islands of the south Pacific had been settled by peoples travelling east by sea from Asia. Heyerdahl believed it would also have been possible for settlers to travel west from South America.

It was Heyerdahl's opinion that the famous stone *moai* statues of Easter Island bore a closer resemblance to the ancient people of South America than to the inhabitants of east Asia. He posited that an Easter Island myth about a battle between two feuding tribes could have been based on actual conflict between settlers from the two continents. Heyerdahl went further, claiming the South American migrants could have travelled further, all the way to the Polynesian islands in the South Pacific.

There was one particularly sizeable and obvious problem with Heyerdahl's theory; the distance from South America to Easter

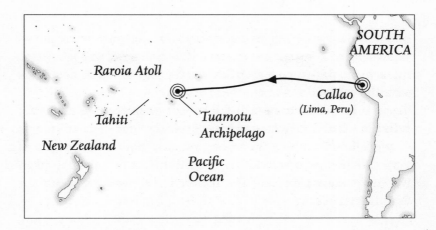

Island was vast. The remote island was more than 3,700 km (2,300 miles) from Peru, the most likely departure point in Heyerdahl's view. The Polynesian island of Tahiti was a further 4,200 km (2,600 miles) distant. Any journey from the Peruvian coast would have involved months of travel across the Pacific Ocean. Modern maps showed the South Sea Islands as tiny pin pricks in the vastness of the planet's biggest expanse of open water. Could the ancient travellers have found their way?

Heyerdahl decided there was only one way to find out. Following the end of the Second World War, he started planning his own voyage from the coast of Peru to the islands of Polynesia, using only materials and building techniques which would have been available more than one thousand years earlier. Heyerdahl assembled a crew of five fellow Scandinavians to join him on the journey, each bringing a particular set of skills to the mission. The first to sign up was Herman Watzinger, an engineer who would chart the seas the vessel sailed on and measure meteorological data. Knut Haugland and Torstein Raaby were radio experts who would make and maintain contact with a land-based support crew and any nearby vessels. Bengt Danielsson was the expedition's 'fixer', arranging equipment for the build of the raft and provisions for the team's time at sea. Erik Hesselberg was a childhood friend of Heyerdahl and, perhaps surprisingly, the only professional sailor chosen for the trip. He served as navigator and later used his artistic skills to create a children's picture book about the adventure.

The team travelled to Peru and set about their work. As a point of reference, the team turned to hand drawings made by the Spanish Conquistadores, who were among the first Europeans to land in Peru. Their illustrations of the traditional sailing craft used by the indigenous people of the region served as a guide for the Scandinavian team's raft.

The team used only materials which could be found locally. Balsa wood, exceptionally light and easy to shape, was used for the main body with strips of pine to provide support. A cabin made of weaved bamboo, 4 m (13 ft) long and 2.5 m (8 ft) wide, would be home for the six sailors during their expedition. The thick leaves of the banana tree were used to roof the cabin and more bamboo was plaited together to form a sail. The mast, nearly 9 m (30 ft) high, was made from sturdy mangrove wood. Rope made from hemp was used to lash the craft together.

The result was a wooden float which may have looked somewhat ramshackle but was, in fact, the result of great care and attention to detail. Over a period of several weeks, the crew had tested various combinations of locally-grown materials before settling on the components which would allow them to create a craft that was large enough to withstand the high ocean but also easy to manoeuvre and repair. The craft was named 'Kon-Tiki' an ancient name for the Incan sun-god, and plans were made for a launch in the autumn of 1947.

The Kon-Tiki was well stocked in preparation for a lengthy spell at sea. Canned goods and water containers were provided by the US military. Traditional water-holding containers were also taken so the crew could test their efficiency and usefulness.

'I jumped on board the raft,' wrote Heyerdahl in his account of the journey, 'which looked an utter chaos of banana clusters, fruit baskets, and sacks which had been hurled on board at the very last moment and were to be stowed and made fast.'

The mood among the crew was incredibly relaxed given the potentially perilous nature of the journey ahead. In fact, Heyerdahl alone was on board when the *Kon-Tiki* was pulled out to open sea by a tug boat on 28 April 1947, his fellow sailors being otherwise engaged in last-minute errands.

'Erik and Bengt came sauntering down to the quay with their arms full of reading matter and odds and ends,' wrote Heyerdahl. 'They met the whole stream of people on its way home and were finally stopped at a police barrier by a kindly official who told them there was nothing more to see. Bengt told the officer . . . that they had not come to see anything they themselves were going with the raft.

'It's no use,' the officer said indulgently.

'The *Kon-Tiki* sailed an hour ago.'

'Impossible,' said Erik, producing a parcel. 'Here's the lantern!'

'And there's the navigator,' said Bengt, 'and I'm the steward.'

Fortunately a boat had been sent back for the missing crewman and the six were united at the mouth of the port.

The distance to their destination was daunting, but Heyerdahl's confidence was high and grounded in two key geographic factors which he believed would be crucial to the expedition's success. The first was the Humboldt Current, a river of unusually cold water in the ocean, which originated off the Peruvian coast and flowed west for a considerable but unmeasured distance. The second was the prevailing trade winds, which blew from east to west and should aid the *Kon-Tiki* on its way.

The most remarkable thing about the *Kon-Tiki's* journey was just how uneventful it was to be. The weather was kind, they made good progress on the Humboldt Current and sea life congregated round the raft, which made for a plentiful supply of food and hydration.

On 30 July, the crew of the *Kon-Tiki* sighted land — the Puka-Puka atoll in what is now known as the Cook Islands. Five days later, they engaged with residents of Angatau Island but were unable to steer the raft in to land. On August 7, their journey ended when the *Kon-Tiki* was beached on a coral reef near the uninhabited islet near Raroia Atoll. The *Kon-Tiki* had been at sea for 100 days and travelled nearly 7,000 km (4,350 miles). Thor Heyerdahl had proved his point.

❛ Land! An island! We devoured it greedily with our eyes and woke the others, who tumbled out drowsily and stared in all directions as if they thought our bow was about to run onto a beach. Screaming seabirds formed a bridge across the sky in the direction of the distant island, which stood out sharper against the horizon as the red background widened and turned gold with the approach of the sun and the full daylight. ❜

Heyerdahl devoted the rest of his life to examining the way ancient civilizations moved around the Earth. He died, aged 87, in 2002. While anthropologists continue to research and debate how the islands of the South Pacific were populated, the extraordinary voyage of the *Kon-Tiki* is evidence that Heyerdahl's theory, however, unlikely, was at least possible.

❛ Civilization grew in the beginning from the minute that we had communication — particularly communication by sea that enabled people to get inspiration and ideas from each other and to exchange basic raw materials. ❜

DR LIVINGSTONE
I PRESUME?
David Livingstone's last journey

*"The mere animal pleasure of travelling in a wild
unexplored country is very great . . . the mind works
well, the eye is clear, the step is firm, and a day's
exertion always makes the evening's repose
thoroughly enjoyable."*

*Livingstone's Journal at the start of his last journey,
26 March 1866*

The source of the River Nile was for centuries a matter of wonder. Where did the continuous flow of water in the Nile come from? South of Khartoum, the river divided. The Blue Nile flowed from the Ethiopian Highlands, and its source was confirmed by James Bruce, a Scottish explorer, in 1770. The source of the White Nile proved more elusive.

David Livingstone set out on his last African journey with the aim of finding what he thought was its source, to the south of Lake Tanganyika. He was unconvinced by John Speke's claim that it was Lake Victoria, a claim first made in 1858 and corroborated by Speke and James Grant in 1860–63 and by Samuel Baker and Florence von Sass in 1863.

Livingstone was born in 1813 at Blantyre, Lanarkshire, in a tenement block for workers at Monteith's cotton mill, and, by the age of ten, he was working in the mill. Even so, he managed two hours of schooling as well, and so grew the steely determination to improve himself and push against the odds. In the 1830s, he decided to be a medical missionary, starting his medical training in Glasgow in 1836, paid for out of his savings. He qualified in 1840, and, supported by the London Missionary Society, was sent to Kuruman, north of the Orange River in South Africa. He went as a missionary and as a campaigner against the slave trade, still actively controlled by Arab traders in eastern Africa.

As he learned local languages and gained a greater understanding of traditional customs, his enthusiasm moved from direct missionary work to exploration. In 1849, he made an extended journey, which took a year. He became the first European to see Lake Ngami, and received a prize from the Royal Geographical Society. He became convinced that exploring and using rivers would open the region.

His first great journey took place in 1853–6. Starting at Linyanti, near the River Zambesi, he travelled northwest, reaching the Atlantic coast at Luanda in Angola in May 1854. He returned to

Linyanti and then followed the Zambesi east to the Mozambique coast at Quelimane, arriving in May 1856. On that journey, in November 1855, he reached the waterfall known locally as Mosi-oa-Tunya (*'the smoke that thunders'*) where the Zambesi, there over 1.6 km (1 mile) wide, plunges down around 108 m (355 ft), more than twice the drop of Niagara Falls. Livingstone named this mighty cataract the Victoria Falls.

He returned to Britain at the end of the year and was greatly lauded by the public. His enthusiasm for making the Zambesi the route into central Africa led to his over-ambitious next journey along it (1858–64). The party was too large, the use of a small steamship problematic, and the six-year length three times as long as originally planned, while the results were relatively small.

After just over a year away in Britain, he returned with support for a smaller expedition to find the source of the Nile. Starting in Mikindani, now in southern Tanzania, he set out as the sole European leading an assorted group of porters, along with donkeys and camels (to see if they fared better against the Tsetse fly than pack horses; they did not). His porters quickly proved unreliable, and within the four months it took to reach Lake Nyasa, he had dismissed some and others had deserted. Livingstone recorded the brutal evidence of Africans killed by slave traders on the route from the coast. By the start of 1867, his chronometers had been damaged, making it impossible for him to accurately fix his location, while another deserter left with the party's medicines.

His hopes of going straight to Lake Bangweulu were thwarted as the rainy season had turned the route into a quagmire, and so he travelled to Lake Tanganyika. He was the first European to visit Lake Mweru (1867) and Lake Bangweulu (1868). Illness struck him and he eventually made it across Lake Tanganyika in 1869 to Ujiji, where some stores sent from the coast awaited him. At the end of that year, with some assistance of Arab traders, he journeyed to the Lualaba River, a previously unknown 'mighty river about 3000 yards broad and deep . . . It flows fast towards the North', as he recorded in his Field Diary. In 1871, he reached Nyangwe, the furthest west any European had journeyed, and hoped to canoe down the river to prove that it was part of the Nile. His porters objected and ensured that no canoes were available, while he refused Arab help after they had taken part in a brutal local massacre. He would have been disappointed, for the river is the largest headwater of the Congo River.

After five months at Nyangwe, he returned to Ujiji. On the journey he was mistaken for a slave trader and was 'waylaid by spearmen, who all felt that if they killed me they would be revenging the death of relations'. When he reached Ujiji, he found that supplies sent by the British government had been stolen by local traders. His desperate situation was quickly saved by the unlikely appearance of H. M. Stanley, the Welsh-born, American-raised adventurer and journalist, who had been sent to 'find Livingstone' by the *New York Herald's* editor, Gordon Bennett. So it was, in November 1871, on the shores of Lake Tanganyika that the famous greeting 'Dr Livingstone, I presume?', was uttered. In his Journal, Livingstone noted 'I am not of a demonstrative turn; as cold, indeed, as we islanders are usually reputed to be, but this disinterested kindness . . . was simply overwhelming . . . I am a little ashamed at not being more worthy of the generosity.' With Stanley for company, they explored the northern end of Lake Tanganyika by boat, and established that there was no outlet to feed Lake Victoria or Lake Albert.

In March 1872, they parted, with Stanley heading back to the coast with his news and a mission to send supplies back to Livingstone. Once these arrived, he planned to find the source of the Lualaba (and hence, he thought, the Nile), to the west of Lake Bangweulu. His certainty wavered and in his Journal he noted: 'In reference to this Nile source I have been kept in perpetual doubt and perplexity. I know too much to be positive.'

However, wet weather, his declining health and the strange boggy nature of the land around the lake thwarted him. Now seriously ill, he had to be carried on a litter and on 1 May he died at the village of Chitambo, now in northern Zambia. Five members of his original party remained, and they arranged for his body to be embalmed and brought it back to the coast, reaching Bagamoyo in February 1874. From there the body was sent back to Britain, and a funeral service in Westminster Abbey was held on 18 April 1874.

Livingstone was an intellectually curious explorer, who recorded in great detail the life and geography of central Africa. Not always easy to deal with, his abhorrence of slavery remained central to him, as did his pre-Imperial dislike of racial superiority, 'the most pitiable puerility'.

THE LAND DOWN UNDER
Captain James Cook and HMS *Endeavour*

*"Do just once what others say you can't do,
and you will never pay attention to their
limitations again."*

Captain James Cook

The genteel city of Newport, Rhode Island, has a proud maritime tradition. Perched on the eastern seaboard of the United States, it was a key strategic naval point during the American War of Independence while today it is renowned as a global centre for yachting. Newport has hosted the prestigious America's Cup competition no fewer than twelve times.

But perhaps Newport's greatest maritime claim to fame can be found in the silt and sand of the harbour's sea bed. It's home to the wreck of an eighteenth century research vessel which opened up the world to one of history's greatest explorers.

For years it was believed that HMS *Endeavour*, the ship which had carried Lieutenant James Cook on his first circumnavigation of the globe, lay somewhere in the waters near Newport. It had been one of a number of ships scuttled by the British navy in 1778 — an attempt to block Newport harbour and deter an attack by French and American forces. It was not until 2016, when the results of a survey by the Rhode Island Marine Archaeology Project were published, that substantial evidence was provided to establish *Endeavour's* final resting place. The timbers of the old ship were said to be among a cluster of five shipwrecks huddled together on the harbour floor — a modest resting place for a ship that was used to change the world.

In 1768, *Endeavour* had sailed from Plymouth harbour under the command of Lieutenant Cook. The three-year circumnavigation of the globe which followed had a profound influence on modern history and was a critical step in Britain's path towards building the largest empire the world has ever seen.

Cook was an unlikely expedition leader. He was from a humble background and had risen through the naval ranks at a time when such progress was far from common. One of eight children, he had an impoverished childhood as a farm labourer's son but was to benefit from the generosity of his father's employer, who paid for young James to attend the local school near the family home in North Yorkshire.

After a brief and unhappy spell as a trainee shopkeeper, Cook moved to the bustling port of Whitby and signed up as an apprentice in the merchant navy. He proved an eager and talented seaman, with an aptitude for mathematical disciplines such as trigonometry and geometry and real ability in navigation and surveying. Cook appeared to be settling into a career in commercial shipping and was offered command of his own vessel but in 1755, aged 27, he volunteered to join the Royal Navy.

Cook served in the Seven Years War where his proficient work in charting the rugged Newfoundland coast was to bring him to the attention of the naval hierarchy. When the British admiralty commissioned a scientific expedition to journey to the southern hemisphere and observe the transit of Venus across the sun, James Cook was chosen to lead the venture. The mission also had a second objective, the orders for which were sealed and only to be opened once the Venus transit had been recorded.

Cook was promoted to Lieutenant, a rank which allowed him to command the expedition, and in the company of a retinue of botanists, astronomers and artists – as well as more than seventy hardened sailors and a dozen Royal Marines – they sailed west into the Atlantic on 26 August 1768. The journey to the south Pacific was not without incident. The master's mate was killed when he became ensnared in chains when the ship's anchor was lowered at port in Madeira, and two naturalists died of exposure while collecting scientific samples on the barren lands near Cape Horn. But in April 1769, the *Endeavour* reached Tahiti where she would stay for three months while her crew carried out their astronomical observations. It was only on completion of this task that Cook was able to open the sealed orders he had brought with him from Britain.

The *Endeavour* was to sail westwards across the Pacific in search of the great, undiscovered southern territory known as *Terra Australis*. The concept of a sizeable land mass on the opposite side of the world from Europe had been a source of keen speculation for some time. Exploratory missions by representatives of the Dutch East India company had charted a coastline which was believed to represent the north, west and southern coast of *Terra Australis* but the east remained uncharted and no European had set foot on the land. Cook and his crew would become the first to do so.

Before then, Cook's party would become the first Europeans to land on New Zealand. The Dutch sailor Abel Tasman had charted the western coast of New Zealand more than 100 years before but had not reached the shore. On 7 October 1769, Cook landed at Poverty Bay and over the next six months he circled New Zealand in its entirety, concluding that the land consisted of two islands rather than one and that it was not sizeable enough to be *Terra Australis*. Cook claimed the islands for Great Britain before setting off westwards again.

On 19 April 1770, a lookout sighted land ahead. Ten days later the *Endeavour* was moored in a large natural harbour with Cook and his company making preparations to make landfall.

Cook had initially called the harbour Stingray Harbour, on account of the shoals of the distinctive fish which surrounded his ship. He changed his mind after exploration of the lush coastal lands yielded a treasure trove of previously unknown plant specimens. Cook renamed the harbour Botanists Bay (later changed to Botany Bay) in recognition of the abundant flora they had discovered. The explorers remained at Botany Bay for eight days. During that time Cook's party also made contact with a small number of the aboriginal people who lived nearby. Relations between the aborigines and the Europeans soured after one of Cook's men fired a musket in the air which, unsurprisingly, prompted a hostile response. The Europeans moved on without making any further attempt at social engagement.

In the weeks that followed, Cook was able to dispel any doubt that he had discovered the eastern coast of *Terra Australis*. He spent four months charting the shoreline of the vast territory but his travels nearly met with disaster on the Great Barrier Reef. The *Endeavour* grounded itself on coral and the expedition was delayed for seven weeks while essential repairs were made to the vessel. By now Cook was eager to return home and report his discovery. He had claimed the land for Great Britain but further exploration, and a great deal more people, would be needed if *Terra Australis* was to come under British sovereignty.

The *Endeavour* anchored at Batavia, the headquarters of the immensely powerful Dutch East India Company, to carry out further repairs. But Cook was anxious to press for home — not least due to a concern that one of his crew might let slip their discovery to their Dutch rivals.

The *Endeavour* rounded the Cape of Good Hope and reached the port of Deal in England on 12 July 1771. Cook's expedition was remarkable not just for the extent of its achievements, considerable as they were, but also for his enlightened approach to leadership. He avoided any outbreaks of scurvy, a potentially deadly condition caused by an absence of vitamin C in the diet, by ensuring his crew ate fresh vegetables whenever practicable.

Shortly after returning to Britain, James Cook was promoted to the rank of Commander. He undertook two further expeditions. From 1772 to 1775 he explored the Southern Ocean and the islands of the south Pacific. He ventured further south than any explorer before him, nearly reaching the Antarctic coast before storms and cold forced a retreat.

In 1776, he embarked on his third and final journey. Cook was charged with finding a sea route between the northern Atlantic and Pacific Oceans — the so-called Northwest Passage. He followed the North American shoreline as far north as the Bering Strait between Russia and Alaska before pack ice forced him to turn round. Cook made for the island of Hawaii where he intended to replenish his stocks, repair his ships and set out again for the north Pacific. He was stabbed to death during a confrontation with Hawaiian islanders on 14 February 1779.

James Cook had achieved incredible things. His expedition on the *Endeavour*, a scientific vessel less than 30 metres (100 ft) long and with a crew numbering fewer than 100, opened up the new continent of Australia for exploration. His skill as a navigator and surveyor was prodigious — some of the maps he drew were still in regular use nearly 200 years after his death.

There is perhaps no better summary of his character and achievements than a quote attributed to the man himself: 'Ambition leads me not only farther than any other man has been before me, but as far as I think it possible for man to go.'

TOP OF THE WORLD
HILLARY AND TENZING: LIVING IN THE DEATH ZONE

"It is not the mountain we conquer but ourselves."

Sir Edmund Hillary

The human body is not built to survive at 8,800 metres (29,000 ft). The air is thin, containing only one third of the oxygen available at sea level. High-speed winds are a near constant presence, even when conditions are benign at lower altitudes. Cold is a deadly threat — the low air pressure sucks any warmth from the atmosphere even in high summer.

Each of these factors in isolation would present a life-threatening danger to any human being and the greater the height, the greater the hardship. When all three elements converge it is impossible for the body to withstand such pressures for any great length of time. The lack of oxygen places enormous strain on the heart and nervous system. The cold and wind will rip through any exposed flesh, causing frostbite and hypothermia within minutes of exposure. When a human being reaches such a destructively high altitude survival is impossible. The only option is to get down as quickly and safely as possible.

On 29 May 1953, there were only two people in the world who truly understood what it was like to try and survive this far above sea level. No other humans had ever climbed so high. They were engaged in the fight of their lives. Each step was an ordeal. Every breath, despite the aid of the oxygen tanks they carried, was a separate torture as their lungs sucked for air. The wind buffeted them and threw shards of ice in their faces. They both knew their lives depended on turning back and reaching the relative safety of their camp several hundred metres below. But first they had a job to do. Edmund Hillary and Tenzing Norgay had to complete their agonizing climb, only a further 48 metres, to the summit of the world's highest mountain and claim their place in history.

The pair had just conquered the last technical climbing challenge on their ascent. They had scaled a sheer wall of rock and ice of around 12 metres (39 ft). If Edmund Hillary had been presented with such a rock face on a mountainside in his native New Zealand, he would have considered it no great challenge. But up in the death zone it was a stern examination of the men's willpower,

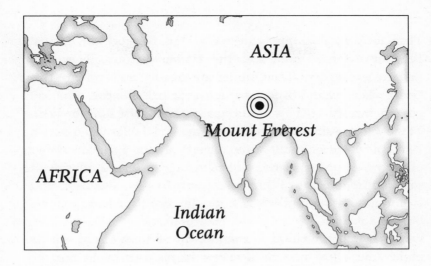

fitness and technical ability. It was also a test of their mental fortitude, for the climbers knew that once they reached the top of the cliff the summit would be theirs — so long as they could continue to keep putting one foot in front of the other.

The rock face would later be named the Hillary Step in honour of the first man to scale it. Today, climbers on their way to and from the summit use a series of fixed ropes to negotiate it, but Hillary and Tenzing had no such luxuries. After hauling themselves up the cliff face, the exhausted climbers were rewarded with a straightforward upward trek along a steadily-rising ridge.

Slowly but surely they made their way onwards. Just before noon, they could climb no higher. They had made the summit of Everest. Hillary turned to Tenzing and extended his hand, expecting Tenzing to reciprocate, only to be enveloped in an enthusiastic bearhug and a solid thump on the back. It was a rare break from 1950s reserve, but reflected the extreme excitement that both men were experiencing on finally achieving their goal.

They took photographs and waved the flags of the United Kingdom, Nepal, India and the United Nations. They also undertook a search of the immediate area for any evidence that George Mallory and Sandy Irvine, two British climbers who had gone missing near the summit in 1924, had made it to the peak. There were no signs to suggest that they had. Hillary then buried a crucifix on the summit at the request of John Hunt the leader of the expeditionary party, while Tenzing left a food offering of some boiled sweets as a Buddhist tribute to the gods. Then, after 15 minutes on the roof of the world, the two friends turned and headed downhill.

By 1953, the competition to conquer the summit of the world's highest peak had become a matter of national pride. For the British expedition, of which the New Zealander Hillary and the Nepalese Tenzing were a part, the late spring of 1953 would probably be their only chance to claim the summit of Everest for their country. A Swiss expedition had come within 250 metres (820 ft) of the summit the year before, and further Swiss and French expeditions would take place over the next two years.

Tenzing and Hillary may have been two small figures set against the vastness of the Himalayas, but they were members of one of the largest mountaineering expeditions ever assembled. The party consisted of 350 porters and twenty Sherpas in support of just ten climbers. They were not the first members of the expedition to strike out for the summit. On May 26, Tom Bourdillon and Charles Evans reached Everest's South Summit – just 101 metres (331 ft) from the peak itself – before exhaustion and dwindling oxygen supplies forced them to abort their bid.

❛ If you cannot understand that there is something in man which responds to the challenge of this mountain and goes out to meet it, that the struggle is the struggle of life itself upward and forever upward, then you won't see why we go. ❜

George Mallory

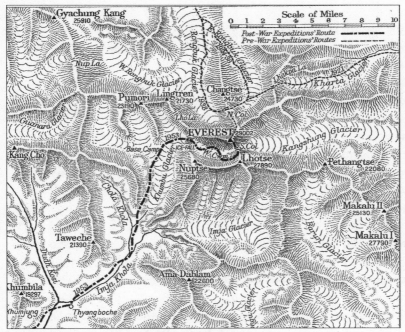

The expedition used nine camps on their way to the summit.

The opportunity then fell to Hillary and Tenzing to strike for glory three days later. Tenzing was by far the most experienced Everest mountaineer in the party. Twelve months earlier, he had been part of the Swiss team that had reached 8,599 metres (28,200 ft) in their Everest attempt. Edmund Hillary was a veteran of several Himalayan expeditions. He made no secret of his confidence in his ability to reach the summit, and was also clear in his preference of Tenzing as his climbing partner. Hillary had reason to trust the Sherpa. At an earlier stage in the climb, Hillary had been plotting a route through an icefall when the ice gave way, plunging him into a crevasse. His life was saved by Tenzing, who managed to hastily fasten a rope round a pin secured in the ice and arrest Hillary's fall.

Now as the pair made their descent down the mountain slopes, John Hunt waited for news of their fate. Hunt was based at Camp VI and watched intently as the two climbers plotted their way towards him. He examined their body language for some clue of whether their bid had been successful and came to the conclusion from the men's demeanour that it had not. Hunt was wrong. He had mistaken their exhaustion for despondency and when Hillary and Tenzing were able to signal from some distance through a variety of finger pointing and arm waving, that they had indeed reached the peak, celebrations broke out within the expedition camp.

For the British, the outpouring of national pride was not diminished by the fact that news of the successful summit expedition reached the United Kingdom on June 2, the day of Queen Elizabeth II's coronation.

Hillary, Tenzing and Hunt returned from the thin air as heroes. All three were given awards for their efforts. Hillary and Hunt both received knighthoods, while Tenzing was awarded the George Medal.

Hunt returned to the UK and became an influential figure in British politics. Hillary and Tenzing remained close until the latter's death in 1986. Tenzing used his prominence to serve as an advocate for the rights of the Sherpa people and to warn against what he saw as the over-commercialization of Everest. Hillary joined an expedition to Antarctica, and in 1958 was part of the first team to reach the South Pole by vehicle after piloting a tractor across the vast polar icefields. In later years, he devoted much of his time to the Himalayan Trust which provided educational and medical support for impoverished communities in the Everest region.

With characteristic modesty, he said: 'I have enjoyed great satisfaction from my climb of Everest and my trips to the poles.

But there's no doubt that my most worthwhile things have been the building of schools and medical clinics.'
Sir Edmund Hillary died on 11 January 2008 in Auckland, New Zealand.

*❛ People do not decide to become extraordinary.
They decide to accomplish extraordinary things. ❜*

Sir Edmund Hillary

A NEW WORLD

CHRISTOPHER COLUMBUS' 1492 VOYAGE TO THE AMERICAS

"YOUR HIGHNESSES . . . ordered that I should not go by land to the eastward; as had been customary, but that I should go by way of the west, whither up to this day, we do not know for certain that any one has gone."

Christopher Columbus

Christopher Columbus became the first known European to reach the Caribbean, making initial landfall on an island in the Bahamas. The year was 1492. On a subsequent voyage, he was the first European to land on the South American mainland, in Venezuela. Not that he fully appreciated the significance, for he always believed he had reached Asia in spite of finding no evidence to support this.

Christopher Columbus (Cristoforo Colombo or, in Spanish, Cristóbal Colón) was almost certainly born in Genoa in 1451, the son of a weaver. Like many Genoese, he went to sea, and he first appears in records having survived a shipwreck off the coast of Portugal in 1476. In the years that followed, he took part in journeys north to England and Iceland and south down the coast of Africa to the Gold Coast as far as Elmina. Columbus became a very accomplished navigator, a skill that was to prove essential in his later voyages.

Like most educated Europeans, he believed that the globe was a sphere and he started to think about travelling to China and India by going west rather than east. He made two important and erroneous assumptions, however — he thought Asia spread much further east and that the world was much smaller than it was, so making such a voyage practical in his view. Others disagreed over the practicality, and initially he failed to gain support from the rulers of Portugal, Spain, France and England.

He moved from Portugal to Spain in 1486, then under the rule of Ferdinand and Isabella. After much lobbying, he was summoned before them in January 1492, shortly after the conquest of Granada that re-established Christian rule across Spain. They agreed to provide assistance for a fleet of three boats to sail west. If Columbus discovered any territories, he would become Admiral of the Ocean Sea and Governor, entitled to 10 per cent of all income generated by these new colonies.

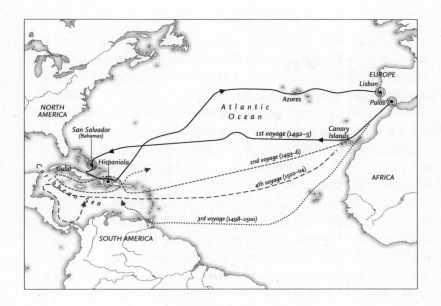

With investment from a group of Italian merchants, he brought together three boats, the *Santa María*, a three-masted, 100-tonne carrack, and two smaller caravels, the *Pinta* and the *Niña*, and prepared for the voyage at Palos, near Cadiz. On the morning of 3 August 1492, the boats set sail from Palos, according to Columbus's journal. Seven days later they reached the Canaries, where they had to wait for the rudder of the *Pinta* to be repaired. A month later they departed 'shaping a course to the west', using the northeast trade winds to head into the unknown.

A week out from the Canaries he noted 'they met with very temperate breezes, so that there was great pleasure in enjoying the mornings, nothing being wanted but the song of nightingales'. After another week, following a number of optimistic notes that land must be near by, Columbus recorded that he 'saw a whale, which is a sign that they were near land, because they always keep near the shore', but he continued to be disappointed. With gentle winds, the crew were beginning to be concerned over when they would reach land, and, more importantly, whether there would ever be any wind to take them home again.

On Sunday 7 October, the *Niña* hoisted a flag and fired a gun, the signal that they had spotted signs of land. By Thursday 11 October they saw more birds and vegetation in the water, including a small branch covered in berries. Later in the day they thought they saw a light, and then two hours after midnight on Friday 12 October, land was seen close by. They waited until dawn and then prepared to land. Columbus was sure they had reached the East Indies, but the island, which Columbus called San Salvador and which the Taino people who lived there called Guanahani, was in the Bahamas. They landed and Columbus 'took possession of the said island for the King and Queen'. Soon the locals came to see what was going on, and in a style oft repeated by European colonizers, Columbus 'gave to some of them red caps, and glass beads to put round their necks, and many other things of little value, which gave them great pleasure, and made them so much our friends that it was a marvel to see'.

He reported that all the islanders were 'as naked as when their mothers bore them' and that they painted themselves in different colours and designs. They were peaceable and 'they neither carry nor know anything of arms, for I showed them swords, and they took them by the blade and cut themselves through ignorance'.

> *(They have no iron, their darts being wands without iron, some of them having a fish's tooth at the end, and others being pointed in various ways.)*

However, Columbus, well aware that his sponsors were seeking gold and other treasures, soon established that the island was poor. Having ascertained that larger and wealthier islands lay to the south, he soon departed to investigate further. Stopping at various islands on the way, he reached Cuba, as the Taino called it, on 28 October. He originally hoped it was Japan, but then decided it was some part of China. He noted the lush vegetation, good harbours and high mountains, but he really wanted to find the gold mines he had been told about. In this and his wish to find the emperor of China, he was disappointed.

Next he sailed to the island called Hayti by the Taino and which he named Isla Espanola (Hispaniola). He visited various places along the coast but disaster struck on Christmas night, as the *Santa María* ran aground on a reef and had to be abandoned. Most of the goods on the ship and some of its timbers were brought to land. He was welcomed by the local chief, who agreed that he could build a fort for his crew. Named La Navidad, it became the first Spanish settlement in the Caribbean, though its exact location on the northern coast of Haiti remains a mystery. On 16 January 1493, he set sail in the *Niña* for Spain, with some captured Taino but leaving behind thirty-nine crew members. After a difficult crossing he reached the Azores on 18 February, where he had to stop for repairs, and then stormy weather forced Columbus to dock near Lisbon on 4 March 1493, which left him with some explaining to do, as he had arrived in a Spanish boat. However, he was soon able to leave and returned to Palos on 15 March 1493. The *Pinta* had returned separately. Columbus was later received by Ferdinand and Isabella in Barcelona and he was able to show off his captives, the gold and exotic goods that had survived the journey.

He was given support for another voyage leaving in September 1493, made up of seventeen boats and around 1,400 people. This is when things started to go wrong for Columbus and also for the indigenous inhabitants. On his return in late November he found that La Navidad had been destroyed and none of his men had survived. The newly arrived Spaniards quickly forced the Taino to be their labourers and their days were to be numbered. Columbus continued his exploration of the Caribbean. On his second voyage he explored more of the coasts of Cuba and Hispaniola and visited Jamaica, while on his third voyage, in 1498–1500, he reached Trinidad and the Venezuelan coast. However, he was an unpopular Governor and had to return to Spain in chains after disputes with the settlers. In his last voyage, in 1502–4, he explored the coast of central America, ending roughly where the Panama Canal now starts. He returned to Spain and died in Valladolid on 20 May 1506, a neglected figure.

GALACTIC EXPLORER
THE VOYAGER INTERSTELLAR MISSION

"These spacecraft have taught us about the wonders of other worlds, about the uniqueness and fragility of our own, about beginnings and ends."

Carl Sagan, astronomer

The Apollo 11 moon landing in 1969 captured the public imagination unlike any other space mission in history. However, in terms of furthering our understanding of the Solar System and the galaxy beyond, NASA's Voyager mission is arguably of far greater significance. Almost 40 years since their launch, the twin *Voyager* 1 and 2 spacecraft are now further away from Earth than anything else mankind has ever constructed, some 20 billion km in the case of *Voyager* 1. Their primary mission was to fly by Jupiter and Saturn and send back data that would ultimately re-write astronomy textbooks. However, the mission has become far more successful than could ever have been imagined at the outset.

In 1964, Gary Flandro was working at the NASA Jet Propulsion Laboratory and was given the task of examining ways to explore the outer planets. During the course of his study, he discovered a rare alignment of the outer planets that occurred just once every 175 years. This alignment would allow spacecraft to travel from planet to planet, utilizing their gravitational pull and thus accelerating them out into deep space. Instead of taking forty years, the mission duration could be reduced to less than ten.
Voyager 2 was the first spacecraft to be launched from Cape Canaveral in August 1977, followed by *Voyager* 1 a few weeks later. On board were an array of instruments including video cameras, magnetometers, plasma detectors, infrared and ultraviolet sensors, and cosmic-ray and charged-particle sensors. Most intriguingly though, gold records were also attached to the side of each spacecraft. Each disk contains scenes, greetings, music and sounds of the Earth. These include 115 images and a variety of natural sounds such as those made by whales, birds and other animals. There are recordings of the wind, thunder and surf crashing on a beach. There are greetings in fifty-five different languages and a selection of music ranging from Mozart to Chuck Berry's Johnny B Good. One day, it is hoped that this record of humanity and Earth will be found by some distant intelligent life-form. In reality though, it would be comparatively less noticeable

in the vastness of space than a single grain of sand on an ocean beach. Nevertheless, it was a clever public relations move and ensured global media coverage of the mission.

On March 3, 1979 *Voyager* 1 reached Jupiter, flying by the giant gas planet some 200,000 km above the planet's cloud tops. *Voyager* 2 passed by a few months later. Although Jupiter had been studied for centuries from Earth – most famously by the Italian astronomer Galileo – scientists were surprised by many of the Voyager findings. Voyager's cameras recorded videos of the Great Red Spot, which is 3.5 times larger than Earth and which was found to be a complex storm that moved across the planet in a counterclockwise direction and has been raging for centuries.
The most unexpected discovery at Jupiter was on the innermost of its four large moons, Io. Here, for the first time, active volcanoes were seen on a body in the Solar System, other than on Earth. The plumes of which reached 240 km (150 miles up), high enough to hit passing satellites. These volcanoes are thought to be caused by the gravitational tug of war between Jupiter and two of the planet's other nearby satellites, Europa and Ganymede. This discovery fundamentally changed our opinion and increased our interest in the moons orbiting other planets. *Voyager* 2 also revealed fascinating details about Europa. This moon's surface is a thick crust of ice, laced with vivid lines and streaks that may indicate that minerals from below the surface have penetrated the ice. Europa's conditions could possibly support alien life, albeit in the form of single-celled microorganisms.

The orbit around Jupiter accelerated both spacecraft towards their next destination, Saturn. In November 1980, and just 7.5 km (12 miles) off course, *Voyager* 1 sent back beautiful close-ups of Saturn's rings, revealing incredible structures within them. The rings are composed of billions of particles, ranging from dust-size to much larger rocks the size of houses. One of the most memorable images of the entire Voyager mission was that of the spinning rings, backlit by the sun like giant spokes on a wheel. *Voyager* 1 then flew within 1,500 km (2,500 miles) of Titan, Saturn's largest moon. It is one of only three moons known to have an atmosphere, made up mainly of nitrogen as well as methane. As a result, the photochemistry is thought to be similar to that of an early Earth, before life took hold.

After this close up view of Titan, *Voyager* 1 then moved out of the plane of the Solar System towards interstellar space, its main mission complete.

By 1986, *Voyager* 2 was now approaching Uranus. It found that the planet spins like the other planets but is tipped on its side. Scientists believe this was caused by a collision with a planet-sized body early in the history of the Solar System. As a consequence, its magnetic field is twisted by Uranus' unusual rotation into a long corkscrew shape behind the planet. Uranus was also found to be the coldest planet in the Solar System. It is not the furthest planet from the sun but it has no internal heat source.

Timeline for Voyager 1 *and* 2.

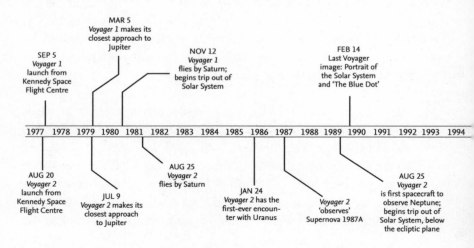

Voyager 2 also discovered ten additional moons to add to the five that were already known. The most interesting of Uranus' moons was Miranda, one of the most bizarre objects in the Solar System with 19-km (12-mile) deep canyons and giant escarpments. Its surface is an assortment of terrains and looks as though it has been glued together. Not surprisingly therefore, astronomers once believed that Miranda was smashed to pieces and re-assembled under its own gravitational pull. This could explain its bizarre configuration but the actual reason is still something of a mystery.

Travelling at 64,000 km/h (40,000 mph), *Voyager* 2 made its rendezvous with Neptune, the last of the outer planets, in August 1989. It was just 35 km (22 miles) off its charted course and 1 second off its projected flyby time. The encounter revealed a storm the size of Earth with the fastest winds ever measured in the Solar System of nearly 1,600 km/h (1,000 mph). This astonished NASA scientists as Neptune is very far from the sun and it was thought that solar energy usually drives atmospheric activity. Having discovered six new moons, *Voyager* 2 then flew by the last solid

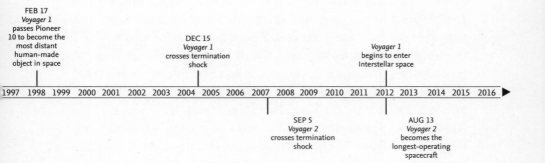

FEB 17
Voyager 1
passes Pioneer
10 to become the
most distant
human-made
object in space

DEC 15
Voyager 1
crosses termination
shock

Voyager 1
begins to enter
Interstellar space

1997 1998 1999 2000 2001 2002 2003 2004 2005 2006 2007 2008 2009 2010 2011 2012 2013 2014 2015 2016 ▶

SEP 5
Voyager 2
crosses termination
shock

AUG 13
Voyager 2
becomes the
longest-operating
spacecraft

body it would encounter in the Solar System, Triton, Neptune's largest moon and the coldest known object in the Solar System. It orbits in an opposite rotation from the planet and it's thought that it may have once been an independent object orbiting around the sun before a cataclysmic collision with another moon smashed Triton into the well of Neptune's gravity. *Voyager* 2 revealed jagged mountains, high cliffs, frozen lakes and active geysers.

The Voyager spacecraft are powered by plutonium radioisotope thermoelectric generators, but to preserve energy NASA have had to systemically shut down Voyager's instruments. In 1990, its cameras were switched off but before doing so, one final image was taken by *Voyager* 1, the 'Solar System Family Portrait'. It was dubbed 'Pale Blue Dot' by the astronomer Carl Sagan as Earth appears as no more than a fraction of a pixel in the image.

With the main mission objectives complete but both spacecraft still functioning, albeit with fewer instruments still operational, the mission now became the Voyager Interstellar Mission. Its objective was to explore the edges of the Solar System beyond the outer planets to the outer limits of the Sun's sphere of influence, and potentially beyond.

In 2012, *Voyager* 1 reached the outer edges of the Solar System and entered the transition into interstellar space. This is the space between star systems within our galaxy. As the ships move further into deep space the effects of the solar wind from our sun decrease and the interstellar galactic wind increases. When the ships' sensors finally detect only a background reading of particles originating from within the Solar bubble, and detect that the direction of the magnetic field has changed, NASA will finally announce that *Voyager* 1 has fully entered interstellar space.

Around 2025, power will finally run out on the spacecraft but they will continue to travel through space long after everything mankind has, or will ever build has gone. Currently, they are 4 light years away from Sirius, the brightest star in the heavens. In just 290,000 years, they will arrive there!

> ❝ Look again at that dot. That's here. That's home. That's us. On it everyone you love, everyone you know, everyone you ever heard of, every human being who ever was, lived out their lives . . . on a mote of dust suspended in a sunbeam. ❞
>
> Carl Sagan, in his book Pale Blue Dot

THE AMERICAN FRONTIER

LEWIS AND CLARK'S CORPS OF DISCOVERY EXPEDITION

*"They collect the wild fruits and roots, attend to
the horses or assist in that duty, cook, dress the
skins and make all the apparel, collect wood and
make their fires, arrange and form their teepees,
and when they travel, pack the horses and take
charge of all the baggage; in short the man does
little else except attend his horses hunt and fish."*

*Meriwether Lewis on the role of the Shoshone woman,
August 19 1805*

Frostbitten, lame and hungry beyond reason, they stood at the apex of a continent. Behind them lay the full length of the mighty river that they had spent sixteen exhausting months paddling, trekking, and rowing up. Ahead of them, they had expected to see another river, one that would give them food and a gentle ride down to the ocean. Instead, they saw a monstrous range of icy mountains. They would need horses and many days' supplies to cross them and the only natives they had found were refusing to offer them anything. This, truly, was the end of their journey. They would never reach their destination.

Then the woman stepped forward. And their fortunes changed forever.

In 1803, the French Emperor was preparing for the seemingly inevitable war with Britain. As part of its overseas empire, France then owned 'Louisiana' — not the US state we know today, but a vast tranche of land comprising all or part of fourteen modern states. This territory was difficult for France to control remotely and, in a war, would be threatened by British forces coming through their territories in what is now Canada. 'Why not simply sell Louisiana to the United States?' counselled Napoleon's minister of finance. They could fill their war chest with cash and divest themselves of an expensive colonial encumbrance at one and the same time. President Thomas Jefferson snapped up the deal and for $15 million (equivalent to $237 million in 2015) he more than doubled the area of the United States. The land cost less than three cents an acre.

Soon after the 'Louisiana Purchase' was made, the president determined to dispatch a party to explore the region, which was then almost entirely unknown. Jefferson simply walked across his office to pick the expedition leader; Meriwether Lewis, an experienced soldier and gifted woodsman who was also the president's aide. Lewis asked his old army commander, William

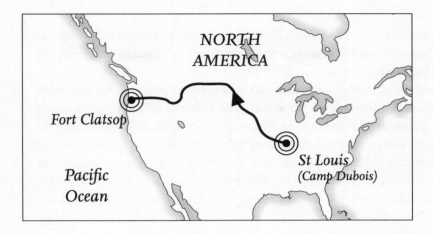

Clark, to be his second in command. Clark was an excellent mapmaker, riverman and leader.

The two friends gathered together the 'Corps of Discovery', a team of soldiers who would help them accomplish their objectives: to explore and map the new territory, and find a viable route across the vast unknown west to the Pacific Ocean. They were also to collect animal and plant samples and, while they were to make only friendly contact with native tribes, they were also to make clear the United States' claims to the territory on which those natives lived.

All of these goals would achieve a grander political point. The independent United States itself was only twenty-seven years old at this time. The expedition was a flexing of the young country's muscles; it would strengthen its authority in the west in the face of the empire-building British and European powers. Lewis was twenty-eight, Clark was thirty-three. They were carrying a lot on their young shoulders.

The expedition left their base, Camp Dubois, near present-day Wood River, Illinois, at 4 pm on 14 May 1804. The plan was to travel the broad Missouri River up it to its headwaters, then cross the continental divide and take another river down to the Pacific. But every day was a back-breaking endurance test. They carried tons of supplies, tools, scientific equipment and gifts for natives and if the wind was not blowing favourably their vessel had to be poled, rowed or towed by hand upstream against the full power of the capricious Missouri.

The lands were unknown to United States citizens but they were home to Blackfoot, Cheyenne, Crow, Ponca and 170 other tribes comprising hundreds of thousands of people. The most powerful and dangerous tribe was the Teton Sioux. They controlled traffic on the middle Missouri and had the numbers and strength to annihilate the explorers. The expedition's very first encounter nearly ended in a bloody battle and there were several more tense standoffs.

In the first five months they travelled 2,575 km (1,600 miles) and had only lost one man, to appendicitis. But the savage prairie winter was nearly upon them, with its bone-chilling cold and constant threat of hunger and frostbite. They built a winter base at Camp Mandan, near present-day Washburn, North Dakota. The area was a relative metropolis: nearby were five villages of native buffalo hunting tribes that had a population of 4,000, more than at that time lived in St Louis.

Lewis and Clark knew that when they reached the high headwaters of the Missouri in the spring they would need the help of the local tribes — the Shoshone people. While camped for the winter, they hired a trapper named Charbonneau as a guide and interpreter. Charbonneau had two young wives, one of whom, Sacagawea, had been kidnapped from the Shoshone when she was a girl of twelve. Still only sixteen, she was also heavily pregnant. Nevertheless, she agreed to accompany the explorers and act as translator. In April, the expedition left Camp Mandan, with two-month old Jean-Baptiste Charbonneau becoming the last member of the party.

The expedition travelled on up the ever-narrowing Missouri in *pirogues*, narrow canoes carved out from single tree trunks. The current and the lessening draught of the river made their work harder every day.

In May, a high wind capsized one boat, and it was Sacagawea who acted swiftly enough to rescue several valuable items, including

Lewis and Clarks' journals. They duly named the Sacagawea River in her honour. It was not the last time she would prove her worth. She showed them edible plants and roots and recognized many places from her youth, which helped keep them on track. But there was a perilous test coming that would try all their strength.

In what is now north Montana, the Missouri River plunges 187 m (612 ft) over five massive cascades. The Great Falls astounded the explorers with their beauty but frustrated them with their size. They would have to be detoured. That meant carrying every single piece of equipment they had on a 27-km (17-mile) trek up steep, rough terrain. They lost a whole month to this portage that left the men limping, sore and faint with exhaustion. They were nearly broken and yet the mountains still lay ahead of them.

Beyond the Falls the river frequently became near-impassable. They ran dangerously low on food and suffered tremendously in the cold and wet. They had no real idea where they were and needed horses and supplies urgently. Rather than running into pugnacious tribes, their problem now was that they could not find the Shoshone. Lewis and Clark were forced to split up, with Lewis heading out with a scouting party to find the natives as Clark and the others trudged on. They would reunite further upstream if Lewis was successful. It was an all or nothing gamble.

Lewis was boosted when he discovered the source of the Missouri. Over the watershed he hoped to see another river rushing westwards. Instead he saw snowcapped mountains — a huge saw-toothed barrier far larger than anyone had expected. The next day he made contact with the Shoshone but now the party's fate was in the hands of people who had never seen a white man. He could not talk to them and the Shoshone seemed disinclined to help.

But when Clark and the rest of the party arrived, an astonishing thing happened. Despite the years of separation since her kidnap, Sacagawea recognized the chief of the Shoshone. He was her brother. Their reunion was very moving and extraordinarily fortunate — Lewis and Clark would have their horses after all.

They recuperated with the Shoshone for two weeks and set out in positive mood. But crossing the mountains was another almost-unendurable hardship. They found hardly any game to hunt and were reduced to eating their tallow candles.

At last, Clark scouted out a way down to green open country. A hospitable tribe helped them make canoes and for the first time in seventeen months they were going downstream. This was the Columbia, the great river of the northwest. Finally, after a year and a half of humbling hardship, they saw it:

'Ocean in view! O! The Joy!'

The sound and smell of the crashing surf must have thrilling beyond description after their trials in the mountains. They built a camp for the winter and made friends with their native neighbours but their happiness was somewhat dampened by the Oregon winter — in four months they only had twelve days without rain. In the spring of 1806, almost two years after first setting out, they headed back upriver. Driven by a fierce urge to see home, and with the help of the maps that Clark had created, the return journey took only six months.

Most people at home had assumed Lewis and Clark were dead. But after a 28-month, 8,000-mile odyssey, the pioneers finally arrived back in St Louis. They brought with them 140 maps of unseen lands, as well as 178 plants and 122 animals new to science. They even had a prairie dog for President Jefferson. Lewis and Clark were the first Americans to cross the continental divide, the first to pass through the Yellowstone region and the first to enter Montana. Their maps gave the first accurate depiction of the relationship of the sources of the Columbia and Missouri Rivers, and the Rocky Mountains.

On a physical level, Lewis and Clark achieved what many had thought impossible — they traversed an unknown land and lived to tell the tale. Even more importantly, they had strengthened the idea that the reach of the United States lay on Pacific shores as well as Atlantic. They had opened the west to their countrymen and blazed the trail of their nation's destiny. But the native way of life would never be the same again.

Despite being made Governor of Upper Louisiana, Meriwether Lewis fell victim to depression and took his own life three years after his return. Clark went on to achieve renown as Governor of the Missouri Territory but he never forgot his great friend and named his first son Meriwether Lewis Clark.

‹ The first white men of your people who came to our country were named Lewis and Clark. They brought many things that our people had never seen. They talked straight. These men were very kind. ›

Chief Joseph

Lewis and Clark were not the first to traverse the North American continent. The Scottish explorer and fur trader Sir Alexander Mackenzie completed an overland crossing of what is now Canada in 1793. This was twelve years before Lewis and Clark reached the Pacific. The Mackenzie River, the second largest river in North America after the Mississippi, is named in his honour.

NOT A SINGLE MAN LOST

Ernest Shackleton's escape from Antarctica

*"When I look back at those days I have no doubt
that Providence guided us, not only across those
snowfields, but across the storm-white sea that
separated Elephant Island from our landing place
on South Georgia. I know that during that long
and racking march of thirty-six hours.......it
seemed to me often that we were four, not three."*

Ernest Shackleton, taken from Shackleton's Epic *by Tim Jarvis*

There has probably never been a more fittingly named vessel than Sir Ernest Shackleton's *Endurance*. When it sailed from South Georgia on 5 December 1914 on the first leg of the Imperial Trans-Antarctic Expedition, the crew were prepared for a tough adventure. They were going to cross the most extreme continent on Earth. Little could they suspect just how much they would be forced to endure. Or how much heroism they would perform to return them all home safely.

Shackleton was leading the crew to Vahsel Bay, the southernmost explored point of the Weddell Sea at 77°49'S. There he would land a shore party and prepare to make the transcontinental crossing. But disaster struck before they could reach their goal. The pack ice was thickening with every mile they sailed south and, by 14 February 1915, the *Endurance* was seized tight in a frozen vice. There was nothing the men could do but sit and wait as, for the next eight months, the drifting ice took the ship back northwards. Then on 27 October, the ice stopped toying with the men and crushed the *Endurance*. The vessel sank from sight on 21 November, leaving the party stranded on the moving ice.

❛ We knew it would be the hardest thing we had ever undertaken, for the Antarctic winter had set in, and we were about to cross one of the worst seas in the world. ❜

Ernest Shackleton

They were not going to cross Antarctica, but the adventure that the continent had thrust upon them was going to be every bit as incredible as what they had planned.

Shackleton's priority now was simply how to save the lives of his twenty-seven-man crew.
In theory they could march across the pack ice to the nearest land and then trek to a harbour that ships were known to visit. But the ice was too broken up and dangerous to travel across. The party

established 'Patience Camp' on a flat ice floe, and waited as the drift carried them further north, towards open water.

Another three months passed. Then, on 8 April 1916, the ice broke up enough to allow them to launch their three lifeboats. For seven perilous days they sailed and rowed through stormy seas and dangerous loose ice, reaching the temporary haven of Elephant Island on 15 April.

They were on solid ground, but their fortunes looked bleak. Elephant Island was not on any shipping routes and it was too far from their planned route to make a rescue likely. Although the island had fresh water and an ample supply of seals and penguins for food and fuel, the savage Antarctic winter was fast approaching. The men only had a narrow shingle beach to call home and this was constantly blasted by gales and blizzards. One tent had already been destroyed and others flattened. Many of the men were mentally and physically exhausted. Somehow, they had to get help.

Shackleton decided to undertake one of the most daring sea voyages in history. They would sail the best of the lifeboats to the whaling stations of South Georgia. The problem was that this island lay some 800 nautical miles (1,500 km; 920 miles) across the Southern Ocean, one of the fiercest stretches of water in the world.

Shackleton's boat party would be venturing into a storm-lashed world where constant gales powered heaving waves – the feared Cape Horn Rollers – that frequently topped 18 m (60 ft) from trough to crest.

We felt our boat lifted and flung forward like a cork in breaking surf.

They took the sturdiest of the three lifeboats, the *James Caird* (named after one of the expedition's sponsors) and got the ship's carpenter to further strengthen it. He raised the sides of the 6.9

m (22½ ft) long boat and added a makeshift deck of wood and canvas. He also fitted a mainmast and a mizzenmast with lugsails and a jib, sealed the craft with oil paints, lamp wick, and seal blood. Finally a ton (1,016 kg) of ballast was added to reduce the risk of capsizing.

Their target was ridiculously small and there was every chance that they would miss the island. The navigation skills of the *Endurance's* captain, Frank Worsley, would be vital if they were to reach South Georgia. Worsley was a New Zealander who had honed his navigation skills as a sailor among the tiny, remote islands of the South Pacific.

On 24 April 1916, Shackleton, Worsley and four other men pushed the *James Caird* out into the hard grey waters that pummelled Elephant Island. They had food for one month, two 70 litre (18 gallon) casks of water (one of which was damaged during the loading and let in sea water), two Primus stoves, paraffin, oil, candles, sleeping bags and 'a few spare socks'.

The wind was a moderate southwesterly, but Shackleton ordered Worsley to set course due north, to get clear of the menacing ice-fields. As they progressed, the swell rose. By dawn, they were 45 nautical miles (83 km; 52 miles) from Elephant Island, sailing in heavy seas and Force 9 winds.

They worked in two three-man watches, with one man at the helm, another at the sails, and the third on bailing duty. It was hard going from the start: the men's clothing had been designed for the dry cold of Antarctic sledging, and was not waterproof. Icy seawater rubbed their skin raw. The only way to rest was huddled together in the tiny covered space in the bows.

Worsley's job was difficult to the point of being almost impossible. To navigate accurately with his sextant he needed to make sightings of the sun. But this was very rarely visible, and when it was the high pitch and roll of the boat made it very hard to be accurate.

After two days, Worsley put them at 128 nautical miles (237 km; 147 miles) north of Elephant Island. They were clear of the dangers

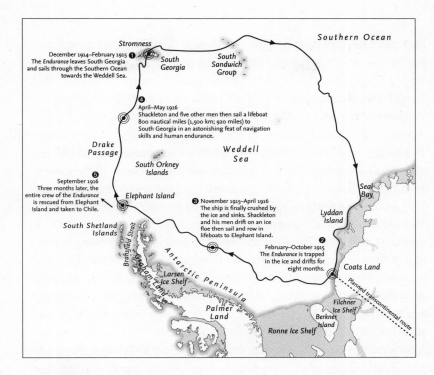

Stromness

December 1914–February 1915 ❶
The *Endurance* leaves South Georgia
and sails through the Southern Ocean
towards the Weddell Sea.

South
Georgia

South
Sandwich
Group

Southern Ocean

❹
April–May 1916
Shackleton and five other men then sail a lifeboat
800 nautical miles (1,500 km; 920 miles) to
South Georgia in an astonishing feat of navigation
skills and human endurance.

*Drake
Passage*

*Weddell
Sea*

South Orkney
Islands

❺
September 1916
Three months later, the
entire crew of the *Endurance*
is rescued from Elephant
Island and taken to Chile.

Elephant Island

❸ November 1915–April 1916
The ship is finally crushed by
the ice and sinks. Shackleton
and his men drift on an ice
floe then sail and row in
lifeboats to Elephant Island.

*Seal
Bay*

*Lyddan
Island*

South Shetland
Islands

February–October 1915 ❷
The *Endurance* is trapped
in the ice and drifts for
eight months.

Coats Land

Bransfield Strait

Antarctic Peninsula

Larsen
Ice Shelf

Planned transcontinental route

*Palmer
Land*

Filchner
Ice Shelf
Berkner
Island

Ronne Ice Shelf

of floating ice but were now in the treacherous Drake Passage, a band of ocean where huge rolling waves sweep round the globe, unimpeded by any land. Shackleton now set a course directly for South Georgia.

After five days' sailing they had travelled 238 nautical miles (441 km; 274 miles), but now the weather deteriorated further. Heavy seas threatened to swamp the boat, and only continuous bailing kept it afloat. It became so cold that spray began to freeze on the boat and the added weight threatened to capsize them. The men had to take turns to crawl onto the pitching deck to chip the ice off the deck and rigging with an axe.

For two whole days the wind was too high for them to raise the sail. But they kept going and by 6 May they were only 115 nautical miles (213 km; 132 miles) from South Georgia. But the two weeks of constant toil in atrocious conditions had worn them down.

Two men were particularly weak, while a third had collapsed and was unable to perform any duties.

> *The bright moments were those when we each received our one mug of hot milk during the long, bitter watches of the night.*

The next day, Worsley thought they were close to their goal but he advised Shackleton that he could be a few miles out. If they were too far north, they could be pushed right past the island by the fierce southwesterly winds. But they soon spotted seaweed and birds including land-loving cormorants, and just after noon on 8 May they saw land. Worsley was dead on and he had accomplished one of the most incredible feats of navigation in maritime history. But, despite being so close to their journey's end, the heavy seas made immediate landing impossible. For twenty-four agonizing hours they were forced to wait offshore in 'one of the worst hurricanes any of us had ever experienced'. The vicious waves threatened to drive them onto the rocky South Georgia shore or the equally dangerous Annenkov Island, 8 km (5 miles) from the coast.

Finally, on 10 May, Shackleton knew that the weaker members of his crew would not last another day in the boat. They had to land, no matter how dangerous the conditions. They found as sheltered an area as they could, Cave Cove near the entrance to King Haakon Bay and, after several near-fatal attempts, landed the *James Caird*. They were on the uninhabited southwest coast. The whaling stations were still 150 nautical miles (280 km; 170 miles) round the coast. Shackleton's plan had been to sail round, hugging the shore. But he knew that the boat would not make such a voyage; nor would two of the exhausted men. After a few days' recuperation, he decided to traverse the island on foot and get help at Stromness. But no one had ever crossed the interior of South Georgia before.

Early on 18 May Shackleton, Worsley and seaman Tom Crean left their three colleagues sheltering on a shingle beach under the upturned *James Caird* and started walking.

Because they had no map they had to improvise a route across mountain ranges and over glaciers. They had no camping equipment so they simply did not stop. They walked continuously for thirty-six hours before reaching the whaling station at Stromness.

By now they were at the edge of total exhaustion, their faces savaged by exposure and wind, their fingers and toes numb with frostbite. The Norwegian seamen must have been staggered to see, as Worsley wrote, 'a terrible trio of scarecrows', walking into their bunkhouse.

Later that same day, 19 May, the whalers sent a motor-vessel to King Haakon Bay to pick up the three other men from the *James Caird*. But the Antarctic winter had now set in, and it was more than three months before Shackleton could retrieve the twenty-two men they had left on Elephant Island. Finally, on 3 September 1916, every single man who had sailed on the *Endurance* reached the safe haven of Punta Arenas in Chile.

Two years later Shackleton headed back to Antarctica on another expedition. On 5 January 1922, he died suddenly of a heart attack in South Georgia.

The *James Caird* was brought back from South Georgia to England in 1919. It is on permanent display at Shackleton's old school, Dulwich College.

THE REAL INDIANA JONES
PERCY FAWCETT: IN SEARCH OF THE LOST CITY OF GOLD

"I expect the ruins to be monolithic in character, more ancient than the oldest Egyptian discoveries. Judging by inscriptions found in many parts of Brazil, the inhabitants used an alphabetical writing allied to many ancient European and Asian scripts. There are rumours, too, of a strange source of light in the buildings, a phenomenon that filled with terror the Indians who claimed to have seen it."

Percy Fawcett, writing in a letter to his son Brian, about the golden city he sought

The world had lost much of its mystery by the start of the twentieth century. The endeavours of Amundsen, Scott et al. had brought the world's attention to the frozen south while most of North America had been explored and settled. Even Africa, the Dark Continent, was opening up to greater exploration.

One of the last remaining unknown wild places was the vast Amazonian basin. This enormous tract straddled the Equator and covered thousands of kilometres in dense tropical forest.

Christopher Columbus had reached the South American mainland in the fifteenth century and European travellers colonized much of the lands near the sea, but South America's green centre remained largely unknown. There were several reasons for this unexplored status. The formidable Andes mountain range presented a huge natural barrier to travel from the west while the vast distances involved in reaching the Amazon basin from the Atlantic coast were prohibitive. Then there was the matter of travelling through the jungle itself. A path had to be cut through thick vegetation in steaming heat. Progress was slow and disease was rife. The region's teeming wildlife caused problems ranging from the constant irritation of biting ants and mosquitoes to the deadly threat of snakes, crocodiles and big cats. Many indigenous tribes

were hostile to the approach of outsiders. Given the treatment South American people had experienced at the hands of European settlers, their hostility was well placed.

Colonel Percy Fawcett was familiar with all the difficulties an explorer in the Amazon must endure. At the ripe age of 39, he undertook his first trip to South America in 1906 to map part of the border territory between Bolivia and Brazil for the Royal Geographical Society. The record of his early exploits in Amazonia made for interesting reading. Fawcett claimed to have stalked and killed a freakishly large Anaconda, more than 20 metres (66 ft) long, and a giant spider known as the Apazauca which was terrorizing the region's tribes with its venomous fangs. His claims were treated with suspicion and were not necessarily offset by his uncontested explorational achievements. Against very little competition he reported to have found the source of the Rio Verde — a tributary of a tributary of a tributary of the Amazon.

Whatever the merits of Fawcett's early discoveries there was no questioning his passion for exploration and he proved himself exceedingly adept at recounting his adventures to others. A distinguished man, with piercing blue eyes and a handlebar moustache, he gave evocative accounts of the dangers of the jungle and the stunning, otherworldly beauty of the Amazon. He gave an account of dramatic plateaued mountains rising from the thick rainforest to Sir Arthur Conan Doyle, which inspired the author's novel, 'The Lost World'. One of the story's key characters, Lord John Roxton, bore more than a passing resemblance to Fawcett. There was no question that Fawcett's early travels had given him a thirst to discover more unknown parts of the South American interior but his plans had to be put on hold by the onset of the First World War.

Fawcett had served in the Royal Artillery and re-enlisted when war broke out. He served with distinction on the Western Front. When the fighting stopped and an armistice announced, Fawcett turned his attention back to the other side of the world. He was determined to return to the Amazon and had a very specific goal in mind.

Fawcett was convinced that one of the greatest myths propagated by the growth of European exploration was in fact true – El Dorado – the city of gold.

Rumours of a city, hidden deep in the jungle and laden with vast wealth, had returned to Europe with the first adventurers to reach South America. The first visitors to the continent heard stories of how tribal leaders in what is now Colombia were caked in gold dust during an annual ceremony. Tales of this 'gilded king' created the idea that vast quantities of gold were to be found. The Spanish conquistadors had already plundered incredible riches from the Aztec and Incan cultures. It appeared further riches were there for the taking.

Among those early venturers was Sir Walter Raleigh. In 1595, he arrived at the mouth of the Orinoco River, ready to head south in search of El Dorado. Raleigh's motivations for undertaking such a trip were complex. He had fallen out of favour with Queen Elizabeth after secretly marrying one of her maids. Finding the fabled El Dorado, capturing its wealth and stealing a march on England's great rival of the age, Spain, would return him to the monarch's favour.

Raleigh left the bulk of his expedition party at the headwaters of the Orinoco. He took a crew of 100 men and they plotted their way against the strong current on a collection of rafts and small boats. He made an alliance with a local chieftain named Topiawari, who told him of a wealthy people living in the mountains. Raleigh pressed on but the fierce Orinoco, fed by heavy rains, quelled his enthusiasm. The team gathered rock samples which they hoped would provide traces of gold ore and he prepared to return home. News of Raleigh's exploits preceded him to the Royal court and, on his arrival, he was dismayed to discover that the South American venture was already regarded as a failure. Raleigh, however, remained convinced that untapped riches and an undiscovered realm were waiting to be discovered in the South American jungle. He endorsed further exploration of the area and in 1616, more than 20 years after his first expedition, Raleigh returned to South America.

The voyage was a disaster. Raleigh, now an elderly man, was among the many travellers to suffer from dysentery. Fifteen men were killed when they were attacked by Spanish forces off the coast of the Canary Islands. Once they reached South America Raleigh's son, also Walter, was killed by Spanish troops in a skirmish at the colonial town of Santo Thome. The expedition's land party found little of interest despite months of foraging in the jungle. Raleigh began the long journey back to England. He had been the master of fourteen ships on setting out in June 1617. The fleet which returned to England one year later consisted of one vessel — the other ships had turned pirate and deserted him on the journey home. Raleigh, one of England's greatest sailor/explorers, was executed at the Palace of Westminster on 29 October 1618.

Raleigh's expedition may have ended in failure but his exploits were all factors in the enduring myth of El Dorado and, some 300 years after Sir Walter's demise, Percy Fawcett was free of his war obligations and ready to continue his search.

Fawcett's own research had led to him to some drastically different conclusions from the established beliefs about El Dorado. Traditionally, the golden city had been notionally placed somewhere in the northern territories of South America with some social and cultural links to the known ancient peoples of the region, such as the Incas.

Fawcett posited that the city of gold, which he called 'Z', was much further south, right in the middle of the continent. In Rio de Janeiro, at the National Library of Brazil, he found an account from a Portuguese who described a beautiful city in the classical Greek style in the depths of the Mato Grosso region. Fawcett also claimed that studies of artefacts found in the Mato Grosso region were similar to archaeological finds around a possible site of the lost Mediterranean city of Atlantis and that 'Z' was culturally distinct from other South American settlements and had more in common with ancient Greece.

It was not a widely held interpretation, but Fawcett's conviction was unshakeable and after several years of exploration in the Mato Grosso he believed he had located the hidden city's whereabouts deep in the Brazilian jungle. Now all he had to do was get there.

It took Fawcett three years to put together a team for what would be his foray into the wilderness. He was joined by his 21-year-old son Jack, and his son's friend Raleigh Rimell. There was widespread interest in the adventure. 'We shall return,' Fawcett told reporters during a stopover in the United States, 'and we shall bring back what we seek.' The three, along with two local guides, set out into the wilderness from the town of Cuiaba on 20 April 1925.

Fawcett Senior, now 57-years-old, had a clear picture in his own mind of the direction he wished to travel and set off at a pace that his younger travelling companions struggled to match. At one point he was so far ahead of the rest of the party that he had to overnight alone and wait for them to reach him.

On 29 May, the party reached Dead Horse Camp. Fawcett had given the camp its unusual name some years earlier. It was the spot where he had been forced to shoot one of his horses and abandon his expedition through fatigue and malnutrition.

The skeleton of the unfortunate horse was still there, stripped clean to the bone by ants and other scavengers. Fawcett instructed his guides to return to Cuiaba. He also had a private word with Rimell and suggested he return, too. Rimell's foot had become badly swollen as a result of bites from ticks and gnats. Percy Fawcett also had concerns that his son's friend may not have the constitution for the undoubted hardship which lay ahead. Rimell refused and vowed to continue with his comrades. Fawcett sent a letter to his wife, Nina, back with the guides. 'Jack is well and fit and getting stronger every day,' it read. 'You need have no fear of any failure.'

It was to be the last time anyone ever heard from Colonel Percy Fawcett, or his son Jack, or Raleigh Rimell. Or, at least, anyone outside of the Amazon jungle.

There was nothing unusual about a prolonged silence regarding Fawcett's expedition. He was travelling beyond all lines of communication and had warned that it may be some time before he was able to relay news of his journey. By the summer of 1927, however, concern as to the fate of Fawcett and his companions was growing. Fawcett had left very clear instruction that, in the event of his disappearance, no search parties were to be dispatched.

This instruction was to be roundly ignored as speculation mounted as to the party's fate. In 1928, George Dyott of the Royal Geographical Survey led a party into the jungle in search of Fawcett. His search was not helped by the fact that Fawcett had been operating in the area for several years. Dyott was to find some of Fawcett's possessions held by various tribes he met, but these were found to have come from earlier expeditions. Similarly, tribespeople who agreed they had seen Fawcett could not be sure whether it had been on his most recent expedition or an earlier occasion.

Dyott concluded that Fawcett and his companions had not survived but he had no firm evidence to support his findings. Over the years, mystique grew around Percy Fawcett and his search for El Dorado. A dozen more search parties followed Dyott into the jungle in search of the explorer and his fellow travellers.

Theories abounded; Fawcett has 'gone native' and was living among a local tribe; Fawcett and his companions had been attacked and killed by a hostile tribe; the group has been taken by starvation, or disease, or animal attack. Some even believed that Fawcett had finally found the lost city and saw out his days in the neo-classical splendour of 'Z'. It was an epitaph which would not have displeased Colonel Percy Fawcett in the slightest.

❛ No one knows what happened to the Fawcetts -- father and son -- and young Mr Rimell. In fact, the Matto Grosso swamps and jungles are such queer places, with records of white men detained by Indian tribes for twenty-five or thirty years and then returning to civilization, that one would not deem it impossible, if improbable, that Colonel Fawcett himself is still alive, perhaps in the recesses of the White Mountains, or the hinterland of the Serra do Roncador, even today, 1945 ❜

Harold Wilkins, in his book Mysteries of Ancient South America (1947)

GOLD FEVER IN THE YUKON

THE KLONDIKE GOLD RUSH

*"...journeys are long and expensive, and can only be
undertaken in summer after the ice has disappeared.
Provisions are very scarce and dear, if procurable at all...
The journeys are difficult and expensive, and no one
should think of going there who is not strong and well
supplied with money for the journey and for food;
nor should anyone go who has not some considerable
experience in prospecting and in roughing it in wild a
nd unsettled countries. All others are strongly
warned against going there."*

The Times *July 29 1897*

In August 1896, a trio of failed prospectors in Canada's Yukon territory decided to try their hands at salmon fishing for a living instead. As one of the men was washing a cooking pan in the stream one evening, he pulled out a gold nugget the size of his thumb. It was 16 August 1896, and George Carmack had just lit the fuse on probably the most explosive gold rush in history.

However, this area – around the Klondike River – was so remote that news of the strike was effectively sealed in by the fearsome winter which soon came howling. It was not until July 1897, when a steamship from Alaska docked in San Francisco, that the story spread. Among the passengers was a gaggle of miners who had spent the long winter in the dark wilds of the north. Filthy and fleabitten they were but in their grubby pockets and knapsacks and the battered boxes and coffee cans that they called luggage, these men carried more than $1,139,000 ($1 billion at 2010 prices) worth of pure gold.

In the last four years, there had been two major financial panics. Unemployment was high. The US and Canadian dollars were then tied to the gold standard, and a shortage of gold had pushed the metal's price up. When those lucky early prospectors landed their gold, it was like a wildfire ripping through a tinder-dry forest, and the media fanned the flames.

Suddenly everyone wanted to be a prospector. A quarter of the Seattle police force handed in their badges and left for the Klondike. They were joined by the city's mayor who not only resigned but bought a steamboat to ferry would-be prospectors north. The event was such a sensation that photographers and writers (including future novelist Jack London) joined the exodus. Over the next two years, at least 100,000 hopeful souls set out for the Klondike gold fields. However, very few of them ever made it rich and many thousands died on one of the most deadly expeditions in history.

The Klondike's climate is the definition of extreme. The short summer is scorching hot and dry. In September, harsh snowstorms herald the arrival of winter. All rivers are frozen solid before October is out. Temperatures in the depths of winter drop to -40°C (-40°F) or even -50°C (-58°F), and the ground is frozen to a depth of 3 metres (10 ft) for at least seven months of the year.

But even reaching the Klondike meant dedicating a whole year of your life to hardship, penury and disease, all for the scanty chance of finding a fortune lying in the mountains. The first danger was the voyage from San Francisco or Seattle. The size of the stampede – 2,800 from Seattle alone in a single week – meant that every old tub was roped into service. These 'floating coffins' had a habit of living up to their nickname.

The Canadian government insisted that each miner must bring enough supplies to last a full year. That way they hoped to limit the amount who perished in the brutal conditions. As well as 12 months' worth of food, prospectors needed to equip themselves with an 'outfit' of tent, stove and tools. In total, these requisites cost around $500 and weighed almost a ton. 'Klondike fever' ran so high that thousands of inexperienced travellers fell prey to conmen selling them Klondike medicines, Klondike gold detectors and Klondike bicycles.

Well-funded prospectors could take a ship directly from Seattle or San Francisco to the west Alaskan seaboard. This all-water route avoided the troubles of the overland trails, but it was 7,600 km (4,700 miles) long and became hugely expensive. In six months the fare rose from $150 ($4,050 today) to $1,000 ($27,000 today). Nor were the rich men immune from suffering. In 1897, only forty-three out of 1,800 prospectors who used this route made it to the Klondike before winter iced the rivers. And thirty-five of those had to return, having ditched their equipment in their hurry.

After a cramped sea journey, most Klondikers were dumped on the mudflats by Skagway, in the southeast 'panhandle' of Alaska.

Skagway was a town of ragged anarchy, a lawless world of saloons, shootouts and cut-throat salesmen. Miners with funds could pay 'packers' to carry their outfits by mule, horse or wagon from here to the gold fields. But many unscrupulous packers would often dump prospectors' equipment in the snow at the trailside if they got a better offer.

The gold fields were still 880 km (550 miles) from Skagway, and the most-used trail was via the notorious White Pass. This had a deceptively gentle gradient but in reality it was a fearsome route. The lower sections had bogs that could swallow a mule whole. Up in the mountains the trail was only 60 cm (24 in.) wide in places, with a 150 m (500 ft) abyss yawning below.

The pack animals were far from thoroughbreds and the conditions killed them by the score. The route became known as 'Dead Horse Trail'. In many places, the fallen animals were not even dragged off the path, but were simply tramped into the trail.

❝ The horses died like mosquitoes in the first frost and from Skagway to Bennett they rotted in heaps. ❞

Jack London, *author of* The Call of the Wild

Despite the deep snow and dead horses, miners were under huge pressure to traverse the trail swiftly. Once over the watershed, they had to reach Lake Bennett, at the head of Yukon, from where they could descend to the Klondike. But if they were tardy, this would have started to ice up and they would have to spend all winter on the lake's frozen shore. The knowledge that they still had 800 km (500 miles) still to go must have ground down on them like a glacier. The whole muddy, bloody nightmare was too much for many miners. They returned to Skagway, sold their outfits and went home broke and broken.

Dyea, the neighbouring town to Skagway, had its own route to the Klondike via the Chilkoot Pass. Too steep for pack animals, this route was used by the poorest prospectors and by others when the

Skagway Trail was blocked by snow. A Klondiker on the Dyea Trail could either hire an Indian packer and pay through the nose or haul their outfits themselves. Since they had so much gear, this had to be done in stages. A miner would sling 45 kg (100 lb) of kit onto his back and trudge off along the trail for a few miles before dumping his gear. He would then trudge back, pick up the next 45 kg of his ton of kit. The 64 km (40 mile) traverse of the pass thus became a three-month odyssey in which every miner would have walked the trail 30 or 40 times, covering 4,000 km (2,500 miles). In the winter of 1897, a constant stream of 20,000 prospectors toiled up the fearsome Chilkoot Pass day and night.

When spring came to Bennett Lake, the prospectors still had to get down the Yukon River to the confluence with the Klondike river. For miners unable to afford a boat ride, this meant hiking into the forest, chopping down trees, shaping them into planks and using them to build a boat of their own. In May 1898, a ragged flotilla of 7,124 rafts and boats floated downstream on the just-melted river. However, the inexperienced sailors had to navigate many miles of fierce rapids. Hundreds of people drowned.

Their goal was Dawson City, a boom town that had winked into existence at the confluence of the Klondike and Yukon rivers. Dawson did not exist in the summer of 1896. One year later, it was among the largest cities in Canada, with a population of 40,000.

But this was no El Dorado for the vast majority who arrived. They had endured a dangerous, diseased sea journey, a sodden hike over mosquito-ridden marshes and had faced frostbite and exhaustion trekking over glaciers only to find every inch of gold-rich river was already staked out. Thousands of dreams died in Dawson City.

Over 100,000 would-be prospectors left for the Klondike; 70,000 returned home without ever swinging a pick. Of the 30,000 who arrived, only 4,000 found gold. Of them, only a handful became wealthy. And a very scarce few of that handful managed to hang onto their wealth; the rest gambled or drank it away. The majority of people who got rich in the Klondike were those who sold food, shelter, tools, and porterage, or those who traded claims. In a particularly muddy thaw, one merchant sold rubber boots at $100 a pair. One packer owned 335 mules and pulled in $5,000 a day, far more than most miners ever earned.

In 1899, the same newspapers that had trumpeted the Klondike proclaimed a new discovery in Nome, Alaska, where the gold could more easily extracted. Almost overnight, miners began to desert the Klondike. In August 1899, 8,000 people deserted Dawson and the great gold rush was over, just three years after it had begun. The boom towns turned to bust.

THE SILENT WORLD

JACQUES COUSTEAU AND CALYPSO

*"The reef of Shab Suleim was an intaglio structure
with porches of coral, winding couloirs and countless
narrow cracks aswarm with beings waiting in the
wings like walk-on players at the opera."*

Cousteau writing about the beauties of the Red Sea reefs

In 1950, the worlds of marine biology, popular science and television documentaries were forever changed by one man and one extraordinary expedition — Jacques Cousteau and his voyage on the *Calypso*.

With a crew of fellow divers, Cousteau steered his remarkable research ship *Calypso* on a two-year underwater odyssey through the Mediterranean Sea, The Gulf, Red Sea and Indian Ocean. Cousteau shot extensive footage – using 25 kilometres of film – of undersea wonders with revolutionary underwater cameras that he had designed himself. This footage was edited into a ground-breaking documentary, *The Silent World*, that was one of the first colour films of the ocean's depths. It stunned audiences. The film won an Academy Award and the Palme d'Or at the Cannes Film Festival in 1956; it remained the only documentary to do so until 2004.

Born in 1910 on France's western seaboard, Cousteau always had a passion for the ocean. He began diving in 1926 using a newly invented breathing apparatus and joined the French navy four years later. After a car crash ended his naval career he spent more and more time exploring underwater, while doing the occasional intelligence mission for the navy. The more he dived, the more unsatisfied he was with his breathing apparatus — it only allowed for dives of 30 minutes duration, and to a maximum depth of 10 m (33 ft).

A few examples of Cousteau's adventures over his career.

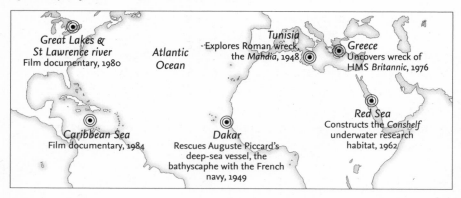

Great Lakes & St Lawrence river
Film documentary, 1980

Atlantic Ocean

Tunisia
Explores Roman wreck, the *Mahdia*, 1948

Greece
Uncovers wreck of HMS *Britannic*, 1976

Caribbean Sea
Film documentary, 1984

Dakar
Rescues Auguste Piccard's deep-sea vessel, the bathyscaphe with the French navy, 1949

Red Sea
Constructs the *Conshelf* underwater research habitat, 1962

In the dark days of the Second World War, Cousteau was in German-occupied Paris when he was introduced to Émile Gagnan, an engineer. Gagnan was trying to solve France's wartime fuel shortage by improving the efficiency of gas generators and had miniaturised an old underwater breathing apparatus to create an automatic regulator. Cousteau instantly saw how useful this new regulator could be to divers; attached to compressed air tanks, it would more than double the potential length of an underwater dive to over an hour. He would also be able to go much deeper than before, making extended underwater exploration possible. The two men patented the device.

In 1943, Cousteau made an experimental undersea film using his revolutionary diving equipment. At the end of the war he was able to convince his navy superiors that his aqualung could be useful and he was made leader of the French Navy's Underwater Research Group. This unit was tasked with clearing minefields from French coasts and the wider Mediterranean, as well as training and testing divers, and conducting underwater exploration. Cousteau and Gagnan also began to manufacture and sell aqualungs in large numbers. The income allowed Cousteau to begin planning a pioneering voyage of underwater discovery.

Cousteau left the navy in 1949 and the following year he set about transforming an old British minesweeping vessel, the *Calypso*, into his scientific dreamboat. Cousteau fitted a bulbous underwater nose to the ship, creating an observation chamber 3 metres (9.8 ft) below the waterline. The *Calypso* had a helicopter landing pad and a wet diving well amidships, so that divers could avoid waves in bad weather. It was equipped with diving saucers, underwater scooters and mini-submarines built to Cousteau's own design. This remarkable craft was a floating laboratory, research base, film studio, dive station and home for twenty-eight crew. For the next two years, Cousteau used it on an expedition that toured the oceans filming marine life, shipwrecks and other undersea wonders.

Cousteau's 1953 book about the expedition, *The Silent World*, sold five million copies and introduced a generation to the marvels of marine biology. Among its many highlights was an accurate prediction of the existence of echolocation in porpoises. Cousteau had seen how the creatures always navigated along the ideal route through the Strait of Gibraltar and concluded that the did so using a form of sonar.

The success of the *Calypso* expedition gave Cousteau the financial security he needed to dedicate his life to exploring and chronicling the secretive wonders of the world's oceans. Cousteau created over 120 documentaries and wrote more than fifty books.

Cousteau himself came across as an ever-curious, charismatic scientific adventurer and his remarkable underwater discoveries captivated the public. Cousteau's explorations in *Calypso* became hugely popular. His documentary television series *The Undersea World of Jacques Cousteau* ran from 1966 to 1976. It introduced audiences around the world not just to the marvels of the oceans but to science itself. Another documentary series, The *Cousteau Odyssey*, ran from 1977 to 1982.

The way he used television to increase the public understanding of science was genuinely novel. Some academics at the time criticised Cousteau's popularisation of scientific concepts but many aspects of his style and methods are now standard practice in documentary-making and broadcasting.

Jacques Cousteau was a pioneering environmentalist, using his films to draw attention to the damage humans were causing to the marine world. He was also a remarkable inventor and innovator. The Aqua-Lung allowed Cousteau and his team to spend more time underwater, to go further and to find more interesting sights. Images of these were captured with underwater cameras that Cousteau himself designed. These included the *Calypso* 35 mm underwater film camera, which was later produced and developed by manufacturers Nikon as a popular series of underwater cameras. Cousteau co-designed the 'Diving Saucer', which could carry two people to depths of up to 400 metres (1,300 ft) and was ideal for exploring the ocean floor.

Cousteau even experimented with living underwater. In 1962, he built a submarine habitat, 'Conshelf', off the coast of Sudan. Here, six 'oceanauts' lived for a full month 10 m (33 ft) beneath the waves of the Red Sea. Between dives, the oceanauts ate and slept in the capsule and breathed a special mixture of oxygen and helium. His experiments with underwater living helped NASA's astronaut training programmes.

Jacques Cousteau died in 1997 at the age of 87. The Cousteau Society, which he founded in 1973, today has more than 50,000 members worldwide and continues the unique explorations of ecosystems, which have helped millions of people understand and appreciate the fragility of life on Earth.

❛ When one man, for whatever reason, has the opportunity to lead an extraordinary life, he has no right to keep it to himself. ❜

Jacques Cousteau

HUNTING
THE MAN-EATER

JIM CORBETT AND THE HUNT FOR THE MAN-EATING
LEOPARD OF RUDRAPRAYAG

*"The word 'Terror' is so generally and universally
used in connection with everyday trivial matters
that it is apt to fail to convey, when intended to do
so, its real meaning."*

Jim Corbett

In the summer of 1926, the people of a remote district in northern India were living in a state of fear. Nightfall brought an unstoppable terror. For eight years, householders in the Garhwal region had bolted their doors and shuttered their windows, never venturing outside once the sun had fallen. Shepherds and goatherds who could not get indoors enclosed their camps in a makeshift circle of protective thornbushes. Travellers on their way to the Hindu shrines at Kedarnath and Badrinath huddled together in pilgrim shelters, listening for any sign of an impending attack.

❛ No curfew order has ever been more strictly enforced, and more implicitly obeyed, than the curfew imposed by the man-eating leopard of Rudraprayag. ❜

Jim Corbett

Their assailant was a rogue leopard which hunted and killed more than 100 victims in the foothills of the Himalayas over an eight-year period. All attempts to curtail the killing proved unsuccessful and the creature's notoriety grew with each attack. As the death toll rose, the British Government came under increasing pressure to help the citizens in the far-off corner of the Empire. Questions were asked in the House of Commons. The Government was called upon to act. A 10,000 rupee bounty was placed on the leopard's head, attracting hunters from around the world. The elite Gurkha regiment were sent in. Ultimately, it fell to the legendary hunter Jim Corbett to track down and kill the big cat. His sustained pursuit of the Leopard of Rudraprayag became one of the most famous of all hunting expeditions.

The Leopard of Rudraprayag was not the first man-eater to terrorize a community on the subcontinent. A rogue male in remote Amora District was held responsible for around 450 deaths between 1907 and 1910. Another was claimed to have killed nearly 100 people over a three-year spell in the countryside north of Nagpur before being shot by a goatherd in 1860. In 1902, a forestry manager shot

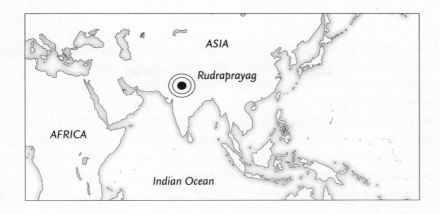

and killed a leopard which he claimed had been responsible for more than thirty fatalities in the Murhel Valley.

Events in the Garhwal were to gain a far greater notoriety than any of these episodes. Improvements in global communication, combined with the staggering details of some of the attacks and the leopard's ability to evade all attempts at capture, made for lurid headlines around the world.

The killing spree may have been the unwitting result of an influenza epidemic which struck India in 1918. The disease claimed between 14 and 17 million lives — around five per cent of the country's population. The sheer scale of death made it impossible for the Hindu custom of cremation to be observed in every case and many bodies were abandoned in isolated gullies and ravines. It was widely accepted that the Leopard of Rudraprayag developed a taste for human flesh in these gruesome stockpiles.

The leopard's first live victim was taken in June 1918 from the village of Benji and the creature swiftly became a seemingly unstoppable force of nature. Pilgrims were snatched as they walked along the road; the leopard clawed through straw and mud walls to take victims from their homes; on one occasion a man smoking his pipe was taken, soundlessly, while his companion sat a couple of feet away in a fog of smoke.

On more than once occasion it appeared the leopard had been captured. Two British soldiers staked out a footbridge over the Alaknada River in the belief that the leopard used it to reach a nearby village. After two months, their vigil bore fruit when the leopard appeared and stalked his way across the rickety structure. Both men opened fire on the animal, which fled across the bridge and into the jungle. When they inspected the scene, they found fresh blood but an extended search found no trace of the killer. On another occasion the leopard was chased into a cavern near an isolated village. The local people created a makeshift blockade of thorn bushes and rocks to keep the leopard in place. For five days they waited for some sign of life from within the cave. Eventually, thinking the leopard must have evaded them once more, the stones and thorn bushes were pulled away only for the leopard to bolt from the cave and run past the onlooking villagers to safety.

It was into this atmosphere of fear and hopelessness that Colonel Jim Corbett arrived. He came to the Garhwal in the summer of 1925 in response to a written plea from William Ibbotson, the region's deputy commissioner, and he was to spend the next nine months locked in a battle of wits with the Leopard of Ruraprayag. Corbett was already a hunter of some renown: born in India in 1875, he had successfully hunted and killed man-eating leopards and tigers across the subcontinent for more than twenty years.

Corbett set out two conditions before commencing his work. He asked that all rewards for the leopard's capture or killing be withdrawn. Corbett regarded the hunting of the leopard as a life-saving obligation and did not approve of killing for sport or fortune. Secondly, he demanded that all other hunting in the area should stop — Corbett was just as wary of other, less experienced, marksmen as he was of a man-eating leopard.

Once his terms had been met, Corbett set out examining the leopard's hunting ground. It was exhausting work. There were recorded attacks across an area of 1,300 square kilometres (500 square miles) of hilly terrain in the thin Himalayan air. Corbett, sometimes accompanied by his friend Ibbotson, covered the ground to get a sense for the killer and its habits. Early attempts at capture ended in failure. Corbett left bait laced with heavy doses of poison. The leopard ate them but, incredibly, suffered no ill effects. On another occasion, he closed in on the killer after an exhausting track through heavy jungle, only for another leopard to scare his prey away.

In his account of the expedition, Corbett describes one occasion when he returned to his shelter after a fruitless night's search. On heading out the next morning he noticed a paw print overlaying his footsteps from the night before. The leopard had followed him home.

Corbett's quest ended on 2 May 1926. Months of careful tracking had revealed a pattern to the creature's attacks and he estimated the leopard would be on the hunt near the village of Golobrai. Corbett and Ibbotson set up a hide in the branches of a mango tree beside an open stretch of pathway and waited. On the tenth night of their treetop vigil, the leopard emerged below them. Corbett used a flashlight to get the leopard in his sights but the torch failed as he pulled the trigger and when the hunters reached the spot where the leopard had been, there was no sign of the animal. Some blood at the site indicated the bullet had found its target and the next morning Corbett tracked the animal to a spot nearby. It was dead. The hunt was over.

The notoriety of the Leopard of Rudraprayag and Corbett's successful odyssey attracted headlines around the world. Corbett felt relief that the killing was over but also sympathy for the animal he had slain: 'His crime was against man, not against nature.'

The leopard, once caught, measured 2.3 m (7 ft 6 in) from nose to tail. It was an elderly male and showed signs of a bullet wound to the foot from its encounter with soldiers on the Alaknada Bridge in 1921. A festival to celebrate the killing of the Leopard of Rudraprayag takes place in the Garhwal on 2 May every year.

In his later years, Corbett used his fame and renown to champion the cause of India's big cats, calling for safe havens to be established for their protection. He was scornful of hunters who killed for sport and mindful of the need for help in ensuring there were fewer conflicts between man and animal. His efforts were not lost on the Indian people and in 1956 the country's first national park was renamed in his honour: the Jim Corbett National Park.

FLYING SOLO

AMELIA EARHART: THE TRANS-ATLANTIC HEROINE

"The stars seemed near enough to touch and never before have I seen so many. I always believed the lure of flying is the lure of beauty, but I was sure of it that night."

Amelia Earhart

The pilot did not know exactly where she was. Looking down at the rocky coastline, she knew where she *was not* — Paris, her intended destination. Nor was she sure how much longer she could stay awake; she had been flying for over fifteen hours without a break. Her plane was leaking fuel and it was now a matter of putting the machine down before it fell down. Thankfully the rocky shore gave way to green fields and she brought the plane down with a few bumps and a skid. As she dragged her weary bones from her cockpit, a man in muddy boots approached.

'Where am I?' the pilot asked him.

'In Gallagher's pasture,' the man replied in a Northern Irish accent. 'Have you come far?' he added.

Amelia Earhart smiled. 'From America,' she replied.

This was not Earhart's first flight across the Atlantic. She had successfully crossed four years previously, but on that trip she was a passenger in a plane piloted by Wilmer Stultz and Louis Gordan. Earhart herself remarked that she had been nothing more than a 'sack of potatoes'. However, Charles Lindberg's incredible solo trans-Atlantic flight of 1927 had ignited a media blaze around aviation. Even carrying a woman over the ocean was noteworthy

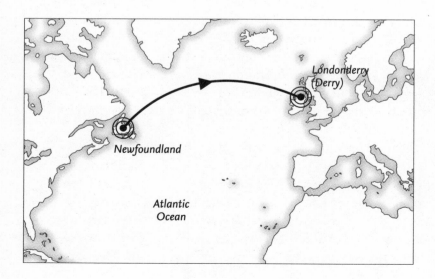

and Earhart became a celebrity. Shrewdly, she capitalized on her moment in the spotlight, writing a book, putting her name to a clothing label and becoming friends with the First Lady, Eleanor Roosevelt. Earhart was as famous and as glamorous as any Hollywood star and her renown helped her raise the money she needed to attempt to fly the Atlantic solo.

Amelia Earhart was an adventurous child who became obsessed with planes after she saw an air show aged 10. She started flying aged 23 and now, at 34, she wanted to go down in aviation history under her own power.

There were many deadly hazards in a solo trans-Atlantic flight. Engine failure was still a realistic possibility despite advances in reliability. Icing – when tiny cloud droplets impact on the leading edges of a plane's wings and tail and then freeze – was a major danger. The ice changes the airflow over the wing and tail, reducing the amount of lift being generated and risking an aerodynamic stall. There was also the risk of running into adverse weather. With no satellites to map the winds and spot potential storms, who knew what fiendish flurries lay lurking out in the middle of the great ocean? If any of these factors forced Earhart into making a splashdown there was no way she would survive.

There was also the sheer exhaustion of piloting a plane; of remaining focused on the controls and conditions in a cramped cockpit with constant vibration and the clattering roar of the great engine that was only inches away. But Amelia Earhart was prepared to endure it all if it meant she had a shot at the prize.

In the dawn light of 20 May 1932, Amelia Earhart piloted her scarlet Lockheed Vega down a runway in Newfoundland, banked to the east and set a course for Paris. It was five years to the day after Lindbergh had made his record-breaking crossing.

But the dangers began almost as soon as she had left land behind. Vicious winds slowed her progress and threatened to swat her from the sky. Her fuselage did indeed ice up. Her altimeter broke; she could no longer be sure of her altitude — an extremely dangerous situation for any pilot to be in. Fuel leaked into the cockpit and the engine exhaust spat flames.

However, she kept her cool and landed in the muddy field near Londonderry. She had flown 3,241 km (2,026 miles) in 15 hours and 18 minutes and had become only the second person and the first woman to fly the Atlantic solo. Americans fell in love all over again with the daring, modest and glamorous young pilot. Earhart was awarded a Distinguished Flying Cross by the U.S. Congress. the Cross of Knight of the Legion of Honour from the French Government and the Gold Medal of the National Geographic Society.

Over the next five years, Amelia Earhart broke several more records. One of the most notable was the first ever solo flight from Hawaii to California, in 1935. In July 1937 she was near the end of an incredible circumnavigation when she and her navigator Fred Noonan disappeared over the Pacific. Her body and plane were never found. That her daredevil nature and tremendous life force should be snuffed out was a profound shock to the public, but her achievements and her attitude lived on.

(The most difficult thing is the decision to act. The rest is merely tenacity. The fears are paper tigers. You can do anything you decide to do. You can act to change and control your life and the procedure. The process is its own reward.)

Amelia Earhart

Amelia Earhart was an inspiration to a whole generation of female aviators, including Beryl Markham. Gutsy and glamorous, Markham became the first woman to fly solo across the Atlantic from east to west in September 1936. This was a significant achievement because going west means heading into the prevailing Atlantic winds, which takes more fuel and time, and demands more endurance from the pilot. No woman before Markham had flown westward solo, but many had died in the attempt.

Charles Lindbergh took off from Long Island, New York, as a nobody and landed in Le Bourget Field, Paris, as one of the most famous men on the planet. It was 1927, and this twenty-five-year-old U.S. Air Mail pilot was the first person to make a solo flight across the Atlantic. He covered 5,800 km (3,600 miles) in his single-seat, single-engine monoplane, *Spirit of St. Louis*, in 33 hours 30 minutes. Lindbergh had never flown over water before.

> *Women must try to do things as men have tried. When they fail, their failure must be a challenge to others.*
>
> Amelia Earhart

INSIDE THE DEADLY CITY

René-August Caillié: The outsider who made it inside Timbuktu

*"It is always dangerous to offend the dignity
of the ignorant."*

René-August Caillié

Tangier, 7 September 1828. A bedraggled traveller staggers into the Moroccan port of Tangiers as night falls. His clothes are little better than rags. His weather-beaten skin bears the ravages of countless hours spent under the Saharan sun. His possessions are held in a sack slung over his back and on the reluctant shoulders of a truculent donkey. His progress is slow. In Arabic, he asks a passer-by how to reach the French Consul building. Following the directions, he slowly walks on to France's official representative in the city.

The unprepossessing figure is René-August Caillié. A Frenchman who has travelled to a destination that has beguiled European travellers for centuries. He has been to the fabled city of Timbuktu. More importantly, he has got out of the city alive. But only just.

Monsieur Delaporte, the French Consul to Tangier, is initially wary of the tattered visitor on his doorstep but over the next few days he comes to recognise Caillié as a man whose exploits have brought great honour and prestige to their motherland. The consul has work to do. His visitor is exhausted and suffering from a potentially fatal dose of scurvy. He must be escorted back to France at once but arranging his transport is not such a simple matter. Caillié has spent four years travelling through northwest Africa disguised as a Muslim — the only way he could safely pass through Timbuktu's city gates. If it was to be discovered that Caillié was an infidel his life would be in jeopardy.

M Delaporte writes to Edme-François Jomard of the Société de Géographie in Paris. Jomard, who took part in Napoleon's commission to Egypt, is initially sceptical about the ground-breaking claim of a relatively unknown explorer but Delaporte's correspondence convinces him that Caillié has visited Timbuktu and earned himself the Society's 10,000 franc reward for being the first European to do so.

'I have introduced to you the French traveller Caillié,' writes M Delaporte on 3 October 1828, 'who has crossed the burning deserts of Africa, and there contracted the scurvy, which has eaten into the bones of his palate. If God, who has been his protector as far as Tangier, should preserve his health, he will reach you two or three months' hence . . . He will present himself to you with authentic labours, with documents and materials taken on the spot, of which he will request you to superintend the compilation. Do not refuse your assistance. This traveller has deserved the prize for the journey to Tumbuctoo [sic] by the route of Senegal . . . he is also entitled to that for the most important discovery in geography, as he will prove by his work. They cannot be refused to him.'

As he waits under Delaporte's care for a French naval vessel to arrive from Cadiz and take him home, Caillié has time to finally reflect in peace on his four-year odyssey.

'After returning thanks to Almighty God,' he was to write later, 'I lay down upon a good bed, rejoicing in my escape from the society of men debased by ignorance and fanaticism. Though all my wants were relieved I found it impossible to close my eyes the whole night, so much was I agitated by the remembrance of the perils I had passed through . . . It would be difficult to describe my sensations on casting off for ever my Arab costume; I retraced in my memory all the privations and fatigues I had endured and the length of route I had traversed in a wild country, amidst a thousand dangers. I blessed God for my arrival in port; but I believed myself in a dream and asked if it was indeed true that I might soon be restored to my country or whether this enchanting hope was but a delusion.'

It was no delusion. Caillié was soon to return home to a hero's welcome in Paris and to fortune and renown. It was a remarkable reversal of fortune for a man whose early years had been inauspicious.

René-August Caillié was born into a poor family in Mauze, western France, in 1799. He became an orphan at age 11 and at 16 he joined a sailing vessel bound for Saint-Louis in French West Africa with a wanderlust inspired, according to Caillié's own account, by reading *The Adventures of Robinson Crusoe*.

Over the next nine years he worked as a hand on sailing trips to various outposts of the French Empire in the Caribbean and West Africa before landing once again in Saint-Louis in 1824 and resolving to undertake a life-changing expedition.

Few places in the world capture the same evocative image of remoteness and mystery quite like the West African city of Timbuktu. A seat of learning and a hub for trade for more than 1,000 years, Timbuktu remained an alluring mystery to Europeans. Speculation of the wealth hidden behind its remote walls had ran rife for centuries. In 1350, King Mansa Manu of Mali arrived in Cairo with so much gold that it depressed the (previously) rare metal's price on the Mediterranean for a decade.

One of the few accounts of Timbuktu available to European readers was given by the Moroccan-born explorer Leo Africanus who visited the city in the early sixteenth century. 'The inhabitants are very rich,' he wrote, 'especially the strangers who have settled in the country . . . But salt is in very short supply because it is carried here from Tegaza, some 805 km (500 miles) from Timbuktu. I happened to be in this city at a time when a load of salt sold for eighty ducats. The king has a rich treasure of coins and gold ingots.'

As a staunch Muslim stronghold, it was no place for unbelievers; any attempts by infidels to breach the town walls and learn the city's secrets were fiercely rebuffed. By the early nineteenth century, explorers were 'discovering' new frontiers around the globe. Timbuktu was in their sights.

Major Gordon Laing, a British Army officer, made it to Timbuktu in 1826 and stayed there for nearly a month, but he was murdered on the day he was due to leave.

By the time Major Laing had met his demise, Caillié, unaware of Laing's fate but keenly aware of the hostility a European visitor to Timbuktu would face, had spent two years immersing himself in the nomadic tribes of the Sahara. He learned Arabic, adopted local dressing customs, joined trading caravans across the desert and presented himself as an Egyptian merchant who had been captured by the French and was seeking to return home. He learned the laws and protocols of Islam during a spell with the Brakna Moors near the Senegal River.

Once Caillié was confident of presenting a convincing cover to the people of Timbuktu, he set out to reach the city itself. He headed east to the upper reaches of the Niger River when ill-fortune intervened. A serious case of scurvy forced Caillié to lay up in a remote village for five months. Upon recovery, he resumed the trail along the Niger River and, in July 1828, found a berth on a vessel shipping nuts to Timbuktu. After three years of preparation and travelling he had made it.

Caillié was somewhat underwhelmed by what he found, describing the settlement as 'a mass of ill-looking houses, built of earth'. There was no obvious wealth or any real evidence of the city's status as the 'Athens of the Sahara'. Caillié was also disappointed to learn that Major Laing had preceded him to the city. He recorded as many details as possible, without arousing suspicion, and even tried to find out what became of the unfortunate Laing and was shown a compass which, it was claimed, belonged to the British explorer.

After two weeks, acquaintances who had travelled with Caillié advised him to get out of the city. The Frenchman needed little convincing. He joined a trade caravan heading north across the desert wilderness and after a 3,200-km (2,000-mile) journey which tested his physical capabilities to the limit, Caillié finally found himself at the gates of the port of Tangier and the route to fame and riches.

Caillié was atypical of the explorers of his time. An outsider, he travelled alone and with little fanfare. His method of travelling, by adopting the mannerisms, clothing and language of his fellow journeymen, did not allow for extensive note taking. He was driven by a curiosity to see the world and had little interest in cataloguing the flora and fauna he encountered, or of capturing the customs and mannerisms of the peoples that he met. Unlike other explorers of the time who tended to romanticize or exaggerate the extent of their discoveries, Caillié's assessment of Timbuktu was downbeat and straightforward.

Upon collecting his 10,000 franc reward, René-August Caillié retired to the French countryside, where he married and became a father to two children. He was awarded the French Legion of Honour and a gold medal by the Societe de Geographie (along with Major Laing) for his efforts but he was not to enjoy the fruits of his exertions for long. In 1838, just ten years after his short stay in Timbuktu, René-August Caillié died at the age of 38.

❝ . . . and as soon as I could read and write, I was put to learn a trade, to which I soon took a dislike, owing to the reading of voyages and travels, which occupied all my leisure moments. The History of Robinson Crusoe, in particular, inflamed my young imagination: I was impatient to encounter adventures like him; nay, I already felt an ambition to signalize myself by some important discovery springing up in my heart. ❞

René-August Caillié

SAVE THE WHALE
ANTI-WHALING CAMPAIGN, GREENPEACE AND THE RAINBOW WARRIOR

"The whale wavered and towered motionless above us. I looked up past the daggered six-inch teeth into a massive eye, an eye the size of my fist, an eye that reflected back an intelligence, an eye that spoke wordlessly of compassion, an eye that communicated that this whale could discriminate and understood what we had tried to do...On that day, I knew emotionally and spiritually that my allegiance lay with the whale first and foremost over the interests of the humans that would kill them."

Paul Watson, early member of Greenpeace

GREAT EXPEDITIONS

The sea was a heaving black mass, topped with angry white wave
caps. A bruised sky threatened to unleash an angry storm. The
three activists tightened their lifejackets and, one by one, climbed
over the rail of the ship and onto the flimsy rope ladder that
bucked and bounced against the hull. Reaching the bottom, they
looked down to the tiny inflatable boat that bobbed like a cork in
the swell. In turn, they timed its movements, took a breath and
stepped from relative safety into the tiny craft that seemed a mere
plaything of the open ocean.
That was the easy part. Now they had to speed out into the path of
a mammoth factory ship and hope they did not get shot.

This was the modus operandi of Greenpeace's anti-whaling
missions, which they established on a remarkable expedition on
board their vessel *Rainbow Warrior*. This vessel was previously
known as the *Sir William Hardy*, a well-travelled fisheries trawler
that was put up for sale by the UK Government in 1977. Greenpeace
had been founded by Canadian environmentalists seven years
earlier, with the goal of protecting life on Earth in all its diversity.
Whaling was an activity that the group was determined to see
banned. Buying the ship to allowed them to set out on a unique
ocean-going expedition of disruption and protest.
Greenpeace spent four months refitting her as their flagship
Rainbow Warrior — a vessel capable of carrying protesters to
the scene of polluting and harmful activities. *Rainbow Warrior*
was relaunched in 1978 and immediately set out on a multi-
year venture which would feature many daring, dangerous and
headline-grabbing escapades around the world's oceans. She
would change the way the world looked at several vital causes
before her seven-year mission was brought to a tragic, murderous
end.

The first destination was the North Atlantic to confront Iceland's
whalers. For a month, *Rainbow Warrior* interfered with whaling

operations in Icelandic waters. There were no serious incidents but that would soon change.

The activists deliberately put themselves in harm's way by clambering down from the *Rainbow Warrior* into tiny, speedy Zodiac inflatable boats and then zooming out to meet the huge whaling factory ships. They then steered themselves in between the whaling vessel and the whales thus, in theory, preventing the whaling ship gunner from firing his harpoon cannon for fear of killing a human rather than a whale. However, gunners sometimes fired directly over the heads of the activists. Footage of such dramatic encounters began to make headline news in the early 1980s, forcing the Save the Whales movement into the public consciousness.

In June 1980, this tactic took them into a more serious predicament. A team of activists from *Rainbow Warrior* took on the Spanish whaling ship, *Ibsa III*. They used their inflatable boats to speed into their disruptive position and continued this activity for several hours before Spanish naval warships appeared on the horizon. These vessels chased the *Rainbow Warrior* and marines eventually boarded the craft, arrested the activists and confiscated the vessel.

The ship's captain was prosecuted and fined $142,000, but he refused to pay. The *Rainbow Warrior* was impounded in a military port and disabled by having the thrust block removed from its engine. The affair now took some twists that would not be out of place in a spy novel. The crew kept the hamstrung vessel ship-shape while at the same time conducting a clandestine hunt for a replacement thrust block. When one was located, it was smuggled into the country and sneaked past the harbour guards by activists pretending to be drunk. The block was fitted and *Rainbow Warrior* sneaked out of port one dark November night. Spanish vessels could not find her before she made it back to the safety of Jersey and a rapturous reception. The admiral of the Spanish Navy later resigned.

In 1982, Greenpeace sent in the *Rainbow Warrior* in to interfere with the activities of a Peruvian whaler. Activists climbed aboard the *Victoria 7* and chained themselves to the harpoon cannon. They remained there till the next day when they were cut out of their chains and arrested by Peruvian marines. The *Rainbow Warrior* was again impounded and the activists were threatened with charges of piracy. However, an outburst of protest from the Peruvian public swayed the government into releasing the activists and the *Rainbow Warrior* just a few days later.

In early 1985, *Rainbow Warrior* sailed to the Pacific to start a campaign against French nuclear bomb tests. In May, she relocated 300 residents from the Marshall Islands; their homeland had dangerously high levels of radioactivity from past American nuclear trials. She then travelled to New Zealand to monitor the impact of nuclear tests scheduled for the Moruroa Atoll in French Polynesia. Activists were planning to break through the French forces' cordon and observe the blasts at close quarters. Unknown to the *Rainbow Warrior* crew, a French intelligence agent had posed as a volunteer to infiltrate Greenpeace's Auckland office and had obtained detailed information about their anti-nuclear plans.

On the night of 10 July, French divers entered the dark waters Auckland harbour, swam to the *Rainbow Warrior* and attached two limpet mines to her hull. Shortly before midnight, the first mine exploded, tearing a hole in the hull and crippling the vessel. The crew were not injured and began to evacuate, but one crewmember, photographer Fernando Pereira, dashed below decks to get his camera. The second mine detonated ten minutes after the first, sinking the ship and drowning Pereira. The mission was codenamed 'Opération Satanique'.

France initially denied responsibility for the attack, and blamed terrorists. But two French agents were captured and the truth soon came out. They pleaded guilty to manslaughter in November 1985 and were sentenced to ten years' imprisonment. The scheduled

French nuclear tests were put on hold. The French Government eventually paid Greenpeace $8.16 million in reparations.

In 1986, the long-fought for moratorium on commercial whaling came into effect. Today, Greenpeace continues to act against whale hunts conducted in the name of science by Norway, Iceland, and Japan.

HEARTBREAK IN THE OUTBACK
BURKE AND WILLS IN AUSTRALIA

"Nothing now but the greatest good luck can now save any of us; and as for myself, I may live four or five days if the weather continues warm. My pulse are at forty-eight, and very weak, and my legs and arms are nearly skin and bone. I can only look out, like Mr Micawber, 'for something to turn up'; but starvation . . . is by no means very unpleasant, but for the weakness one feels, and the utter inability to move oneself."

Extract from the journal of William Wills, 26 June 1861

Robert O'Hara Burke and William John Wills traversed Australia from south to north. It was a staggering feat; the two men and their companions crossed 3,250 km (2,000 miles) of barren expanse on foot in deadly conditions, withstanding all manner of deprivations. They tramped through the coarse deserts of Australia's hard centre and the cloying mud of the tropical mangrove swamps of the continent's far north, then turned and retraced their steps. They overcame monsoon conditions, searing heat and bitter cold. It was an achievement founded on pure, unbending will. Their expedition has an iconic place in the history of the Australian state.

But the expedition of Burke and Wills is also a story of starvation, incompetence and bitter death. Burke's leadership was characterized by poor judgement and a succession of bad decisions which led to his demise in the Australian wilderness. Burke and Wills set off on their grim journey to answer a question that had intrigued and perplexed European settlers since they first made landfall in Australia; what lay beyond the frontier? The Australian interior was a vast, unknown land. Few settlers ventured far from the continent's coastal fringes. Those that headed inland

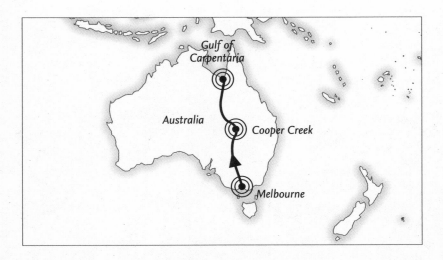

found little to encourage them onwards into the vast, scorched expanses of the undiscovered country.

In 1860, the Royal Society of Victoria funded an expedition into the great unknown. A party was selected to head north across the wilderness from Melbourne to the Gulf of Carpentaria, a journey of approximately 3,250 km (2,000 miles). Time was of the essence. In Adelaide, the Scottish explorer McDouall Stuart was also planning to traverse Australia from south to north.

The Society selected Burke, an Irish emigrant, to lead their party. It was an unorthodox choice. Burke was a police officer and former soldier who had little experience of exploration or wilderness survival skills. He was not helped by the Royal Society of Victoria's haphazard approach to planning the venture. The route from Cooper Creek – the final staging point for the trip north into the interior – and the Gulf of Carpentaria was agreed only one month before the journey's start. The mission's objectives were not agreed until after Burke and his party had left Melbourne; a messenger bearing instructions had to be dispatched to catch Burke en route.

While the expedition may have been somewhat lacking in detail and scrutiny there was no shortfall in financial support. The estimated 15,000 people who lined the Melbourne streets on 20 August 1860 to cheer the Victorian Exploring Expedition on its way witnessed an extravagantly funded venture; a contingent of nineteen men, twenty-six camels, twenty-three horses and six wagons which carried enough provisions to sustain the group for up to two years.

Ill-fortune and questionable decision-making blighted the expedition from its earliest stages. Early progress on the 'easiest' part of the journey was painfully slow. Burke declined a proposal to have heavier supplies shipped ahead to a staging point up the Murray-Darling River because the offer came from Captain Francis Cadell, a member of the Royal Society of Victoria who had opposed his appointment as expedition leader. One of the wagons broke down before the expedition had left Melbourne.

It took the party nearly two months to travel the 756 km (470 miles) to Menindee on the Darling River. By comparison, the regular mail coach managed the journey in scarcely more than one week. At Menindee there was a further setback when George Landells, camel-master and the expedition's second-in-command, resigned after quarrelling with Burke. He was replaced by William Wills, a surveyor, with some bushcraft experience. A Menindee local named William Wright was promoted to third officer. It was to prove a poor choice.

Agitated by the expedition's sedate progress, Burke took a series of fateful decisions. He went with the advance party to Cooper Creek and awaited the arrival of the main group, led by William Wright. Anticipating the arrival of Wright's group did nothing to ease Burke's restlessness and when the wait reached its fifth week, he decided on a radical change of plan. A small, hand-picked group would leave the main party and strike out for the Gulf of Carpentaria. They would take three months' worth of provisions, six camels and a horse. The remaining advance party would wait for them at Cooper Creek, where they would be joined by Wright, bringing the rest of the supplies.

Burke left the men at Cooper Creek under the charge of William Brahe. He instructed them to wait there for three months then to head back to Menindee if Burke and his companions had failed to return. Burke expected that in the time it took his group to cross Australia and come back again, William Wright would have finally arrived at Cooper Creek with a full stock of supplies.

It was a reckless gamble; born of frustration, ill-conceived and poorly executed. Burke, Wills and two other men – Charles Gray and John King – set out from Cooper Creek on 16 December 1860, at the height of the summer heat. On the trek north the expedition benefitted from its first, perhaps only, piece of good fortune. Heavy rains had hit the Sturt Stony Desert, leaving plentiful water supplies, negating time-consuming searches for water. Their luck was to run out as their destination approached, however. Gray and King, and the camels, were labouring on the north country's hilly terrain. With just a few miles to go, Burke and Wills left their companions and battled on together for the final push to the coast. Salt marshes and thick mangrove swamps blocked their route to the sea at the Gulf of Carpentaria. The pair, running low on supplies, were forced to turn back. Before doing so they observed tidal changes in the swamps, confirming they had reached the northern coast.

The gruelling return journey was to prove Burke's plan for a three month journey had been hopelessly optimistic. It had taken nearly eight weeks to reach the coast. They were now in a grim race against time to return to Cooper Creek before, as per Burke's instructions, Brahe and his group left camp and headed back south. Their progress was hampered by stormy weather, fierce desert heat and depleting rations. The men were forced to slaughter their animals for food. Charles Gray, who had been suffering from dysentery, was caught stealing flour from the rations and beaten by Burke. His health deteriorated and he died on 17 April 1861. Burke, Wills and King spent several exhausting hours digging a grave for their companion before moving on.

Four days later the surviving three men and two bedraggled camels made it back to Cooper Creek and the cruellest of discoveries. Brahe had stayed at camp for an extra month in the hope that Burke's party would return, only to depart for Menindee a few hours earlier. The embers of the camp fire were still warm. In the time it had taken Burke and Wills to traverse the continent, William Wright had been unable to shepherd his support party and the bulk of the provisions the 645 km (400 miles) from Menindee to Cooper Creek. Brahe had held on for as long as he could. His food supplies were running out and several men were suffering from scurvy (four of the expedition party died of the disease. The lime juice which could have saved them had been earlier jettisoned to save on cargo). Brahe buried a case of food under a tree at the camp, carving instructions on its whereabouts into the bark, then headed south with his men and the rest of the expedition's supplies.

Burke, Wills and King were faced with an unappealing choice. Brahe's supplies gave them some sustenance but not enough provisions for the 645-km (400-mile) journey to Menindee. The nearest settlement was 240 km (150 miles) southwest at Mount Hopeless. Should they head south in Brahe's wake or take the shorter, uncharted route to Mount Hopeless? Wills and King proposed heading south after Brahe but Burke decided on Mount Hopeless. Although Burke had no way of knowing, it was to be yet another wrong decision.

On the road to Menindee, William Brahe had had a change of heart. On meeting William Wright's group on the trail, he decided to return to Cooper Creek and check for signs of Burke's party. Fifteen days after he departed camp, Brahe returned to find the scene exactly as he had left it. There was nothing to indicate that Burke, Wills and King had returned, or that they had set off towards Mount Hopeless. In fact, Burke had left a note explaining the decision to head for Mount Hopeless and buried it under the same tree where Brahe had left the supplies. However he failed to mark the tree to show he had been there and Brahe did not think to check the supplies he had left.

Burke, Wills and King staggered on. The men were in a terrible condition; clothed in rags, drinking brackish creek water and eating barely enough to ward off starvation. The Aboriginal people who lived near Cooper Creek took pity on the dying men and gave them fish and bread made from seeds. Their goodwill was lost, however, after an altercation with Burke ended with him shooting his pistol in their direction. The last people who could have helped the beleaguered group to survive disappeared into the outback.

The three men made little progress on their forlorn journey towards Mount Hopeless and retraced their steps towards the Cooper Creek camp once it was clear the 240-km (150-mile) walk was beyond them. Wills was the first to succumb. In his final letter he wrote: 'We have been unable to leave the creek. Both camels are dead and our provisions are done . . . we are trying to live the best we can . . . but find it hard work. Our clothes are going to pieces fast. Send provisions and clothes as soon as possible. W J Wills.'

Burke and King walked on but within days the expedition leader became too weak to continue. He died, propped against a tree and pistol in hand, with King in attendance.

King survived. He was discovered by a rescue party on 15 September 1861 — nearly five months after his return to Cooper Creek camp with Burke and Wills. The Aboriginal people whom Burke had scared off had returned and helped him to live in the wilderness. The bodies of Burke and Wills were recovered and taken to Melbourne where the two pioneers were given a state funeral. They had achieved the primary goal of the expedition and had become the first people to cross the vast Australian interior.

It is a great consolation, at least, in this position of ours, to know that we have done all we could, and that our deaths will rather be the result of the mismanagement of others than of any rash acts of our own. Had we come to grief elsewhere, we could only have blamed ourselves; but here we are, returned to Cooper Creek, where we had every reason to look for provisions and clothing; and yet we have to die of starvation, in spite of the explicit instructions given by Mr Burke, that the depot party should await our return . . .

Extract from the journal of William Wills, 21 June 1861

TRAVELS IN THE ORIENT
Marco Polo's journey to the fabled Xanadu

"Ascending mountain after mountain, you at length arrive at a point of the road, where you might suppose the surrounding summits to be the highest lands in the world. So great is the height of the mountains, that no birds are to be seen near their summits."

Marco Polo describing his journey across the Pamir mountains on the way to China.

Marco Polo was not the first westerner to travel to China — the first known named traveller was a Syrian, named Alopen, a Christian Nestorian missionary, whose presence in the Tang dynasty capital of Chang-an (now Xi'an) was recorded in an elaborate carved stone in AD 635. However, Marco Polo was the first European to travel to, from and widely around China (between 1271 and 1295), and to record his impressions.

Marco was born around 1254, almost certainly in Venice into a merchant family. He was brought up at a time when Venice was the European centre for trading with the Middle East and beyond: the best place to purchase exotic silks, fragrant spices, and much more besides. Six years after Marco's birth, his father, Niccolò, and his uncle, Maffeo, set off on a trading mission, initially to the western edges of the Mongol Empire on the river Volga. They then travelled to Bukhara (now in Uzbekistan), where they became trapped by a local civil war and left with a party of traders heading towards China, the best route of escape. Thus they arrived accidentally in Dadu (now Beijing), recently established by Kublai Khan, the grandson of Genghis Khan, and from where he ruled the newly conquered China.

After a year there, Kublai Khan sent them back to Europe as his ambassadors to the Pope with a letter requesting a hundred men 'of the Christian faith . . . learned in the seven arts and qualified to demonstrate that idols were of the devil'. He also requested some holy oil from the Church of the Holy Sepulchre in Jerusalem. Their return journey, which took three years, was greatly eased by the use of Kublai Khan's network of horses, lodgings and guides. They had travelled further east than any previous European travellers.

They waited two years before returning to China, this time with Niccolò's seventeen-year-old son, Marco. In 1271 they left Venice for Acre and then headed north to Laiazzo on the Mediterranean coast (now Yumurtalik in Turkey, close to the Syrian border).

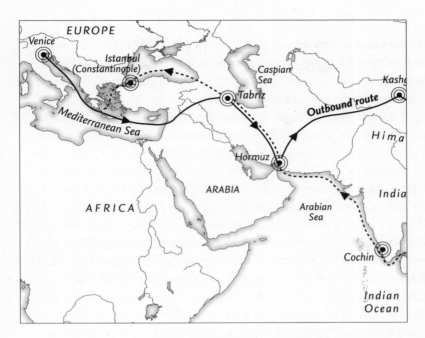

Map continued from above at same scale

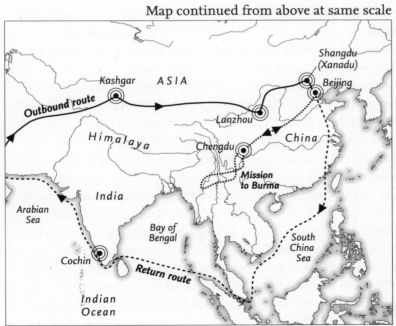

At the time it was one of the main trading ports at the western end of the Silk Road. They set off with a letter from Pope Gregory X and the holy oil from Jerusalem, but with just two Dominican monks, who quickly found reasons to turn back.

Their first destination was Hormuz, on The Gulf, initially with the thought of going by boat from there. To reach Hormuz, they travelled to Layas and past Mount Ararat, the reputed resting place of Noah's ark, but Polo noted: 'the ascent is impractical on account of the snow towards the summit, which never melts, but goes on increasing by each successive fall'.

He did hear accounts of a fountain of oil near Baku, and the popularity of its use in lamps ('people come from distant parts to procure it'). They travelled on south, through Mosul and Baghdad, 'the noblest and most extensive city to be found in this part of the world'.

They reached Hormuz, but, faced with ships 'of the worst kind, and a danger to navigation', they headed inland again, after a little trading, as Hormuz received a great variety of goods from India ('spices, drugs, precious stones, pearls, gold tissues, elephants' teeth'). Their route took them through deserts. For one desert crossing he recorded that 'during the first three days but little water is to be met with, and that little is impregnated with salt, green as grass, and so nauseous that none can use it as drink.' Eventually they arrived at Balkh, in northern Afghanistan, where they stayed for upwards of a year, recuperating from their gruelling trek.

Then began the journey across the Pamirs, the most arduous and isolated part of their journey. After nearly two months they made it to the great oasis town of Kashe (Kashgar), at the western end of the Taklimakan Desert, where Polo took a dislike to the locals, 'in truth, they are a covetous, sordid race, eating badly and drinking worse'. The Polos continued on the well-used Silk Road route along the southern edge of the Taklimakan Desert and then around the Gobi Desert.

Their destination was Shangdu, Kublai Khan's summer palace, now in Inner Mongolia, and known throughout the world as Xanadu, thanks to Coleridge's poem, 'Kubla Khan'. Forty days out from Shangdu, the party was met by a troop of soldiers and they were led ceremoniously into the presence of the Great Khan, prostrating themselves on the ground when they first meet him. He was disappointed that they had not returned with a hundred Christians, but was much pleased by the presence of Marco, and soon all three Polos were helping Kublai Khan's administration. Marco made many journeys through the new empire, travelling as far as Burma (Myanmar) and Vietnam, and reporting back the sights he saw to the emperor.

By 1291, with Kublai Khan now aged over 80, the Polos became concerned over what their status might be after his death, and they persuaded him to let them join a naval expedition that was to take a Chinese princess to Hormuz, as a new wife for the Khan's widowed great nephew, Arghun, the Mongol ruler of Persia. They sailed in a fleet of four-masted boats, stopping in Vietnam and on Sumatra, where unfavourable winds kept them for five months. From Sumatra they sailed to Ceylon (Sri Lanka) and then up the Indian coast, reaching Hormuz in 1293. By then Arghun had died (and the princess married his son), and when they reached Venice in 1295, via Trebizond and Constantinople, Kublai Khan had also died.

Three years after returning, Marco Polo was captured in a naval battle with the Genoese and was imprisoned, sharing a cell with Rustichello da Pisa, a writer of romances and expert on chivalry. Marco dictated his adventures to him, who recorded it in Franco-Italian. The resulting work is known as *Livre des Merveilles du Monde* ('Book of the Marvels of the World'), better known in English as *The Travels of Marco Polo* and in Italian, as *Il Milione*, a reflection on Marco's ability to exaggerate.

The book was remarkable for it provided the first detailed account of a country so different from any European experience. While he may have exaggerated, many of the places and habits he described were so alien to his readers that some conjectured that it was all fantasy. It is certainly puzzling that it contains no mention of the Great Wall or of drinking tea or of Chinese calligraphy or even of the compasses that would have been used on their return trip, but then, as death approached in 1324, he said that he had not told 'the half of what I saw'. His interests are clear, however, with his detailed descriptions of trade and transport, his delight in the imperial buildings, and the pleasure he gained from living in China, while he also recounted the use of paper money, the manufacture of porcelain, the burning of coal and the making of asbestos, all unknown in the west.

Marco Polo died in 1324 and is buried in an unmarked place outside the church of San Lorenzo in Venice.

ON HER OWN IN DARKEST AFRICA

MARY KINGSLEY: TRAVELS IN THE HEART OF AFRICA

"The grim, grand African forests are like a great library, in which, so far, I can do little more than look at the pictures, although I am now busily learning the alphabet of their language, so that I may some day read what these pictures mean."

Mary Kingsley

Mary Kingsley set out on her first expedition at the age of thirty. Tragically, just seven years later she was dead, falling victim to typhoid in a South African hospital, but the journeys she made in those seven years broke new ground.

She was an explorer in uncharted territory, making contact with tribes which were regarded as hostile to outsiders and discovering flora and fauna which were unknown to European science.

Her achievements established her as an explorer of some repute; the fact she was a woman travelling alone made her unique.

Mary Henrietta Kingsley was born in 1862. She came from a literary family. Her uncles Charles and Henry Kingsley were both novelists (Charles authored the popular fantasy *The Water Babies*) and her own father, George, was a keen writer and an insatiable collector of books. The family home in north London boasted a sizeable library. George Kingsley was a doctor with a hopeless case of wanderlust. He travelled round the globe as a medic on various overseas tours and chronicled his experiences in Australia, New Zealand and the islands of the south Pacific.

Mary's mother had been a servant in the Kingsley house. The couple were married four days before Mary was born and also had a son together. Kingsley's mother suffered from poor health for much of her life and, as the only daughter, Mary assumed many of the household responsibilities. She was schooled at home, albeit with the benefit of the household's copious supply of reading material, and when her father became ill, too, Mary dutifully tended to her parents. She was ambitious for more and yearned to see the wider world she had learned of from her father's own globe-trotting adventures. Kingsley's parents died within a few weeks of each other, in 1892. She was released from her familial obligations and came into an inheritance sizeable enough to fund her thirst for exploration.

Kingsley considered various destinations before settling on the west coast of Africa. Her preparation was meticulous. She ordered custom-made containers to store any interesting plant and animal specimens discovered on her travels. She studied navigation and began to correspond with British settlers on the West African coast; missionaries, traders, government officials and army clerics. The letters would offer some idea of the landscape she would face, the tribes she would meet and, crucially, the possessions which the indigenous peoples may wish to trade.

In August 1893, Mary Kingsley arrived on the coast of what is now Sierra Leone. She skirted the coast as far south as Angola before returning to England.

The expedition had been a success of sorts. She had collected several previously unknown specimens of tropical insects and fish for the British Museum; had traded trinkets with tribes who had had little contact with Europeans, and had successfully dealt with the privations of travel in Africa, all the while dressed in a manner befitting an unmarried English woman in her thirties. Amending her dress by, for example, swapping a voluminous skirt for gentlemen's trousers or making do without a corset was never a consideration for the upright Kingsley. A lady had, she said, 'no right to go about in Africa in things you would be ashamed to be seen in at home'.

To Kingsley this was not merely a matter of Victorian propriety. She believed the people she met in Africa were just as deserving the care and attention it took her to dress properly as the people she met in London.

Initial accounts of a solo woman's travels on the 'Dark Continent' earned Mary Kingsley some prominence but she had little interest in enjoying her new found status in Great Britain. She was already making plans for a second, more ambitious, expedition.

This time she would venture further from the coast in search of encounters with the indigenous people of West Africa. She was particularly intrigued by a mysterious tribe believed to inhabit the rainforests of what was then known as the French Congo: the Fang. Few Europeans had encountered the Fang but second-hand

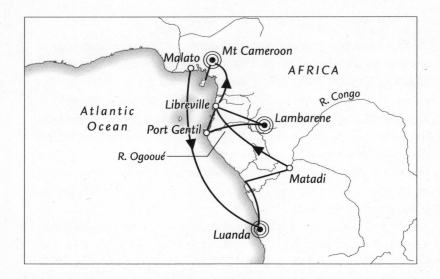

tales of a warlike tribe who engaged in cannibalistic feasts had reached the colonial outposts when Kingsley made her first visit to West Africa. She vowed to educate herself better on the peoples of the region, and the Fang in particular, when she returned.

Kingsley departed from Liverpool in December 1894 and arrived in what is now Gabon in early 1895. She retained the services of a handful of local guides and plunged forward into the jungle. The expedition headed up the Ogooué River into uncharted territory. Kingsley took the view that a missionary or cartographer might be received with hostility by local tribes but a trader, bringing objects of interest, would be able to pass through the country in peace. It was a theory on which she was willing to stake her life. The expedition struggled east against the river's currents. At one point a crocodile launched itself onto Kingsley's canoe — she sent the animal on its way with a paddle blow to the snout. On another occasion she took shelter behind a boulder during a thunderstorm. A bolt of lightning briefly illuminated the area and showed a full-grown leopard taking shelter behind the same rock, barely a metre away.

Her first encounter with the Fang came on the banks of a tributary of the Ogooué and involved no small measure of good fortune for Kingsley. A posse of weapon-wielding Fang charged down towards the explorer's canoe only to stop short when one of the local men recognised a member of Kingsley's party as a man he'd traded with on previous occasions. Introductions were made and Kingsley was able to stay.

The Fang belied their hostile nature and proved stimulating company. Kingsley was invited to stay in the hut of a village chief but was unable to sleep due to a pungent aroma coming from two bags hanging from the ceiling.
'Waking up I noticed the smell in the hut was violent . . . and it had an unmistakable organic origin,' she wrote. '. . . I investigated, and tracked it to those bags, so I took down the biggest one, and carefully noted exactly how the tie-tie had been put around its mouth, for these things are important and often mean a lot. I then shook its contents out in my hat, for fear of losing anything of value. They were a human hand, three big toes, four eyes, two ears, and other portions of the human frame. The hand was fresh, the others only so-so, and shriveled.'

Kingsley decided to sleep in her own tent instead.

The expedition moved on through the deep jungle, wading through fetid swamps and dense underbrush. For a traveller with no formal scientific training, Kingsley again proved adept at collecting unfamiliar species. She secured specimens of a new type of snake and several previously unknown river fish.

As she ventured back towards the coast Kingsley decided to take on one final, formidable challenge. At 4,040 metres (13,255 ft), Mount Cameroon was the highest peak in West Africa and a testing climb for even an experienced mountaineer. Kingsley had no mountaineering experience to speak of but did possess deep reserves of determination. One-by-one the guides accompanying her were forced to quit the ascent as heavy rains, dense forest and the thin air of high altitude took their toll. Kingsley alone made the summit – only the third person recorded to have done so – and certainly the first woman.

Almost a year after her departure, Mary Kingsley returned to Great Britain. Her journey had resulted in the discovery of several new species (to Europeans, at least) and her notes and observations on the people of West Africa helped to change perceptions of native African cultures, showing them to be far removed from the 'uncultured savages' of popular myth. She wrote two best-selling books and thousands attended public events to hear her stories. At the Liverpool Geographical Society, she sat and listened as a male member of the organization read extracts from one of her books. While it might have been possible for a lone female to befriend cannibal tribes in the unexplored African rainforest, addressing an audience at a gentlemen's club was clearly an unsuitable role for a woman.

A third venture to Africa was to be Mary Kingsley's last. She travelled to South Africa and volunteered to treat injured prisoners during the Boer War. The conditions in the military hospital were appalling and disease was rife. She contracted typhoid and died on 3 June 1900, aged thirty-seven. She was buried at sea in accordance with her wishes.

❛ It is merely that I have the power of bringing out in my fellow-creatures, white or black, their virtues, in a way honourable to them and fortunate for me. ❜

DESCENT TO THE CENTRE OF THE EARTH

Norbert Casteret: Into the abyss at Pierre Saint-Martin

"No man has gone before us in these depths, no one knows where we go nor what we see, nothing so strangely beautiful was ever presented to us, and spontaneously we ask each other the same question: are we not dreaming?"

Édouard-Alfred Martel, the 'father of modern speleology' and inspiration to Casteret

Pierre Saint-Martin, French Pyrenees, 3 August 1954 a man stands on a remote mountainside more than 1,800 metres (6,000 ft) up in the French Pyrenees. Before him is a depression about 30 metres (100 ft) deep. At the foot of the depression is a narrow gash of pitch blackness. It gives no indication of what lies below. A small cross is planted at the chasm's mouth. This simple marker is barely two years old but the harsh Pyrenean weather has already stripped away much of the painted inscription. The name 'Marcel Loubens' is just about legible on the weathered wood.

Loubens was a 29-year-old who, two years earlier, had travelled to this wind-beaten spot in the mountains between France and Spain on a mission to explore the labyrinth of caves in the heart of the mountain. He was the first of the expedition to journey down hundreds of metres into a world of complete darkness. He had exhausted himself over four days of scrambling, climbing and crawling in the cold stone and was returning to the surface by winch when a clip on his belt snapped. Loubens plunged helplessly back to the cave floor. The injuries were severe. His fellow cavers tried to assist but he fell into a coma. A doctor who was sent down fought desperately to save his patient, even managing to carry out a blood transfusion in the cramped confines of the deep, but there was nothing to be done. Marcel Loubens died on 13 August 1952.

Now, two years later, the man who had led that fatal expedition stood again at the mouth of the chasm. Norbert Casteret returned to the abyss with two burning ambitions. Firstly, he wanted to recover the body of Marcel Loubens so that his family could give him a Christian burial. Secondly, Casteret's in-built sense of adventure made him want to delve even deeper into the unknown blackness and unlock the mysteries of the cave that had claimed his comrade's life.

Part of the inscription which had been lost on Loubens' wooden cross stated, 'fallen in the battlefield of speleology'. It was a phrase which summed up Casteret's approach to underground

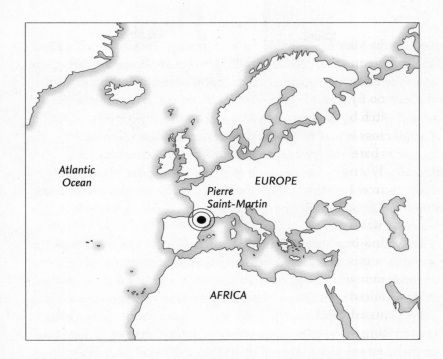

Atlantic
Ocean

EUROPE

Pierre
Saint-Martin

AFRICA

exploration. For three years he had fought in the trenches of the Western Front during the First World War and had seen the horrors of conflict. He did not lightly describe speleology – the study of underground spaces – as a 'battle'. In his younger years, Casteret had been reckless and headstrong, having risen to prominence within the caving community in 1923 during an exploration of the Grotte de Montespan. His route to that discovery had been bold, to say the least. He had descended to the banks of an underground lake and, feeling confident of finding an underwater route to further caverns, had plunged into the freezing water and forged ahead into the unknown. Casteret's gamble had paid off as he emerged onto dry land to discover something special; a series of prehistoric drawings etched on the stone walls of the cave.

Speleology proved to be a brutal pursuit. As the years progressed, Casteret's passion for this demanding branch of exploration was undimmed but the human cost was heavy. Loubens was one of several companions he was to lose underground. The confined spaces and constant risk of rockfall presented a constant threat. An injury which impeded the caver's mobility could make a return to the surface impossible and sending down the apparatus necessary to rescue an injured person was fraught with difficulty.

Casteret continued to go deeper and make new discoveries; each major breakthrough he regarded as a 'victory' against the cave. With his wife Elizabeth, he explored the caves at Cigalère to a depth of more than 400 metres (1,300 ft); with Marcel Loubens he went down into the Henne Morte (the 'Dead Woman') reaching a depth of 446 metres (1,460 ft).

The complex at Pierre Saint-Martin was on a different scale to anything that had gone before. From that narrow opening high on a Pyrenean ridge, a chasm reached down for several hundred metres. It then opened out into a complex labyrinth of large caverns and deep pools. A single cavern, now known as La Verna, is 250 metres (820 ft) in diameter and 194 metres (636 ft) high, making it one of the largest underground chambers on Earth. To speleologists such as Casteret and Loubens the lure of winning one more battle against the cave had been irresistible.

10 August 1954. Casteret and his five fellow cavers are exhausted, having found the remains of Marcel Loubens, placed them in a coffin, and readied it to be winched to the surface, hundreds of metres above them.

The stated objective of that August expedition had been to recover Marcel Loubens and take him home to his final resting place. But it had always been Casteret's intention to do battle once more with the caves. It was a matter of honour.

He wrote: 'We had been categorically forbidden to do any more exploring, and were supposed to limit our activities to recovering Loubens's body. From the start we had considered these instructions as an unjustifiable abuse of authority; we had signed no undertaking, and it was therefore with an easy conscience that I decided upon my own responsibility to ignore them . . . Pierre Saint-Martin was in a very real sense "ours" and to go home without trying to explore upstream would have been a miserable surrender of our rights.'

Casteret stayed with the coffin while three of his comrades headed off to explore. They came back with reports of further openings extending deep into the rock. It was agreed that Casteret and his companions would head out the next day.

The party set off at 8am. Progress was slow. They had to use ladders and climbing gear to negotiate steep cliff faces; they roped themselves together to traverse a fast-flowing underground river and had to squeeze through constrained spaces in the dark. Fierce gusts of wind convinced the men that they were heading towards an open space of significant proportions and, sure enough, after hours of toil they were to find what they were looking for.

Casteret wrote: ' . . . we reached the summit of a rise which we had to descend with the help of an electron ladder. This manoeuvre brought us out from the labyrinth into a colossal chamber, so vast and tortuous that we could make out neither its size nor its shape. It was perfectly stupendous, exceeding all conceivable dimensions, far transcending human architecture.'

Over the next few days Casteret's team continued exploring the natural wonders of Pierre Saint-Martin before returning to the surface with their fallen comrade Marcel Loubens. A priest who had descended held a Mass that remains the deepest in history.

The mission was to cement Norbert Casteret's place in history as one of the great underground explorers. The Pierre Saint-Martin cave system that he helped open up is now known as one of the largest on Earth, with over 435 km (270 miles) of explored tunnels and at least thirteen major underground rivers. Casteret continued to explore, and report vividly on his discoveries, for a further thirty-three years. His written works inspired a new generation of cavers and taught the world that, even as the surface of the planet was becoming increasingly familiar, a whole new avenue for exploration lay waiting in the world beneath us.

‘ *Lying in the absolute darkness, wrapped in our sleeping-bags under the frail and illusory shelter of our canvas tents, the consciousness of our weak and helpless state in the presence of this awful demonstration taught us an eloquent lesson of humility.* ’

A LONE VOICE IN THE WILDERNESS
JOHN MUIR: A THOUSAND MILES TO SAVE THE WILD PLACES

*"I only went out for a walk, and finally concluded
to stay out till sundown, for going out,
I found, was really going in."*

John Muir

The young man's hands worked the wood surely, carving out the curves and smoothing the grain. By the time he'd finished, another chunk of raw timber would be transformed into an elegant wagon wheel. Though he was good at it and it paid well, the young man did not like his job. His heart, soul and spirit yearned to be in the outdoors, which he had loved with a passion since childhood. His mind drifted as he worked, from the wood in his hands to his beloved trees, from whence that wood had come. And in a heartbeat it happened. In a single lost moment of concentration, the tool slipped. Its edge skipped free of the wood's surface. The man's weight carried him forwards. The sharp metal caught him in the eye. He fell to the ground, bloody and blind.

The trauma of the wound caused him to lose vision in both his eyes. For the next six weeks he sat in a darkened room, unsure if he would ever see his beloved woods and mountains again. Painfully slowly, the grey fog lifted and his sight returned. When it did, the young man took it as a sacred gift, and he vowed to 'be true to [himself]' and follow his dream of exploration and study of plants. He wrote, "This affliction has driven me to the sweet

fields. God has to nearly kill us sometimes, to teach us lessons.' The man's name was John Muir, and in 1867 he set out on an expedition that would change not only his own life but that of millions of Americans – and millions more further afield – far into the future.

John Muir was born in the small coastal town of Dunbar in Scotland before moving at the age of 11 to Wisconsin, America with his family in 1849. His father was staunchly religious and a harsh disciplinarian. This upbringing had a huge impact on Muir throughout his life. From an early age, however, he had a fascination for nature and a particular interest in the flora and fauna of the United States.

Whilst working for his father on the farm, he taught himself mathematics, geometry, literature and philosophy. After finishing his studies at university, he became an industrial inventor, but in March 1867, aged twenty-nine, he had his horrendous accident. Whilst laid up, he made plans to 'see as much of creation as he could'. In September 1867, Muir set out on a walk of 1,600 km (1,000 miles) from Kentucky to Florida.

To say that Muir's preparation before his huge undertaking was minimalist is an understatement: he packed little more than his compass and a few books, which included Paradise Lost, the poems of the Scottish poet Robert Burns, The Bible and a textbook on botany. He did not even work out a route, except to go by the 'wildest, leafiest, and least trodden way I could find'. His walk took him across the Cumberland Mountains and down through Georgia and Florida until he reached the Gulf of Mexico.

Muir did not carry a gun, he did not hunt and seemed to survive only on the bread he took with him and wild berries he came upon. This ability to go several days without eating properly was nothing new to Muir. He once said that as a child he was rarely given enough food to eat and lived in a perpetual state of hunger.

This was not a journey to discover new places and fill blanks on a map. Instead, it was a pilgrimage to unlock the shackles of his religious upbringing and to free his mind so that he could see the world in a new way. In the course of his walk, he began to think that people were in no way superior to any other living thing on the planet. Rather than being at the centre of nature, mankind was but one small piece of the giant jigsaw of creation. More importantly, this was nothing to fear or be despondent about.

After this, Muir headed west to California and, having arrived by boat in San Francisco in March 1868, famously asked a local carpenter what was the quickest way out of the chaotic city. The carpenter asked him where did he want to go. 'Anywhere that is wild' was Muir's reply. And with that, he started walking east towards the Sierra Nevada Mountains. His route took him through meadows of wild flowers and up into the high country for the first time.

Reaching Yosemite in June, he was awestruck by the grandeur of the valley — the thundering waterfalls, towering cliffs and ancient Sequoia trees. Muir instantly fell in love with the place. At the time, the 12 km (7.5 miles) or so of the main valley had some state protection but there was already a working community there when Muir arrived. He found work locally at a sawmill and built his own cabin. He explored as much of the valley and beyond as he could during his spare time. In time, he would become one of America's leading climbers, though his own safety was never at the top of his priority list. He climbed without any proper equipment and took risks all the time. During one night climb up the valley's largest waterfall, Yosemite Falls, which drop the equivalent height of the Eiffel Tower through a series cascades, he climbed behind the falls so he could view the moon through the cascade. Unfortunately, the wind direction changed, sending water crashing over him. Fortuitously, Muir managed to hold on and crawl out to safety. He also had a lucky escape whilst completing the first recorded ascent of Mount Ritter. Nearing the 4,006-m (13,143-ft) summit of the mountain, he froze with fear, unable to go on or climb down. He would later write:

> ❛ At length, after attaining an elevation of about 12,800 feet, I found myself at the foot of a sheer drop in the bed of the avalanche channel I was tracing, which seemed absolutely to bar further progress... After gaining a point about halfway to the top, I was suddenly brought to a dead stop, with arms outspread, clinging close to the face of the rock, unable to move hand or foot either up or down. My doom appeared fixed. I must fall. There would be a moment of bewilderment, and then a lifeless rumble down the one general precipice to the glacier below. ❜

Luckily, he did not fall. Muir clung on precariously for minutes until, in a moment of clarity that he ascribed to the visit of a guardian angel, his nerves settled, the strength returned to his muscles and he was able to pick a safe route upwards.

By now he was writing letters to his friend Jeanne Carr, who was the wife of his old university lecturer. He wrote to her and described in eloquent detail the scenery, wildlife and especially the giant Sequoia trees, some of which were thought to be as much as four thousand years old. Muir pointed out that if individual trees were of such an age, how old was the species? Millions of years most likely. He studied the rocks in the valley and was introduced to the idea of glaciation around this time.

The lure of the High Sierra grew stronger and by 1871, his trips into the wilderness were becoming longer as he hiked further into the mountains. That year he discovered an active glacier at the eastern end of the valley. As a result, he wrote an article for a newspaper in New York, describing how, over time, glaciers had sculpted Yosemite Valley, and not earthquakes as was previously thought.

Muir was now a man on a mission. He wanted to fundamentally change the way Americans viewed the wilderness. He wanted them to experience what he had, instead of just being consumed by work and unrelenting economic progress. So, in 1873, he moved to Oakland and started writing for a local newspaper and other publications where he slowly began to gain a considerable reputation. During this period, he solo-climbed the highest mountain in the contiguous United States, Mount Whitney, the first recorded ascent via the eastern route among many other firsts.

By 1875, he was writing for several periodicals with national circulations. One of the main threats at this time was to the Sequoia trees in the High Sierra. Due to their size, they were a lumbering company's dream. He bombarded Congress with letters demanding their protection. For the next four years, Muir continued to write, travel and explore, venturing as far north as Alaska. On one later trip there, he completed a 10-day solo-expedition with dog sleds across what is now called Muir Glacier. In 1880 he married the daughter of a successful fruit farmer — whom he'd met a few years before, having floated 400 km (250 miles) down the Merced and then San Joaquin rivers to Martinez near San Francisco on a raft he had constructed. He would later write to her to say:

❛ Only by going alone in silence, without baggage, can one truly get into the heart of the wilderness. All other travel is mere dust and hotels and baggage and chatter. ❜

They had children and Muir helped to manage the fruit farm in Martinez. During this decade he stopped writing. Although he loved his family, he yearned for the wilderness. In 1889, he was contacted by Robert Underwood Johnson, the editor of 'Century', a magazine with a readership of around 1 million. He wanted Muir to start writing again and to persuade him, the two of them returned to Yosemite to find that the valley was under siege. There were ploughed fields, a large pig farm and talk of attempts to divert some of the waterfalls. Muir was horrified and it was clear that state protection was not enough.

Sixteen years before, the world's first national park had been created at Yellowstone in Wyoming and Muir and Johnson wanted the same status for Yosemite. Muir's writing touched a chord with the public in a way that no other author's could at the time and in 1890 Yosemite, largely as a result of Muir's lobbying, was given national park status. Muir demanded that a total of 3,100 square kilometres (1,200 square miles) of land around the main valley should also be protected. Within one month, Congress passed the bill and it became law. Muir also requested protection for the giant Sequoias of the Sierra. Such was Muir's influence by now that President Benjamin Harrison responded personally and established 53,000 square kilometres (20,000 square miles) of land nationally as forest reserves. Around the same time, Sequoia National Park was born.

After this, Muir co-founded the Sierra Club and became lifetime president. Today, the Sierra Club has around 2.5 million members and is the most important grassroots environmental organization in America.

After the turn of the century, Theodore Roosevelt, seeking re-election for the presidency, visited Muir in Yosemite and the two of them spent three days camping in the valley, hiking and talking. Following his re-election in 1904, Roosevelt set aside well over 800,000 square kilometres (312,000 square miles) of National Parks across the nation as well as 18 National Monuments and more. Crucially, in 1905, the main valley in Yosemite was finally taken under federal control and included in the park.

Muir's goal was to make America see the wilderness, not as a resource that could be harvested, but as something to be treasured and preserved for future generations to enjoy. He died in 1914, but the Sierra Club went on to establish a series of new National Parks and a National Wilderness Preservation System. John Muir remains today an inspiration for environmental activists everywhere and is known as 'The Father of the National Park System' in America.

(Most people are 'on' the world, not in it – have no conscious sympathy or relationship to anything about them – undiffused, separate, and rigidly alone like marbles of polished stone, touching but separate.)

From Muir's journals

FAIR TRADE
ZHENG HE'S TREASURE VOYAGES

*"We have traversed more than one hundred
thousand li of immense water spaces and have
beheld in the ocean huge waves like mountains
rising sky-high, and we have set eyes on
barbarian regions far away . . . traversing
those savagewaves as if we were treading a
public thoroughfare."*

From a commemorative stele erected by Zheng He in 1433

Zheng He was the Chinese admiral who led seven voyages of Chinese treasure fleets over the period 1405–33. The fleets travelled as far as Malindi in Kenya, as well as visiting the Red Sea, The Gulf, southern India, Sri Lanka and south-east Asia. Together, the voyages comprised a cultural expedition unprecedented in its ambition. Despite the colossal scale of the enterprise, its incredible achievements were hidden from the wider world for centuries, as China isolated itself from the world shortly thereafter.

Around 1371, Ma He was born into an ethnic Hui Muslim family near Kunming in Yunnan province, an inland province in southwest China. It was a tumultuous time in Chinese history as the new Ming dynasty arose from the collapse of the Mongol Yuan dynasty. Ma's father was killed in 1381 when Yunnan, which had remained loyal to the Yuan dynasty, was conquered. Ma was captured, castrated and sent as a eunuch to the household of Zhu Di, Prince of Yan and son of the emperor.

Ma He grew into an imposing figure, though not the 2.1-m (7-ft) giant of some accounts and had a 'voice like a bell'. He rose in the service of the Prince and became known for his military and diplomatic skills. After the Prince's father, the Hongwu emperor, died in 1398, his nephew became the Jianwen emperor, to the Prince's disgust. He successfully overthrew him, becoming the Yongle emperor in 1402. Ma had become a close confidant of the emperor and, after winning a battle at Zhenglunba near Beijing, the emperor gave him the honorific title of Zheng He.

Yongle, as part of his plans to confirm the power of the Ming dynasty, wished to assert Chinese maritime dominance in what China regarded as the 'Western Oceans', and he chose Zheng He to lead this enterprise, which was truly magnificent in its scale. Zheng He was instructed to take imperial letters to the rulers of the countries of the Western Ocean along with gifts of porcelain, silks, gold and silver, and bring back tribute goods from the lands he visited.

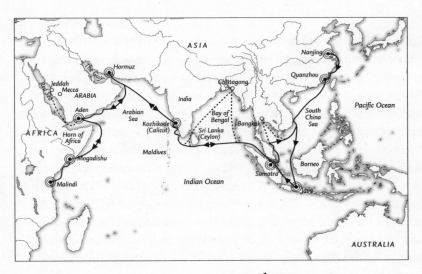

A silhouette of one of Zheng He's giant ships – of which he had 300 – relative to Christopher Columbus' Santa Maria.

His fleet, at its peak, consisted of around 300 vessels, manned by 28,000 people, not just sailors and navigators but soldiers, astrologers, interpreters, traders, doctors and many more professionals besides. The largest boats were the treasure boats and upwards of sixty of these massive vessels were built. They had nine masts, five or six decks, were over 122 m (400 ft) long and weighed at least 1,500 tonnes (Columbus's *Santa Maria* was about 26 m (85 ft) long and weighed around 100 tonnes). The design included watertight bulkheads in the hold so that damaged areas of the boat could be sealed off, not a feature of western naval architecture until the nineteenth century.

The first voyage commanded by Zheng He left Nanjing in the autumn of 1405 and returned in 1407. He sailed down the coast of China, making his first major port of call Vijaya, the main port of the Champa kingdom in southern Vietnam. From there he sailed on to Java, to Malacca (on the Malay peninsula), to Sri Lanka, sailing across the Bay of Bengal rather around the coast, and to

Calicut in South India. Some of his ships also visited the Nicobar and Andaman Islands. His activities were mostly diplomatic, exchanging gifts with rulers and allowing the merchants in his fleet to trade. The second voyage (1407–9), took a similar route and the main purpose was to attend the inauguration of a new king of Cochin at Calicut. The third voyage (1409–11) also covered similar ground, though this time he subdued a local ruler on Sri Lanka who opposed him, killing many of his supporters and bringing the king back to China. He also visited Siam. The fourth voyage (1413–5) extended the range of his journeys, for this time he reached Hormuz, on The Gulf and on the fifth voyage (1417–9) he reached the East African coast, travelling as far south as Malindi, now in Kenya. His sixth voyage (1421–3) covered a similar route.

The further west he went, the more exotic the gifts he brought back to the Yongle emperor. On his voyage from Hormuz he brought 'lions, leopards with gold spots and large western horses'. From Aden came a 'qilin [a mythical Chinese creature that brings good luck] of which the native name is culafa [giraffe], as well as the long-horned animal maha [oryx]', and the city of 'Mogadishu presented huafu lu [zebras] as well as lions. The country of Barawa [Somalia] presented camels which run one thousand li as well as camel-birds [ostriches]'. The regularly arriving treasure ships were, one can only assume, beginning to prey on the local rulers, whose gifts and homage became more extravagant as it was recorded that: 'They all vied in presenting the marvellous objects preserved in the mountains or hidden in the seas and the beautiful treasures buried in the sand or deposited on the shores.'
Zheng He continued to be a practising Muslim (and may have visited Mecca on one of his voyages). He also respected Tian Fei, the goddess and protector of sailors, who would have been honoured by many in his crews. While the fleet was waiting at Changle, in Fujian province, in 1433, Zheng He erected a commemorative stele giving thanks for Tian Fei and describing his voyages (as quoted in this account).

The Yongle Emperor died in 1424, and his successor, the Hongxi emperor, ordered that no further voyages should take place, believing that China had no need to look beyond its own borders. His rule was short, and his son, ruling as Xuande, allowed Zheng He to undertake a further voyage in 1431. It repeated the journey to Hormuz, and sections of the fleet sailed down the Somali coast while others reached the Maldives and Jeddah (to visit Mecca).

Zheng He died in 1433 as the fleet returned to Calicut and he was buried there or at sea. The main fleet then returned to China and no major voyages were undertaken by the Chinese thereafter. In the late 15th century, imperial administrators began to destroy records of the voyages, and Zheng He's exploits were forgotten until the late twentieth century.

Zheng He is now honoured in China and speculation of what more these voyages might have achieved has been extensive, suggesting that Chinese boats passed beyond the Cape of Good Hope reaching North and South America, finding the Strait of Magellan, crossing the Pacific and also reaching Australia. However, even without this speculation, Zheng He's voyages were a major maritime achievement but were not exploited in the ruthless way Europeans did later in the fifteenth century when they reached the places previously visited by Zheng He.

WITH A CAMEL AND A COMPASS

GERTRUDE BELL AND HER JOURNEY TO HA'IL

*"From a little rock above my tent I have spied out the land
and seen the towers and gardens of Hayyil [Ha'il]. . .
I feel as if I were on a sort of pilgrimage, visiting
sacred sites. And the more I see of this land the more
I realise what an achievement that journey was."*

Gertrude Bell's diary for 24 February 1914

Gertrude Bell was a traveller, mountaineer, archaeologist and Arabist. Her journey from Damascus across deserts to Ha'il, now in northern Saudi Arabia, won her the Royal Geographical Society's gold medal in 1918, while her work with the Arab Bureau from 1916 led to the creation of Iraq and her role as adviser to King Faisal I, its first ruler.

She was born in 1868 into a prosperous family in northeast England, whose fortune was based on family businesses in the iron and chemical industries. Always bright, she studied at Oxford University and gained a first in modern history after only two years of study. She then travelled widely and also became a notable mountaineer, achieving many successes between 1899 and 1904, including ascents of Mont Blanc and the Matterhorn.

It was the Arab world, however, that really drew her, ever since a visit to Persia in 1892. In 1900, she made the first of her desert journeys, visiting Petra, Palmyra and Baalbek, and spent much of the first decade of the twentieth century as an archaeologist in Anatolia and Mesopotamia. At the same time, she became well-informed on contemporary regional politics, and informally provided information on what she saw to the British government. After a spell in England in 1913, Gertrude returned to the Middle East in November, planning to make a journey into the Arabian Desert. She arrived in Beirut on 21 November, all her baggage going through customs without a check ('I need not have hidden the cartridges in my boots!') and by 25 November she was in Damascus. She ascertained that the desert area known as Najd was quiet and its tribes were at peace with each other. She was then able to take on an experienced guide and to buy seventeen suitable camels for a desert trip.

Accompanied only by her guide and camel riders, she set out on 16 December. The journey started in the rain and once into the desert the party suffered from the cold winter nights and early morning frosts. She quickly felt at home again in the desert: 'Already I have dropped back into the desert as if it were my own place; silence and solitude fall round you like an impenetrable veil.'

The journey progressed through the desert with the occasional exploration of ancient ruins. At one point they were attacked by a group of Druze shepherds, but their guns and possessions were returned after two Druze sheikhs recognized members of her party. In early January, they met Turkish officials who had been trying to stop her since she left Damascus, a situation she resolved by travelling to Amman and using her influence to allow her to carry on.

Soon the party was back in the featureless desert: 'for most of today there was nothing on which to take a bearing but my camel's ears which are not a good line'. By the middle of February, they had reached the Najd, an area of sand hills that would take over a week to cross. A furnace in summer, Gertrude knew that January was a good time to make the crossing: 'All the plants are greening and putting forth such flower as they know how to produce and our camels eat the whole day as they march. But the going is very heavy — up and down endless ridges of soft pale yellow sand.'

On 25 February, Gertrude rode into Ha'il. The Amir was away hunting and his uncle, who was left in charge, detained her in one of the summer palaces of the Amir. She spent much time with Turkiyyeh, a Circassian woman who had been given to the Amir's great uncle: 'under her dark purple cloak she was dressed in brilliant red and purple cotton robes and she wore ropes of rough pearls round her neck. And she is worth her weight in gold, as I have come to know.' After a number of fruitless negotiations, she finally was allowed to leave on 8 March for Baghdad. While at Ha'il she recorded and photographed daily life in the court and its harem: 'there was nothing but me myself which did not belong to medieval Asia.'

After finding out that it would not be safe to travel south, court officials managed to persuade her to travel west to meet the Amir. Her view that any meeting would be unlikely proved true and

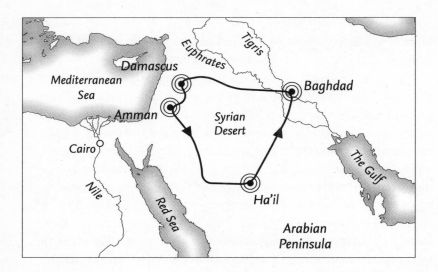

after a few days she headed to Najaf. The journey took the party through more desert until they reached Najaf. From there she drove to Baghdad, arriving on 29 March.

After making various visits around Baghdad, she went to Fallujah and met up with her camels and servants. As a small camel party, they headed off over the Syrian Desert to Damascus, travelling nine or ten hours a day in weather now much hotter than when they set off. Passing close to Palmyra, they reached Damascus on 1 May, as she described in her diary: 'And today through the vineyards and orchards to Damascus. I cannot tell you what they looked like in the bright morning to eyes weary with deserts — you must think of it, the rushing water and the deep green corn, the grey shade of olive trees and the rustle of sweet smelling chestnut leaves, the pale Damascene roses.'

After a brief rest and selling her camels, she headed for Beirut and Constantinople and was back in Britain before the end of the month. She had intended to write up her journey in a book but the First World War intervened. Her diaries and letters provide a valuable account of desert life before the collapse of the Ottoman empire, while the information and mapping she undertook gave useful informal intelligence for British military planners.

At the start of the First World War, Gertrude Bell worked for the Red Cross but by November 1915, she was back in Cairo to assist with British military intelligence. She became part of the Arab Bureau and in 1916 she was in Basra as assistant political officer with the Mesopotamian Expeditionary Force. She moved to Baghdad after its capture in 1917 and had special responsibility for contact with the local population. She played an important part in the discussions over the form of government for the new country of Iraq, and was an adviser to Faisal ibn Hussein, who became the first king of Iraq in 1921. She continued to play a central part in the development of the country (including the agreement of its borders with Jordan, Saudi Arabia and Turkey), but her influence waned after constitutional changes in 1924. She established the Antiquities Museum and became Director of Antiquities. She died in Baghdad in her sleep having taken an overdose of sleeping pills on the night of 11 July 1926.

TAKE WITHOUT ASKING

Francisco Pizarro: The raider who ended an empire

*"This city is the greatest and the finest ever seen in
this country or anywhere in the Indies . . .
We can assure your Majesty that it is so beautiful
and has such fine buildingsthat it would be
remarkable even in Spain."*

Francisco Pizarro

November 16 1532. An exalted figure in ceremonial regalia is carried on a brightly decorated litter into the centre of the Peruvian town of Cajamarca. He is resplendent in gold and jewels and flanked by thousands of subjects, who chant exhalations in his praise. The man is Atahualpa, the Inca Emperor. He has recently vanquished his brother after a vicious civil war and earned the right to succeed his father and rule the kingdom. En route to the ancient city of Cuzco to claim his crown, he has paused at Cajamarca to meet with a small party of Spanish explorers.

Atahualpa is not worried. He has left his army, many thousands strong, camped outside the city walls. His retinue is unarmed, save for *lassos* and ceremonial daggers. He settles in the town's central plaza and awaits an approach from the Spanish visitors.

A Spanish priest emerges from one of the stone buildings on the edge of the square. Friar Vincente de Valverde speaks to Atahualpa through an interpreter. He offers the emperor a book explaining the tenets of the Catholic faith. Atahualpa is dismissive and throws the book to the ground. Then all hell breaks loose.

Four small cannon, concealed at strategic points around the square, are brought forward and ignited, supported with musket fire and a charge of sword-wielding cavalry in heavy armour.

Thousands of Incas are trapped in the square at Cajamarca. Their leather armour is no defence against bullets, steel and cannon shot. They are butchered. Atahualpa is captured.

An estimated 5,000 people were slaughtered by a party of 160 conquistadors at Cajamarca on 16 November 1532. The killing started in the mid-afternoon and lasted until the daylight faded but in the short span of those brutal hours, an ancient empire was condemned to oblivion.

The architect of the destruction is a man of humble origins; the illegitimate son of a soldier, with no formal education to speak of. He has risen through the ranks of the conquistadors and is about to seize a haul of riches the like of which the world has never seen before. His name is Francisco Pizarro.

He was born in the Castilian city of Extremadura. Records vary as to the year of his birth but it is believed he would have been in his twenties when he made his first journey to the Americas as a soldier on a colonization expedition in 1502.

Over the next 20 years, Pizarro made a name for himself among the conquistadors — professional warriors from the Iberian peninsula who were to claim much of Central and South America for the Spanish crown.

It would be more accurate to describe the conquistadors as colonizers rather than explorers. Spanish settlers began establishing communities in the Caribbean in the early sixteenth century and spread inexorably west to the mainland of Central America.

❮ We Spaniards know a sickness of the heart that only gold can cure. ❯

Hernan Cortes

Hernan Cortes, a distant relation of Pizarro's from Extramadura, was a leading figure in the conquest of Mexico. The indigenous civilizations he encountered had no match for the modern weaponry available to the conquistadors. Through a combination of cunning alliances with local tribes and brute force, Cortes and his army were able to harvest the region's riches for Spain.

Pizarro himself was involved in the conquistador activity in Mexico and rose to prominence as the Spanish settlers extended their reach to the south. He was present at the foundation of what is now Panama City and made a prosperous life for himself as the settlement grew into a bustling port, but he wanted more. Pioneering travellers returned to Panama with tales of a land to the south where riches abounded among a cultured civilization. They called it Viru, or as it came to be known 'Peru'. Pizarro prepared himself for a new venture.

He found two partners to help lead an expedition to South America. Diego de Almagro was a fellow conquistador. His main

role would be to recruit men and ensure there was a solid chain of supplies and soldiers from Panama to the expedition team. Hernando de Luque was a priest but his position on the South American venture was more worldly. He acted as an agent to ensure money provided by investors was productively used.

The first expedition embarked in 1524. It was a disaster. The travellers found it impossible to reach the shore on the mudflats and mangrove swamps of the Colombian coast; their provisions ran low and they had the worst of violent exchanges with fractious tribes — de Almagro lost an eye to an arrow during one skirmish. The conquistadors limped home but Pizarro's resolve was unbowed. He petitioned the local authorities and received permission to launch a second expedition which left port in 1526.

For several months Pizarro skirted the western coast of South America. Conditions were difficult. They struggled to restock their dwindling provisions and the crew were ravaged by disease. Their first real progress came with the capture of a balsa craft carrying Inca sailors. The vessel contained enough gold, silver and jewels to suggest an advanced and wealthy civilisation lay nearby. Further examination of the coast revealed sizeable towns and evidence of comparatively advanced cultures. Pizarro wanted to stay and make for the mainland but stories of the mission's difficult progress had reached Panama and the governor ordered an end to the expedition. Francisco Pizarro would not hear of it.

He drew a line in the sand on a beach and said: 'There lies Peru with its riches. Here, Panama and its poverty. Choose, each man, what best becomes a brave Castilian. For my part, I go to the south.' His words had little effect. Only thirteen crewmates opted to stay, with the vast majority heading for home. Pizarro followed them back to Panama within months but his powers of persuasion were to prove more effective when he convinced King Charles of Spain to grant him permission for a third expedition to Peru.

Pizarro and his conquistadors arrived at the Inca mainland in May 1532. It quickly became clear they were entering a war zone. The paramount Inca ruler, Huayna Capac, had died after a bout of illness. His sons, Atahualpa and Huascar, fought for control of the kingdom. Atahualpa had won. Little did he know but it was to be a short-lived victory.

The Spanish party was almost laughably small in comparison to the fighting men at Atahualpa's disposal. Around 160 conquistadors, including sixty horsemen, headed south through Peru on the trail of Inca riches. They made contact with Atahualpa's men and arranged to hold discussions at Cajamarca, where Pizarro took his audacious, bloody gamble and ordered the slaughter.

The massacre at Cajamarca was a desperate gamble on Pizarro's part but there was some logic to his thinking. The conquistadors were hopelessly, ridiculously outnumbered by Atahualpa's troops. They could not win a direct confrontation or prolonged fighting.

The Incas were unfamiliar with the conquistador's weaponry or military style. Innovations such as fighting men on horseback were unknown to them. Atahualpa had ordered his troops to stay outside the city walls as a gesture of goodwill. An ambush could just work. And Pizarro's options were limited. The gamble paid off and, incredibly, not a single Spanish fighter was injured.

Atahualpa survived the carnage. He was kidnapped and held captive by Pizarro's troops. The Incas deduced that the conquistadors could be bought with precious metal and their ruler offered a deal. The 'king's ransom' was to be the stuff of a conquistador's dreams. Atahualpa showed his captors a room 6.7 m (22 ft) long and 5.2 m (17 ft) wide. In return for his freedom, he offered to fill the room with gold to the height of his raised arm, around 2.4 m (8 ft). He also offered to fill the room in a similar fashion, twice, with silver. Pizarro was stunned by the offer and he agreed to the deal.

It took eight months for the Incas to gather their haul. Pizarro and his men took Atahualpa at his word and made sure every space of the chamber was packed with treasure. Once the price had been met, the conquistadors melted down their haul — 15 tons of gold and silver.

With the riches received, Atahualpa had outlived his usefulness. He was charged with treason – accused of trying to source an army to rescue him – and garrotted after a brief trial.

❛ We have been displeased by the death of Atahualpa, since he was a monarch, and particularly as it was done in the name of justice. ❜

King Charles writing to Pizarro

The eight month delay had a silver lining for Pizarro. It allowed for more reinforcements to arrive from Panama. It also allowed the conquistadors to forge alliances with groups who had been on the losing side of the Inca civil war. The conquering party marched on Cuzco, the capital city of the leaderless Incas. Pizarro sent ahead a detachment of 40 warriors on horseback, led by his brother Juan, to quell any further resistance. They promptly overcame an Inca force which was waiting for them outside the city gates.

As much gold and silver as could be found was gathered up, melted down and shipped out. The Incas attempted to rally but their uprising was easily dealt with by Spanish troops. Their rule had ended.

It is perhaps fitting that the fortune which had been gained in such blood-soaked circumstances was also to be the root cause of the bitterness that followed for the victors. Pizarro had been the expedition leader and as such he claimed the lion's share of Atahualpa's treasure, much to the chagrin of his long-time partner Diego de Almagro. Pizarro set up a new colonial seat of government on the coast at Lima and left the ancient capital of Cuzco in the command of his brother Hector.

Disappointed with his share of the spoils, de Almagro set off on a new expedition in search of new civilisations to conquer. He journeyed south to Chile but found nothing to compare with the riches of Peru. He joined forces with Manco, a young Inca leader, and hatched a plan to seize control of Cuzco. The assault on Cuzco was a failure. Diego de Almagro was captured and executed by Hector Pizarro in 1538. The death was to be avenged. On 26 June 1541, a group of armed men, acting on orders from de Almagro's son, stormed Pizarro's home in Lima and stabbed the aging conquistador to death.

JOURNEY TO LHASA
ALEXANDRA DAVID-NÉEL'S TREK ACROSS THE HIMALAYAS

*"The first white woman has entered forbidden
Lhasa and shown the way. May others follow and
open with loving hearts the gates of the wonderland,
'for the good, for the welfare of many', as the
Buddhist Scriptures say."*

The last words in My Journey to Lhasa, *published in 1927*

Stories about Tibet began to circulate in the West in the seventeenth century. Visitors to China reported on what they had heard about the region and a few Christian missionaries had short-lived missions there. By the mid-nineteenth century, those few travellers who wished to visit found that the region was closed to them. Tibet unwittingly became part of the 'Great Game', the competition for influence in Central Asia played out between Russia and Great Britain. Around 1900, Russia appeared to be gaining influence in Lhasa and Britain responded by sending around 1,000 soldiers under the command of Colonel Francis Younghusband into Tibet in December 1903. With British assistance, Tibet still remained effectively sealed off from the outside world.

The influence of what was regarded in the West of the 'other-worldliness' of Tibet grew in the late nineteenth century and captivated the mind of Alexandra David-Néel. She was born in Paris in 1868, the daughter of Louis David, a French Protestant teacher, and his Belgian Catholic wife, Alexandrine. In 1873, the family moved to Belgium, where Alexandra was brought up. A free and unconventional spirit, as a teenager she escaped from an unloving family home to travel and to explore new areas of thinking; as she noted 'I dreamed of wild hills, immense deserted steppes and impassable landscapes of glaciers!'.

With her fine soprano voice she studied at the Royal Conservatory of Brussels and dabbled in many alternative ideologies. In the 1890s she travelled to India and Southeast Asia. She met Philippe Néel, a French engineer, in Tunis in 1900, when she was singing at the opera house there. They married in 1904. However, she was too independent to be happy in a conventional marriage and, while remaining close throughout their lives, they soon lived independently. In 1911, she left for India and did not return to Europe until 1925.

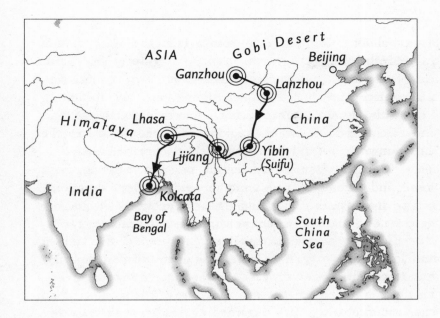

She studied at a Buddhist monastery in Sikkim, and in 1912 she met the Dalai Lama, who was living in exile in Kalimpong in north-eastern India. David-Néel was one of the first western women to meet the Dalai Lama and the meeting made a huge impression on her. She now focused on learning the Tibetan language and her studying became more intense and austere. She befriended a young monk Aphur Yongden, whom she would later adopt as her son. Together in 1916 they made a secret (and, as far as the British administration was concerned, illegal) trip into Tibet as far as Shigatse and met the Panchen Lama. On their return, she was expelled from Sikkim and India by the British.

She spent much of the following years in China, including three years at the Kumbum monastery in Qinghai province, close to Tibet. Her thoughts moved to making a secret journey with Yongden to Lhasa: 'what decided me to go to Lhasa was, above all, the absurd prohibition which closes Thibet [her preferred spelling]'.

They set off in autumn 1923 from a French mission station in Lijiang, in northwestern Yunnan province in China, close to Tibet. Initially accompanied by two coolies, they assured everyone that they were going on a plant-hunting expedition. However, within two days, they managed to lose their coolies, changed into disguises, and made for the Dokar Pass, the entrance into Tibet and the start of their journey to Lhasa.

They travelled disguised as beggar pilgrims, Yongden as a monk and David-Néel as his mother undertaking a devotional pilgrimage, a familiar Tibetan sight. As pilgrims they would not be expected to have possessions or travel with anyone else. David-Néel also had to disguise herself, wearing Tibetan clothes and hat and 'I rubbed a wet stick of Chinese ink on my own brown hair. I hung large earrings on my ears, and they altered my appearance. Finally I powdered my face with a mixture of cocoa and crushed charcoal, to obtain a dark complexion.' Hidden in their clothes they had compasses, two pistols and money belts.

Once they had made it over the Dokar Pass: 'a gust of wind welcomed us — the violent, icy kiss of the austere country whose severe charm has held me so long bewitched and to which I always return.'

David-Néel recorded their journey in her book *My Journey to Lhasa* (which is quoted from here). It contains accounts of being awoken by leopards, of enduring extreme cold and snow storms on mountain passes in winter, of fending off bandits by firing a pistol or invoking Buddhist curses, and of the fear that they would be unmasked and expelled. As the journey progressed they became more comfortable in their roles as pilgrims. They travelled during the day, and Yongden frequently performed rituals for farmers and others and was rewarded with accommodation and, sometimes, gifts.

In February 1924, after four months of walking, they approached Lhasa. 'The weather was clear, dry, and cold, the sky luminous. In the rosy light of the rising sun, we sighted the Potala, the huge palace of the lamaist ruler, still far away, yet already majestic and impressive ... As we advanced, the Potala grew larger and larger. Now we could discern the elegant outlines of its many golden roofs. They glittered in the blue sky, sparks seeming to spring from their sharp upturned corners, as if the whole castle, the glory of Thibet, had been crowned with flames.'

They spent two months in Lhasa, exploring temples, visiting the Potala (where her disguise almost failed as she had to remove her hat, revealing brown hair), and enjoyed the many festivals and celebrations linked to the Tibetan New Year. She wondered whether she should leave quietly, but felt she wanted people to know about her travels, so headed for Gyantse, a British outpost in southern Tibet. With relish, she went straight to the Resident's bungalow. As she recalled, 'The first gentleman who saw me and heard a Thibetan woman addressing him in English was dumbfounded ... When I said that I came from China, that for eight months I had wandered across unknown parts of Thibet, had spent two months at Lhasa and enjoyed in the Forbidden City all the New Year's festivities, no one could find a word to answer me.'

After her return to India, she made her way back to France, arriving in May 1925. She settled in the south of France, wrote books about her journey and about Tibetan Buddhism, which she also taught, supported by Yongden. They made a further eastern trip between 1936 and 1945 spending much of their time in Tibet. Yongden died in 1955 and she died, just short of 101, in 1969. Their ashes were then scattered in the Ganges.

FACE OF DEATH
THE FIRST SUCCESSFUL ASCENT OF THE NORTH FACE OF THE EIGER

"It was much worse than we ever thought and had anticipated. We underestimated the whole thing, the height, the difficulties, the snows, the storms . . ."

Heinrich Harrer

Shattered Pillar; Difficult Crack; Brittle Ledges; The White Spider; Death Bivouac — even to non-mountaineers, these names conjure up an aura of dread and danger. But to those who know the Eiger they generate an exceptional, almost primitive, feeling of fear and respect.

The Eiger is a 3,970-metre (13,020 ft) mountain in Switzerland. Its north wall is the largest in the Alps and the most notorious mountain face in the world. This is a vertical mile (1,800 metres, 5,900 ft) of crumbling limestone and sheer ice, whipped by howling winds, known as the Nordwand ('north wall'). Since 1935, at least sixty-four climbers have died on this face, earning it another nickname Mordwand — 'murder wall'.

The mountain's summit can be attained relatively easily along its sharp ridges and in 1858 it was climbed for the first time by Irishman Charles Barrington with local guides Christian Almer and Peter Bohren. But the north face is something else entirely. It faces due north and is therefore always in deep shadow. It is concave, so it embraces bad weather, trapping it in close to itself. And it gets more than its fair share of storms — its geographical location means it is the first major Alpine peak that any weather system coming in from the north west will meet. The Eiger is often shrouded in heavy cloud when the air is clear in the valley and has its own private storms.

In spring, the Eiger starts 'shedding', when regular avalanches of ice, snow and rock cascade down its walls as the mountain shrugs off its winter coat. These deadly cascades are a regular feature of summer afternoons, as the air warms. The whole face can seem to be in motion with thunderous waterfalls carrying murderous rocks and great shards of ice.

Humbled at its base is the resort town of Kleine Scheidegg. In the café terraces, skiers and day-trippers sit eating and drinking and watching climbers through telescopes as they inch upwards

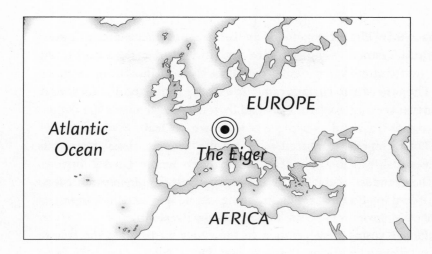

through the dangers. No other great mountain occupies such a public position.

⟨ I think the fact that every ledge on the Eiger is covered in the sediment of history makes it very special. It adds to that sense of awe. You know when you get to the Hinterstoisser Traverse what terrible scenes unfolded there. And that's bound to instil an anxiety, a nervousness. ⟩

Stephen Venables, mountaineer

The British dominated Alpinism in the nineteenth and early twentieth centuries. By the early 1930s, all the major peaks had been climbed in their classical style. As the British began turning their attention to the Himalayan peaks, young local, working-class men with nothing to lose and instant fame to gain began undertaking bold and breathless climbs that redefined what was possible. They turned their attention to the great north faces and particularly the greatest of them all — the Eiger.

Two German climbers were the first to try. At 2 am on 21 August 1935 they started their attempt. As no one had done this before they had no conception of how truly dangerous or difficult it was. After two days of climbing they had reached the top of the second of the great icefields on the face. But the next night a great thunderstorm engulfed them. On the fifth day, the cloud lifted, and the diners in the cafés could see them still battling upwards. Then the storm curtain came down once more and the men were never seen alive again. They had frozen to death on a ledge at 3,300 metres (10,800 ft) — a place now known as Death Bivouac.

This tragedy captured the public imagination; here was a real-life show of death and glory being played out on the grandest of stages. It was like an inverted colosseum; instead of looking down at the tragic spectacle, people were looking up at it. And, for climbers, the Eiger was now irresistible.

Twelve young men camped in the valley waiting for the face to come into condition the next year. On 21 July, a four-man team made a promising start, with Andreas Hinterstoisser making a traverse that would make the rest of the attempt on the Eiger possible. He climbed up onto an impassable slab and lowered himself to then pendulum across to the other side, securing a rope and enabling his companions to also cross. This traverse still bears his name today. But foul weather set in on the second day. They were showered by near constant ice and rock falls. They were seen descending on the third day. One climber had been severely injured. The party became stuck on the face when they could not re-cross the difficult Hinterstoisser Traverse. They were ultimately swept away by an avalanche, with only one man, Toni Kurz, surviving, dangling on a rope above an overhang. Incredibly, a mountain railway runs inside the Eiger, and it has viewing windows and doors cut into the rock face itself. Rescuers were able to exit these and pass ropes to Kurz. But, after a brutal night spent hanging in the open, his hands were too frozen to work the ropes. Kurz slowly froze to death.

In 1938, the British editor of the Alpine Journal, the oldest and most prestigious mountaineering journal in the world, wrote that the face was 'an obsession for the mentally deranged' and 'the most imbecile variant since mountaineering first began'.

Two young Austrians, Heinrich Harrer and his friend Fritz Kasparek, did not share that editor's opinion. After sitting their university finals in summer 1938, they headed to the Alps, and on 21 July they started their ascent. The attempt did not start well — Harrer forgot his crampons and the colossal wall began shedding ice and rock in earnest. Harrer later said, 'We had given a promise never to climb during the afternoon . . . In the afternoon it is hell on the second icefield, you hardly can avoid getting hit by a stone.' A day later, two German climbers, Anderl Heckmair and Ludwig Vörg started an ascent. They were more experienced, with better equipment that included the latest 12-point crampons. The Germans soon caught the Austrians; they decided to join their forces and roped together as a single group of four.

Avalanches and rock falls constantly rained down upon them. Every time this happened, they had to push themselves against the cliff face and hope for the best. When the falls stopped, they had to climb as quickly as possible before the deadly cascade began again. A storm hit on the third day, adding whipping wind and intense cold to the list of difficulties. Swirling spindrift made route-finding extremely difficult.
The four men were on the White Spider, a series of snow-filled cracks running out from a steep ice-field on the upper face, when a serious avalanche hit them. Harrer later said, 'Kasparek shouted at me, "an avalanche is coming!". And so I just pressed my body to the ice-slope and just had time to push my rucksack above my head, and that saved my life.' Somehow all four managed to cling on. But a final danger awaited them.

The prize was right in front of them. The four men were in the exit cracks that would bring them out at the very top of the face. But then Heckmair, who was the most experienced climber on the team, and who had led the most difficult pitches in the ascent, suddenly slipped. He dropped straight down and would have kept going were it not for Ludwig Vörg who thrust his hands upward and caught his feet. Heckmair was coming straight down on top of Vörg, and a crampon point stabbed clean through his gloves and the flesh of his hand, sending blood flying and exposing muscle and sinew.

'I bore straight down on him in a lightning swift slide. Wiggerl [Ludwig Vörg] let the rope drop and caught me with his hands, and one of the points of my crampons went through his palm. The force with which I came down on Wiggerl knocked him out of his holds, but he, too, had been able to save himself and there we were, standing about 4 feet below our stance on steep ice without any footholds. Our Friends . . . hadn't even noticed anything had happened. If we hadn't checked our fall we would have hurled them out from the face with us in a wide arc.'

Vörg's bravery had saved the whole party from certain death. Soon after, at 4 pm on the 24th of July 1938, they hauled themselves up over the lip of the great wall and found themselves on the knife-edge summit. Elated, but utterly exhausted, they then descended a ridge through a raging blizzard.

Instant worldwide fame awaited them at the bottom. The north face of the Eiger – climbing's most deadly challenge – had been conquered.

THE SOLAR FLIGHT
THE QUEST TO FLY AROUND THE GLOBE WITHOUT FUEL

"A Jules Verne dream of today means the urge to explore the unknown and the force to do good, which must continue to inspire human beings. Take your time, be patient and determined, wrote my great grandfather Jules Verne, for everything great that has ever been achieved in the world, is the result of exaggerated ambitions. And it is this spirit that Bertrand Piccard symbolizes best in this project, which is ambitious but of universal benefit to mankind."

Jean Verne

Hawaii. Lush, welcoming islands that promise rest, warmth and a haven from the storms of the vast Pacific. But for Bertrand Piccard and André Borschberg it was a land of frustration and disappointment. Would their pioneering dream die here, in this wonderful place? Considering the difficulties they had already faced and the sacrifices they had made, that would be the bitterest of ironies.

Bertrand Piccard has an adventuring pedigree that no one on the planet can match. His father, Jacques Piccard, was on the first expedition that reached the deepest part of the world's oceans, the Mariana Trench. His grandfather, Auguste Piccard, was a record-breaking balloonist. Bertrand was born into a family that had the unique distinction of breaking world records for both the highest balloon flight and the deepest dive. Bertrand's first major adventure was to win the first transatlantic balloon race. He then launched the Breitling Orbiter project which, with Brian Jones, made the first non-stop, round-the-world balloon flight in 1999. In doing so it also set the record for the longest flight in the history of aviation, both in time and in distance.

In 2009, Piccard conceived a new and very simple expedition with fellow pilot André Borschberg: to fly around the world with no fuel. If they succeeded they would not only capture the public imagination with their daring and pioneering feat, they would make the wider point that clean technologies can accomplish incredible things. But to do so they would have to overcome technical, human and operational challenges that have never been faced before.

'The question now is not so much whether humans can go even further afield and populate other planets, but rather how to organize things so that life on Earth becomes more worthy of living.' (Auguste Piccard, 1931)

'The public has not yet woken up to the extent and seriousness of the problem of pollution.' (Jacques Piccard, 1972)

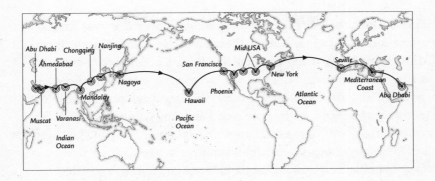

'Adventure in the 21st Century consists of applying human creativity and the pioneering spirit to developing a quality of life which present and future generations have a right to expect.' (Bertrand Piccard, 2004)

Like all great firsts, there were no benchmarks. No one had flown a solar aircraft across an ocean. The team had to create from scratch strategies that would keep a fuel-less plane flying across the Pacific for five consecutive days and nights.

They built a prototype, *Solar Impulse 1*, that could stay aloft for up to thirty-six hours. But their vision was for a plane of perpetual endurance. A second aircraft was completed in 2014, which had more solar cells and more powerful motors. *Solar Impulse 2* is a single-seat aircraft with a wingspan greater than that of a Boeing 747 — 72m (236 ft). Despite this huge span, the aircraft weighs only 2,300kg (5,100 lb), about the same as an unladen family car. The wing surfaces are packed with 17,248 solar cells that feed four batteries with electricity at a rate of 38.5 kW. These batteries power four electric engines of 13.5 kW each, which spin propellers endlessly. The plane gorges itself on sunlight during the day to fill its batteries, which it then uses to power its night flights. By using no fuel at all, *Solar Impulse 2* could in theory fly forever. The pilot might have different ideas.

The cockpit has a capacity of just 3.8 cubic metres, and is unpressurized and unheated. Temperatures inside range from -20°C to 35 °C. Piloting in such conditions is tough but there is no room for a co-pilot. This is a solo flight, even on a five-day mission. To rest, the pilot can lower his seat back just enough to lie down and take a 20-minute nap. He can raise one leg at a time to stretch and do yoga exercises with his upper body to stay alert and keep blood moving through their restricted limbs.

Solar Impulse 2 is a tortoise, not a hare: its top speed is a little over 100 km/h (62 mph), but its average cruise speed is around 75 km/h (46 mph). At night it flies more slowly to conserve power. Another useful tactic the pilots deploy is to gain height during daylight hours and use that as potential energy to gain more distance.

The expedition team for *Solar Impulse* 2 included meteorologists and mathematicians to calculate flight parameters, taking into account weather data, the availability of sunshine and air traffic restrictions.

There would be twelve stops on the route, to allow the pilots to swap over and to give the plane a chance to sit out any stormy weather. The first six legs went as planned. The plane flew from Abu Dhabi to Nanjing, in China, via Muscat in Oman, Ahmedabad and Varanasi in India, Mandalay in Myanmar and Chongqing in China. Leg 7 of the expedition was planned to go from Nanjing to Hawaii, a trip of 9,132 km (4,931 nautical miles). But appalling weather conditions forced the pilots to divert to Nagoya in Japan.

After a month long stop in Japan, the moment arrived for the team's second attempt to get to Hawaii. André Borschberg kissed his wife Yasemine adieu and climbed into the cockpit. *Solar Impulse* 2 eased down the runway and took off into the Japanese night on the 7,000 km journey. But the aircraft had only been in the air a few hours when engineers at expedition HQ in Monaco radioed Borschberg to tell him there were problems. The plane's batteries had been heavily insulated to protect them from the cold. But there was too much insulation; the batteries were overheating and would soon burn out.

When the technical team realized how serious the battery issues were, Borschberg had just sixty-five minutes before he reached the point of no return. The engineers recommended that he turn back to Japan. There was little that they could do if André decided to go on. The pilot felt sick to his stomach. He would ditch in the ocean if the aircraft lost power. He might die. But he also felt quietly determined. The weather was good. The plane would not have to be pushed. At the point of no return, André kept going.

After five days and nights aloft, Borschberg touched down in Hawaii on 2 July, 2016. This single mammoth leg was a triple world record breaker. It was the world's longest solar-powered flight both by time (117 hours, 52 minutes) and by distance (7,212 km; 4,481 miles). It was also the longest duration of a solo flight by any type of aircraft, ever.

However, the celebrations were short-lived. The plane's batteries were found to be damaged beyond use. They could not be repaired; new batteries would have to be built. There was no way that this could be done before the stormy winter season arrived. So the plane was wheeled into a hangar to hibernate.

Christmas came and went and the crew can hardly have felt festive. They finally got the new batteries installed in February 2016 and tried them out with a few test flights. But the northern hemisphere winter did not offer nearly enough daylight to keep them powered up for night flights. With the US mainland still a very long way off, Piccard and Borschberg could only keep on waiting, checking the weather and their own impatience.

Finally in April 2016, the forecasts looked good enough and the days were long enough for marathon expedition to be restarted. The plane taxied out onto the Hawaiian tarmac, trundled smoothly towards the east and lifted quietly into the air, heading out once more across the vast emptiness of the Pacific Ocean.

Solar Impulse 2 landed gently at Moffett Field, in Mountain View near San Francisco, on 23 April 2016. The Pacific Ocean was finally behind it. By early summer it had reached New York and then on 23 June it completed its Atlantic crossing, landing in Seville, Spain. The lofty dream of flying around the globe without fuel was almost complete.

ONE WAY TICKET
FERDINAND MAGELLAN'S CIRCUMNAVIGATION OF THE WORLD

"We found, by a miracle, a strait which we called the Cape of the Eleven Thousand Virgins, this strait is a hundred and ten leagues long, which are four hundred and forty miles, and almost as wide as less than half a league, and it issues in another sea, which is called the peaceful sea."

From Antonio Pigafetta's journal of the voyage

Ferdinand Magellan led the first successful circumnavigation of the globe. His fleet of five boats left Spain in 1519 with around 270 men, but returned in 1522 with only one boat and just eighteen of those who had departed. Magellan himself was killed in the Philippines in 1521. The journey confirmed that the Earth was a globe and established its size (larger than expected), as well as adding to Spain's colonial empire.

Ferdinand Magellan (in Portuguese Fernão de Magalhães and Spanish Fernando de Magallanes), was born into the Portuguese nobility in 1480, and he became a page to the Portuguese royal family. In 1505, he travelled to India to help install Francisco de Almeida as Viceroy at a time when Portugal was establishing land bases in support of the sea route to the Spice Islands. He helped secure Malacca, on the Malay peninsula, and by 1511 was thought to have sailed as far as the Moluccas, the centre of the spice trade. He was a man of firm opinions, and the following year had to return to Portugal having disobeyed orders. He next sailed to Morocco and, in a battle against the Moors at Azamor in 1513, suffered a leg wound that left him with a limp. He returned to Lisbon in hope of receiving a pension for his injury, instead of which Manuel I accused him of selling captured spoils of war back to the Moors. Magellan disputed the charge in vain, and in 1516 the king told him that his service to Portugal was no longer required.

He then moved to Spain, effectively switching sides in the contest for control of trade routes. He knew that the route east was dominated by the Portuguese, so, in 1518, he offered Charles I of Spain an expedition that would sail west to find a route around South America to reach China and the Spice Islands. The king agreed to support him. Five old ships, the *Trinidad, San Antonio, Concepión, Victoria* and *Santiago* were prepared and he put together a crew of Spaniards, Portuguese, and other assorted nationalities. Antonio Pigafetta, an Italian, wrote a journal of the whole voyage.

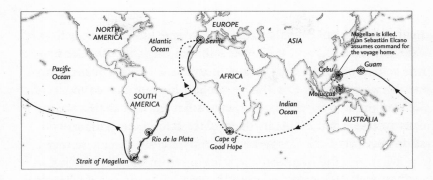

They left the port of Sanlúcar de Barrameda, near Cadiz, on 20 September 1519, initially heading to the Canaries. From there they sailed west and by the middle of December were near Rio de Janeiro. They carried on down the coast, and from the estuary of the River Plate onwards, they probed all major inlets in the hope of finding a channel through to the other side of South America. By the end of March 1520 they had reached San Julian, in the far south of Argentina, where they overwintered. Some of the captains and crews were not happy with the privations and rationing imposed by Magellan, and they mutinied. Magellan crushed it — executing one of his captains and abandoning another there when the fleet moved on in August. Before reaching the tip of South America, he lost the *Santiago* which was wrecked while undertaking some surveying.

After many false starts, on 21 October he reached the entry to what is now known as the Strait of Magellan between the South American mainland and Tierra del Fuego. As they began to sail through, the *San Antonio* deserted and returned back to the Atlantic. On 28 November 1520, the three remaining boats emerged from the strait into the Pacific. For three weeks or so, they sailed up the coast and then they headed northwest into the Pacific, which Magellan so named because 'we met with no storm'.

After leaving the Strait of Magellan they did not touch land for ninety-nine days until they reached Guam (apart from two small, uninhabited islands). This epic voyage was far longer than Magellan expected and the crews suffered mightily. For the first time scurvy was recorded: 'this misfortune which I will mention was the worst, it was that the upper and lower gums of most of our men grew so much that they could not eat, and in this way so many suffered, that nineteen died.' All fresh food was gone and the rations became fairly desperate: 'we only ate old biscuit reduced to powder, and full of grubs, and stinking from the dirt which the rats had made on it when eating the good biscuit, and we drank water that was yellow and stinking. We also ate the ox hides which were under the main-yard . . .'

Finally, they reached what is now Guam on 6 March 1521 and were able to restock. Then they sailed southwest to the Philippines, which Magellan claimed for Spain. Warmly welcomed by one local ruler on the island of Cebu, the crews recuperated from their crossing. To help this ruler, who had been converted to Christianity, Magellan agreed to subdue a rival who lived on the island of Mactan, but the attack, on 27 April 1521, did not go as planned: 'then the Indians threw themselves upon him [Magellan], and ran him through with lances and scimitars, and all the other arms which they had, so that they deprived of life our mirror, light, comfort, and true guide.'

There now remained only enough crew to man two boats, so the *Concepción* was scuttled and the *Victoria* and *Trinidad* sailed on to the Moluccas and began to load up with spices. The boats were now in a poor state. The *Trinidad* started to sail back across the Pacific, but soon returned, as it was no longer seaworthy, and its crew were captured by the Portuguese. Juan Sebastián Elcano, now captain of the *Victoria*, decided it would be safer to return westwards, and sailed from the Moluccas south of Java and directly across to the Cape of Good Hope, successfully avoiding Portuguese ships. Sailing back up the west coast of Africa, their need for supplies was so great that they had to stop at the Portuguese Cape Verde

Islands. The *Victoria* made a swift departure when they feared being taken by the Portuguese, leaving some crew behind.

They then made it back to Spain: 'At last, when it pleased Heaven, on Saturday the 6th of September of the year 1522, we entered the bay of San Lucar. . . From the day when we left this bay of San Lucar until our return thither, we reckoned that we had run more than fourteen thousand four hundred and sixty leagues, and we had completed going round the Earth from East to West.'
In his conclusion, Pigafetta summarized Magellan's achievements:

❛ *One of his principal virtues was constance in the most adverse fortune. In the midst of the sea he was able to endure hunger better than we. Most versed in nautical charts, he knew better than any other the true art of navigation, of which it is a certain proof that he knew by his genius, and his intrepidity, without anyone having given him the example, how to attempt the circuit of the globe, which he had almost completed.* ❜

SCIENTIFIC EXPLORATION IN THE AMERICAS
Alexander von Humboldt, the father of geography

*"People often say that I'm curious about too many things
at once: botany, astronomy, comparative anatomy.
But can you really forbid a man from harbouring
a desire to know and embrace everything that
surrounds him?"*

Alexander von Humboldt

As the eighteenth century drew to a close, the Old World and the New World were, for better or worse, more familiar with each other. The Age of Discovery had seen travellers from Europe sweep the globe. Some explorers were driven by a lust for wealth, or glory. Some were compelled to travel by an incurable wanderlust. Some were following the orders of their monarch; others were fleeing from persecution.

For the people who already lived in the New World, the boom in exploration signalled the sudden end of one way of life and the start of another. The newcomers brought previously unknown diseases, such as smallpox, resulting in catastrophic loss of life. Centuries-old civilizations and cultural practices were replaced. Treasures and natural resources were plundered; by the end of the sixteenth century silver imports from the Americas accounted for 20 per cent of Spain's total budget.

Alexander von Humboldt was a different kind of explorer. He was fascinated with the world around him and determined to find out how it worked. In 1799, he embarked on one of the greatest expeditions; a five year journey through the Americas.

He drew on seemingly endless reserves of curiosity and enthusiasm. He made a succession of important scientific discoveries; he carried out ground-breaking anthropological studies; he claimed genuinely significant feats in exploration. By any measure, the breadth of Humboldt's achievements were truly exceptional. He changed the way humankind looked at Planet Earth.

More than 100 animal species are named in his honour, from squid to skunk, along with more than 300 species of plant. His name has been given to mountain ranges, salt marshes, rivers, glaciers and national parks.

Other explorers measured their success in wealth and influence. The greatest reward for Humboldt was the attainment of knowledge itself and the way it informed his understanding of the world around him.

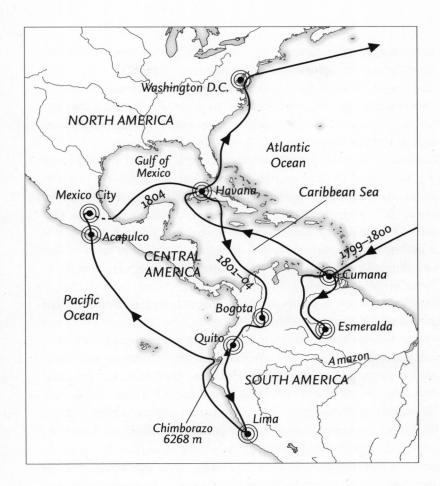

Alexander von Humboldt was born to a well-to-do family in Prussia in 1769. His father died when he was nine years old and, together with his brother Wilhelm, he was educated by private tutors under the supervision of his mother. It was a lonely and confining childhood.

His early academic career was unremarkable for a man whose exploits were to have such a profound impact on modern science. He studied briefly at the Universities of Frankfurt an der Oder and Gottingen but did not graduate from either. He spent two years at a recently formed School of Mining but, again, left before completing any formal qualification.

The conventional career path for a young man from Humboldt's background was clearly defined; a profession such as the law, accountancy or medicine would be seen as appropriate, or perhaps a career in the civil service.

Humboldt yearned for something different. He had a real passion for the natural world and also showed aptitude in the fields of mineralogy and geology while studying at Gottingen. He believed these skills could all be put to use on a scientific exploration. This belief was bolstered by discussions with Georg Forster, a naturalist who had served under Captain James Cook on his second voyage on the HMS *Resolution*, who encouraged young Humboldt to broaden his horizons.

Humboldt took a position as an inspector of mines with the Prussian Government, but all the while he continued to be a voracious learner, acquiring the skills he would need for a career in exploration. He studied foreign languages, astronomy, anatomy and geology. He purchased scientific instruments and received training in how to use and maintain them. He described his state of restless excitement in a letter to a friend: 'There is a drive in me that often makes me feel as if I am losing my mind.'

In 1796, Humboldt's mother died and he came into a considerable inheritance. He was now able to resign from his government post and fund his expedition.

It took three years, and the agreement of King Carlos II of Spain, for Humboldt to finally secure the equipment and permission required to visit the Spanish American territories. He set sail on board the ship *Pizarro* from La Coruna, Spain, on 15 June 1799.

Joining Humboldt on the expedition was Aime Bonpland a Frenchman who would oversee the expedition's botanical collections. Together the two men were to change the face of naturalism. They matched the dynamism of the best explorers with academic rigour. They pushed themselves to the limits of physical endurance without compromising the thoroughness of their note-taking. They had no orders to follow. Humboldt self-funded the entire venture. His only obligation was to his own spirit of discovery.

The explorers started as they meant go to on. An early stop in Tenerife saw Humboldt use his new equipment to take a longitudinal measurement for Santa Cruz harbour (it turned out that the existing measurement, taken by Captain Cook, was wrong) and scale Mt Tiede, the island's highest point, defining five different zones of vegetation as he went. This last discovery epitomized Humboldt's unorthodox approach. He was the first naturalist to classify plants by the climate in which they were found rather than the taxonomy of the species. It led him towards the theory that flora and fauna coexisted in distinct ecosystems and that species depended on each other to survive and grow. The expedition then headed west across the Atlantic and Humboldt, with Bonpland at his side, immersed himself in years of punishing exploration.
Landing in Venezuela, they traced the mighty Orinoco River to its source then pressed on into the waterways of the heavy jungle, along the Casiquiare River, until it met with tributaries of the Amazon itself. Bonpland and Humboldt had discovered a natural canal linking two of the continent's great river systems.

The explorers moved on, swapping the cloying heat and humidity for the cold and thin air of the Andes. They trekked along the mountain range from Bogota in Columbia to Trujillo in Peru, a distance of some 2,300 km (1,430 miles). They recorded everything and anything that interested them on the way from the colour of the soil to the shape of a leaf. The volcanic peak of Chimborazo, in Ecuador, was at the time thought to be the world's highest mountain. Humboldt decided to climb it.
Chimborazo would have presented a challenge to even the most experienced mountaineer. Humboldt was not an experienced mountaineer. He also insisted on taking much of his scientific equipment on the climb. The ascent was hair-raising. At some points the party had to crawl on all fours along crumbling,

wind-whipped passes flanked by sheer drops measured in hundreds of metres. At others they shuffled sideways along ledges just a few centimetres deep. The local porters abandoned their headstrong clients when the climb reached the snowline and heavy fog settled in. Going any further, they explained, would be reckless. Humboldt, Bonpland and two brave companions ventured on into the thin air.

At 5,500 m (18,000 ft), Humboldt recorded the last signs of vegetation in his notebook, a few strands of lichen on an exposed boulder. He also catalogued the effects of altitude sickness on the party — the first time the condition had been scrutinized in this way. The fog cleared and Chimborazo's summit unveiled itself. To the party's dismay, a deep crevasse, some 20 m (66 ft) across, blocked their route to the top. Disconsolately, Humboldt recorded the altitude — 5,917 m (19,413 ft). No human had ever stood so high on Earth before and it would be another 30 years before Humboldt's altitude record was surpassed.

The expedition moved on to Mexico, where Humboldt developed an interest in the indigenous Aztec and Inca peoples. He studied their languages and customs and sought out accounts of what life and been like in the time of these ancient civilizations. He was particularly interested in the effect of climate on agriculture and how these communities had developed before the arrival of European settlers.

In 1804, five years after leaving Spain on the *Pizarro*, Alexander von Humboldt was finally readying for a return to Europe. He did, however, make time to stop at Philadelphia and Washington D.C. where he had an audience with Thomas Jefferson, the President of the United States of America.

Humboldt's incredible journey ended at the French port of Bordeaux on 3 August 1804. Humboldt had undertaken his expedition because he wanted to understand how the world worked. In the Amazonian rainforests and the volcanic Andean peaks, and the high plains of Mexico, he found some of the answers he was looking for.

Humboldt noted similarities between the Old World and the New. The leaf structures of plants he found in the high Andes were reminiscent of those he had seen years earlier in the Swiss Alps; the grasslands of Peru resembled those of northern Europe; he discovered moss in Ecuador similar to a species that was common in the forests of his native Prussia. He also started to consider the impact of human activity on the natural world. He was the first person to recognize that intensive deforestation could have an impact on the climate.

Alexander von Humboldt moved to Paris and undertook the not-inconsiderable task of writing up his notes. The resulting works, stretching to 30 volumes, were to prove hugely influential on the generation of scientists that followed. Humboldt's work, wrote Charles Darwin, 'stirred up in me a burning zeal to add even the most humble contribution to the noble structure of Natural Science'.

He undertook one other expedition, across Russia in 1829, and returned to Prussia where he lectured at the University of Berlin, served as a counsellor to the royal court and started writing a treatise which would encompass his beliefs about the natural world and humankind's place within it. *Kosmos* stretched across five volumes which were linked by a theory that Humboldt had spent a lifetime considering. He saw the world as a single organism where the actions of one species had a cascading impact on others around it. 'Everything,' he said, 'is interaction and reciprocal.'

Kosmos was a success but the fifth volume was to be published posthumously. Alexander von Humboldt died, aged 89, on 6 May 1859.

> ❛ The most dangerous worldview is the worldview of those who have not viewed the world. ❜
>
> Alexander von Humboldt

RUNNING THE RAPIDS

JOHN WESLEY POWELL'S EXPLORATION DOWN THE COLORADO RIVER

"On my return from the first exploration of the canyons of Colorado, I found that our journey had been the theme of much newspaper writing. A story of disaster had been circulated, with many particulars of hardship and tragedy, so that it was currently believed throughout the United States that all the members of the party were lost save one. A good friend of mine had gathered a great number of obituary notices, and it was interesting and rather flattering to me to discover the high esteem in which I had been held . . . ."

John Wesley Powell, in his memoirs

The Colorado River is 2,330 km (1,450 miles) long, rising 3 km (2 miles) high in the Rockies and draining parts of seven US and two Mexican states on its way to the Gulf of California. It is a natural barrier *par excellence*. Sheer cliffs on both sides run for hundreds of kilometres forming a series of deep canyons, including the Grand Canyon, a mile-deep scar in the earth cut by the river over millions of years. There are also wild meanders, deadly rapids, waterfalls and whirlpools. In 1869, most of its length was still a total mystery; no white explorer had dared to pass down it in a boat. The Native Americans believed the gods had made it purposely impassable and anyone who tried to enter the mighty canyons would perish.

To John Wesley Powell it was simply irresistible.

Powell was an imposing character and charismatic leader. As a youth, he had spent many happy hours rafting on the Mississippi and exploring the mountains of Wisconsin. He had a meteoric rise in the Union army before a bullet shattered his right arm and forced its amputation at the elbow. After the Civil War, he worked as a geology professor and museum curator in Illinois. He also lectured on botany, physiology, zoology, geology, and mineralogy. Although he was a passionate student of the natural sciences, he had inherited his preacher father's skills of oratory. Powell found it easy to persuade backers to fund an expedition to explore the then unexplored Colorado River. He even persuaded the railroad company to give his team and their equipment free passage to their starting point in return for publicity.

Powell's ten-strong team was comprised of war veterans and hardy mountain men, and included his brother. The expedition had three large boats: *Maid of the Canyon*, *Kitty Clyde's Sister*, and *No Name*, which each carried over 1 tonne (2,200 lb) of food and supplies — enough to last them ten months. There was also a smaller fourth boat, the *Emma Dean*, which was under Powell's personal command. They were armed with rifles and had scientific equipment including two sextants, four chronometers, thermometers, compasses and several barometers. The barometers were needed to assess their altitude, an absolutely essential measurement for map-making.

They set off from Green River Station, Wyoming, on 24 May, 1869. Their route would take them down that river to join with the mighty Colorado, then on through five states to the confluence of the Colorado with the Virgin river, just east of modern day Las Vegas. But they had no real idea how long it would take to reach their destination; no one knew how many meanders the river had, or how deep the canyons were.

The expedition was only two weeks into its trip down the Green River when disaster struck. It was 9 June, they were cruising through a peaceful canyon when suddenly Powell noticed white water ahead. He pulled in to the shore and ordered the other pilots to follow, but the crew of the *No Name* missed his warning and floated on past. By the time they heard his frantic shouts it was too late — the current seized them and pulled them down a series of crashing rapids.

The three crew were thrown overboard into the maelstrom. When the boat smashed into a boulder and was momentarily pinned they managed to climb back on. But the current won out and plucked the boat from its rock, pulled it over another set of raging falls, and smashed it clean in two against a fist of boulders.

Horror-struck, Powell and the others scrabbled over the rocks to follow the *No Name* round the bend. At first, the three men were nowhere to be seen, and their colleagues feared the worst. Then, one by one, the men managed to haul themselves dripping onto the rocky bank. They had survived a near-drowning but many of the party's clothes, guns, personal possessions, and large amount of food were at the bottom of the river. They had also lost all their barometers.

Powell located the wreck the next day, a little downstream. Two men were able to rescue Powell's precious barometers, as well as some provisions and a 3 gallon (16 litre) keg of whiskey that had

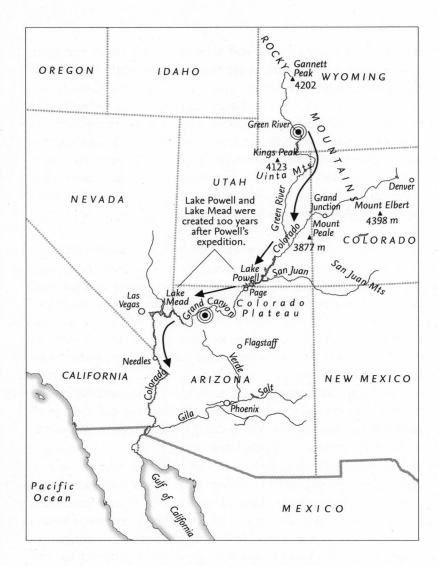

zbeen sneaked aboard without Powell knowing. Happily, he let the battered and weary men enjoy the contents of their illicit keg. Powell named the rapids Disaster Falls and the island that the boat washed up on Disaster Island.

These rapids were a typical example of one of the problems the men faced on the expedition. There was no level place to camp on either cliff-lined shore and they spent the night shivering and soaking wet from the spray that was constantly flung up by the crashing water. In the morning they found what footing they could on the bank and started a portage that lasted several days.

A week later, they were on a portage round yet more rapids when the *Maid of the Canyon* broke loose, was grabbed by the current and whisked away from them, out of sight. They knew they were now in serious trouble. However, on this occasion, fortune smiled on them. A little further on they found the vessel; she had been captured by an eddy and was calmly spinning in a pool by the river's edge.

On 28 June, the expedition reached the confluence with the Uinta River, in Utah. Here, the only Englishman in their party, Goodman, proclaimed that he had 'seen danger enough' and promptly departed.

Several weeks went by and the world at large had had no news or sighting of the party. So the press simply made up their own tales, recounting the evidence of a trapper who had seen all four boats plunge over a waterfall. Then an attention-seeking hoaxer named John Risdon claimed to be the sole survivor of the Powell expedition. Newspapers trumpeted his tale of woe across the nation. The party was assumed dead.

During the expedition Powell liked to ride high up on the *Emma Dean*'s prow, from where he would watch for white water and listen for the sound of falls. If he sensed danger, he would order the boat to the shore and scale the cliff – amputated arm be damned – to survey the peril ahead. They would then either continue or start the laborious process of a portage. On one occasion, though, he got stuck on the rock face, unable to move up or down. One man, Bradley, managed to clamber to a flat rock above Powell. But he could see that his leader's toe-holds were slipping. There was no time to get a rope. There was no branch nearby. Powell was beyond his reach. So the quick-thinking Bradley removed his trousers.

Powell wrote: 'I hug close to the rock, let go with my hand, seize the dangling legs, and with [Bradley's] assistance am enabled to gain the top.'

And so they fell into a strength-sapping rhythm of battling rapids and making back-breaking portages in 38°C (100°F) heat during the day, then shivering the night away in sodden clothing on narrow rock ledges.

> ❛ We are now ready to start on our way down the Great Unknown. Our boats, tied to a common stake, chafe each other as they are tossed by the fretful river… We have but a month's rations remaining. The flour has been resifted through the mosquito-net sieve; the spoiled bacon has been dried and the worst of it boiled… We have an unknown distance yet to run, an unknown river to explore. What falls there are, we know not; what rocks beset the channel, we know not; what walls rise over the river, we known not. Ah, well! we may conjecture many things. ❜
>
> Powell's diary, 13 August

Deep down at the base of the winding cliffs, rarely lit by the sun, it must have felt like they were passing through a great snake. The constant pounding of the current and the shortened rations strained the temper of some in the expedition party. Powell wrote that three men thought the group '…had better abandon the river here…' and they had '…determined to go no farther in the boats.' Powell asked the whole expedition whether they would stand by him. The rest agreed to continue but the trio departed in high dudgeon, taking rifles but refusing any rations. The groups would never see each other again.

At this point, Powell left the damaged *Emma Dean* behind. He also stopped making any attempt at scientific observation; for one thing, the instruments were shattered, but he knew that their focus must now be on simply surviving.

Finally, after all those months running the gauntlet of towering stone walls, the cliffs simply fell away. At both sides now was open country. They could see the sun rise from the horizon and set below it again. And there, where the river widened and slowed, three white men and a native American were fishing in the shallows. Except, when they introduced themselves, the four strangers admitted that the net they were hauling was not to catch fish, but to snag debris from the Powell expedition which for weeks had been assumed crashed to smithereens.

Fresh bread, blessed butter, cheese and ripe melons were thrust in the famished travellers' hands. And soon the telegraph wires were buzzing with the news. The Powell party was found. They had ridden 1500 km (900 miles) of wild virgin river in thirteen weeks. They had conquered the Colorado.

Six of the ten expedition members that started out from Green River Station finished the whole journey. Goodman survived and lived out his life in peace. The trio of mutineers were killed by natives. Powell enjoyed a hero's welcome but no sooner was he back in civilization than he began making plans for a second trip down the Colorado River, which he completed in 1871.

The Powell expedition produced the first detailed descriptions of large parts of the unexplored canyons of the Colorado Plateau. It also named many landmarks along the Green and Colorado rivers, including the Flaming Gorge, the Gates of Lodore, and Glen Canyon. It was Powell who first used the term 'Grand Canyon'; it had till then been called 'Big Canyon'.

FARTHEST NORTH
Fridtjof Nansen's crushing expedition in the Arctic

*"[Nansen made] almost as great an advance as has
been accomplished by all other voyages in the
nineteenth century put together."*

Edward Whymper, celebrated British mountaineer

Fridtjof Nansen was an explorer with a very bold plan. It was 1890 and no man had yet made it to the North Pole. Nansen proposed a mission to do just that, by sailing a boat into the pack ice and using its natural drift to journey north.

There was a scientific basis for this theory. In June 1881 the US Arctic exploration vessel *Jeannette* was crushed and sunk off the Siberian coast. Wreckage from this ship was later found on Greenland.

Henrik Mohn, a distinguished Norwegian meteorologist, predicted the existence of an ocean current that flowed east-to-west across the polar sea, possibly over the pole itself. If a ship could be built strong enough it could, in theory, enter the ice by Siberia and simply drift to Greenland via the pole.

Nansen kept this idea in the back of his mind for the next few years as he cut his adventuring teeth. He made a triumphant expedition to Greenland then began to develop a serious plan for a polar venture in earnest.

In February 1890 he presented his plan to the Norwegian Geographical Society. He needed a small, manoeuverable and immensely strong ship. It must be able to carry fuel and provisions for twelve men for five years. He would sail this ship through he Northeast Passage to where the *Jeannette* sank and then enter the ice. The vessel would then catch the ice's natural drift west towards the pole and beyond, eventually coming out into the sea between Greenland and Spitsbergen.

Many other experienced explorers laughed at him, including Adolphus Greely, Sir Allen Young and Sir Joseph Hooker.

But Nansen was driven, passionate and eloquent. He persuaded the Norwegian parliament to give him a grant. Several private investors also chipped in and the remaining balance came from a public appeal. Crazy idea or not, he was going to do it.

❛ *An illogical scheme of self-destruction* ❜

Veteran polar explorer Adolphus Greely on Nansen's plan

Nansen asked Norway's top shipbuilder, Colin Archer, to create the unique vessel that would take him to the pole. Archer rose to the challenge, building a squat, rounded ship that the ice could not grip. He used South American Greenheart, the hardest timber available. The hull was 24 and 28 inches (60–70 cm) thick, increasing to 48 inches (1.25 metres) at the bow. The ship was launched by Nansen's wife Eva at Archer's yard at Larvik, on 6 October 1892, and was named *Fram* ('Forward' in English).

Thousands of men applied to join the expedition, but only twelve could go. Competition for places was so intense that the dog-driving expert Hjalmar Johansen had to sign on as ship's stoker. Nansen appointed Otto Sverdrup from his Greenland expedition as captain of *Fram* his second-in-command.

Fram left Christiania (now Oslo) on 24 June 1893, cheered on by thousands of wellwishers, and headed north round the coast of Norway. After a final stop in Vardø, the expedition set out through the North-East Passage along the northern coast of Siberia.

These waters were largely uncharted and their progress through the treacherous fog and ice floes was slow. They also spent days hindered by 'dead water' where a layer of fresh water lying on top of heavier salt water creates enough friction to stop a boat.

Eventually, they passed Cape Chelyuskin the most northerly point of the Eurasian continental mass. Then, on 20 September, *Fram* reached the area where the *Jeannette* had been crushed. Nansen followed the pack ice northwards to 78°49'N, 132°53'E, before cutting the engines and raising the rudder.

It would be two and a half years before they were back on the open sea.

To Nansen's frustration, the ship zigzagged for the first few weeks, rather than moving towards the pole. On 19 November, *Fram* was actually further south than where she had entered the ice. It was only in January 1894 that she started to progress more steadily north. On 22 March they passed 80° of latitude. But the drift was slow: just a mile (1.6 km) a day. At this rate it would take them five years to get to the pole.

Nansen thought of a new plan — to leave the ship at latitude 83° with Hjalmar Johansen and drive a dog sledge to the pole. They would then make for the recently-discovered Franz Josef Land before crossing to Spitsbergen and picking up a ship home. The *Fram* would meanwhile continue its drift until it popped out of the ice in the North Atlantic.

Preparing the clothing and equipment for this plan took up the whole of the 1894–95 winter. The crew built kayaks, which the polar pair would need when they reached open water on the return journey. Nansen also had to master dog-driving, which he practised on the ice.

On 14 March 1895, with the ship's position at 84°4'N, above Greely's previous Farthest North record of 83°24, Nansen and Johansen set out. The men had 356 nautical miles (660 km; 410 miles) of ice between them and the top of the world, and fifty days' worth of provisions. That meant a daily trek of seven nautical miles (13 km; 8.1 miles).

At first they set a good pace, averaging nine nautical miles a day, (17 km; 10 miles). But the ice became rougher and their progress slowed. They were also marching against the same drift that had previously carried their ship, in effect pushing them two steps back for every three they took forward.

It was soon clear that they did not have enough food to make it to the pole and on to Franz Josef Land. Nansen's heart must have been breaking when, on 7 April, he saw that the way ahead was nothing but 'a veritable chaos of iceblocks stretching as far as the horizon'. That was the final straw. The men turned south. They were at 86°13.6'N, almost three degrees further north than any man had previously ventured.

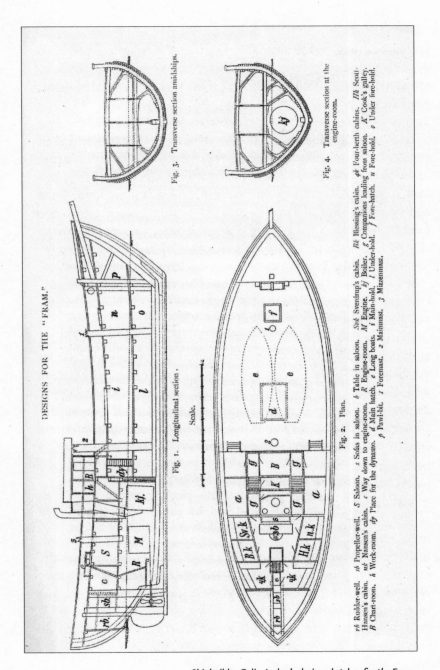

DESIGNS FOR THE "FRAM."

Fig. 1. Longitudinal section.

Scale.

Fig. 2. Plan.

Fig. 3. Transverse section amidships.

Fig. 4. Transverse section at the engine-room.

rb Rudder-well. *sh* Propeller-well. *S* Saloon. *s* Sofas in saloon. *Svk* Svedrup's cabin. *Bk* Blessing's cabin. *Hk* Scout-Hansen's cabin. *nk* Nansen's cabin. *c* Way down to engine-room. *R* Engine-room. *bj* Boiler. *fjk* Four-berth cabins. *K* Cook's galley. *B* Chart-room. *h* Work-room. *dy* Place for the dynamo. *d* Main hatch. *e* Long boats. *i* Main-hold. *l* Under-hold. *n* Fore-hold. *o* Under fore-hold. *g* Companions leading from saloon. *b* Table in saloon. *p* Pawl-bitt. *1* Foremast. *2* Mainmast. *3* Mizzenmast.

Shipbuilder Colin Archer's design sketches for the Fram.

For a week they moved smoothly south, but then on 13 April both of their watches stopped. This made it impossible for them to calculate their longitude and find their way accurately to Franz Josef Land.

Two weeks later they crossed the tracks of an Arctic fox, the first trace of a living creature other than their dogs that they had seen since leaving the *Fram*. Within the next few weeks they also came upon bear tracks, and started to see seals, gulls and whales. But they could not catch any and were running low on food. They had no choice but to start shooting their dogs, starting with the weakest. They then fed this animal to the others, allowing them to eke out their rations a little further.

At the end of May, Nansen calculated that they were only 50 nautical miles (93 km; 58 miles) from Cape Fligely, the northernmost known point of Franz Josef Land. But their luck turned again: the weather was getting warmer and the ice was breaking up.

On 22 June they camped on a stable ice floe, resting there for a month. The day after leaving this camp they spotted land, far in the distance. Whether this was Franz Josef Land or a new discovery they could not be sure, but it was their only hope. On 6 August they ran out of ice — they would have to trust their lives to the homemade kayaks. They shot the last of their dogs, lashed their two kayaks together and sailed for land.

❝ *At last the marvel has come to pass—land, land, and after we had almost given up our belief in it!* ❞

Nansen, in his diary, after sighting Franz Josef Land

Nansen soon identified Cape Felder, which lay on the western edge of Franz Josef Land. But time was against them, and towards the end of August the weather grew colder again. They would have to spend another winter in the frozen north. They found a sheltered cove where they built a hut from stones and moss. It would be their home for the next eight months.

Their food supplies were long gone, but they still had ammunition and now there was plenty of bear, walrus and seal around. Although they would not go hungry, the feeling of settling in to a long arctic winter in their tiny refuge must have been disheartening in the extreme. Christmas and New Year came and went, and the severe weather continued through the early months of 1896. Finally, on 19 May, they restarted their journey south.

In mid June their kayaks were attacked by a walrus. After scaring the beast off, Nansen and Johansen stopped to make repairs. Cursing their luck, Nansen was astonished to hear a dog barking and then, human voices. He rounded the headland and to his amazement saw a man approaching.

It was Frederick Jackson, the British explorer who was leading an expedition to Franz Josef Land. Jackson was equally dumbfounded and it was some moments before he asked: 'You are Nansen, aren't you?' and heard the reply Yes, I am Nansen.'

Jackson took the Norwegians to his camp at nearby Cape Flora on Northbrook Island. As they recuperated from their ordeal, Nansen came to thank the feisty walrus; had it not been for that beast they might never have encountered Jackson.

Nansen and Johansen boarded Jackson's supply ship Windward on 7 August and set sail for Vardø which they reached a week later. To their surprise they were greeted by Hans Mohn, the polar drift theorist, who just happened to be in the town. Telegrams were dispatched to tell the world about Nansen's safe return.

Nansen and Johansen caught a mail steamer south to reach Hammerfest on 18 August. There they learned that the Fram had emerged from the ice north and west of Spitsbergen, as Nansen had predicted. The men immediately sailed for Tromsø, where they joined their old shipmates.

On 9 September 1896, Fram sailed into the harbour at Christiania. The quays were thronged with the largest crowds the city had ever seen. Nansen was reunited with his family more than three years after setting out and they spent the next few days as special guests of King Oscar. He may not have reached the North Pole, but Nansen's epic tale of survival ensured his lifelong celebrity.

HIDDEN IN PLAIN SIGHT
Jeanne Baret: The first woman to circumnavigate the world

"She dared confront the stress, the dangers, and everything that happened that one could realistically expect on such a voyage. Her adventure, should, I think, be included in a history of famous women."

Karl Heinrich von Nassau-Siegen, co-passenger

In 1784, the French Ministry of the Navy made an announcement to address a remarkable feat of exploration which up to that point had scarcely been acknowledged. Jeanne Baret, a peasant's daughter from Burgundy, was to be awarded a government pension of 200 livres per year in recognition of her services to France.

M Baret, a missive from the ministry stated, was an 'extraordinary woman' who had shown 'great courage' while serving as a member of an expedition led by the famed seaman Louis Antoine de Bougainville. She had played a part in journeys that had mapped previously unrecorded islands in the Pacific Ocean and she had helped to catalogue hundreds of plant species which had previously been unknown in Europe.

More importantly she had also become the first woman to circumnavigate the globe. Baret's journey was far from straightforward. It took her ten years to complete her circle and return to France. Along the way she had to endure a multitude of sorrows and challenges. It was an epic journey.

Jeanne Baret was born to farm workers in 1740. Little is known about her early years, but by 1764 she was employed as the housekeeper of Philibert Commerson, a widower twelve years her senior who had a home in the town of Toulon-sur-Arroux. In that same year, Baret filed a 'certificate of pregnancy' as all unmarried mothers-to-be in France were legally obliged to do. Shortly after filing for the certificate, Baret had moved to Paris with Commerson and given birth to a son, Jean-Pierre, whom she gave up to a foundling hospital in the city.

Baret and Commerson shared a keen interest in naturalism and had worked together on creating and tending a botanical garden while living in the country. The success of this project brought Commerson to the attention of eminent naturalists including the noted Swedish botanist Carl Linnaeus. The move to Paris increased Commerson's profile further and when, in 1766, de

Bougainville was given permission to form a French expedition to circumnavigate the world, he was approached to be the party's botanist.

It was at this point that a degree of plotting took place. Jeanne Baret was to be part of the expedition, too, but her identity would have to be a secret. Women were not allowed to serve as crew on French naval vessels. If Baret was to make the journey she would have to disguise herself as a man.

It remains unclear exactly why the pair risked the wrath of the French Government to ensure Baret made the trip but there were several considerations which may have played a part. Commerson had suffered from pleurisy since moving to Paris and was still recovering when he was offered a place on the expedition. Commerson had authored several botanical works but it is not clear how much assistance he had received from Baret, both in collecting and recording specimens in the field and in cataloguing them and documenting the collections. It also seems clear that Baret was a closer companion to Commerson than most housekeepers were to their employers.

The plot to get Baret aboard was brilliantly simple. Commerson was given an allowance to pay for an assistant to accompany him on the voyage. He stalled in finding a suitable candidate for the role until just a few days before the expedition was scheduled to depart from the port of Nantes. At this point, Commerson was to tell his fellow travellers, a young man named Jean Baret presented himself at the quayside and seemed to adequately fit the bill. Baret was in.

Louis Antoine de Bougainville's expedition set sail from Nantes on 15 November 1766. The expedition consisted of two ships, the French navy frigate *Boudeuse* and the former trading ship *Etoile*. Although several other countries had already conducted successful circumnavigations, the French mission had a distinctly more scholarly emphasis than any of the preceding ventures. Joining Commerson, the botanist, would be the astronomer

Pierre-Antoine Veron and the historian Louis-Antoine Starot de Saint-Germain. While other nations may have been first to reach Earth's unexplored territories, de Bougainville claimed his expedition would bring the goals and teachings of the Enlightenment to the 'new world'. He also promised King Louis XV to claim any undiscovered lands for France.

Commerson and Baret were quartered on the *Etoile* and immediately enjoyed a stroke of luck. Commerson was accompanied by so much bulky scientific equipment that he was offered the captain's quarters for the duration of the expedition. Crucially, the larger space included a private washroom and bunk space for his assistant, which meant Baret would not be required to share quarters or toilets with the ship's crew.

The first significant challenge to Baret's disguise came in the form of an age-old seagoing tradition. All sailors were expected to pay tribute to Father Neptune when they crossed the Equator for the first time. This custom usually involved participants being stripped to the waist and 'baptised' in a vat of seawater by their crewmates. Clearly this would not be an option for Baret. An entry in Commerson's journal notes: 'We did not wish to refuse the lavabo . . . and prepared for this.' The implication being that bribes were paid to avoid any disrobing.

The expedition landed in Brazil, where Commerson and Baret took samples of a plant which they named Bougainvillea in honour of their leader, before heading through the Strait of Magellan and into the Pacific Ocean. The French ships sailed on to Tahiti, where Baret's cover was finally blown.

At Tahiti Commerson and Baret landed on shore to conduct fieldwork only to be approached by several islanders, one of whom pointed directly at Baret and remarked at the presence of a woman in the party. In truth this probably only confirmed suspicions which already existed about the gender of Commerson's assistant, but the bald statement of fact in a public space made it impossible for de Bougainville to turn a blind eye to the deception. He discussed the situation with François Chenard de la Giraudais, the captain of the *Etoile*, but in truth there was little to be done about Baret's presence until the expedition returned to France.

'I admire her determination,' wrote de Bougainville. 'I have taken steps to ensure that she suffers no unpleasantness. The Court will, I think, forgive her for this infraction to the ordinances. Her example will hardly be contagious.'

As the party continued to traverse the Pacific, more pressing issues came to the fore for Baret and her fellow crew. The expedition was running low on supplies. Food shortages were becoming a serious problem, so much so that the crew were required to trap and eat rats which they found on the ship. Veron, the astronomer, succumbed to illness and died on the island of Timor.

Meanwhile Commerson's health was deteriorating too, and when the ships reached the French-held island of Mauritius in late 1768, it was agreed that Baret and Commerson would stay and assist with botanical research. To de Bougainville, it probably represented a chance to rid himself of a potentially tricky problem when he returned to France. For Commerson, the stay was an opportunity for him to recuperate. For Baret, however, the stay in Mauritius was to be a difficult one.

Commerson never did recover and he died, aged 45, in 1773. Jeanne Baret stayed on, finding work as a housekeeper and running an inn, before she met and married a French soldier named Jean Dubernat in May 1774. Together, the newly-married couple returned to France.

There is no record of when Jeanne Baret, the first woman to travel round the world, arrived back on French soil but it was some time before the spring of 1776. This is known because she claimed the inheritance which was due to her from Commerson's will in the April of that year; 600 livres and the contents of the apartment they shared in Paris.

Baret did not leave a record of her adventures or of the struggles she faced on the high seas. Little is known of her later life, save for the instatement of her pension at the prompting of de Bougainville. Much of her life was left unrecorded but she was respected by the men who shared her voyage.

Karl Heinrich von Nassau-Siegen, a French aristocrat who had paid to join de Bougainville's expedition, gave her tribute: 'I want to give her all the credit for her bravery, a far cry from the gentle pastimes afforded her sex,' he wrote. 'She dared confront the stress, the dangers, and everything that happened that one could realistically expect on such a voyage. Her adventure, should, I think, be included in a history of famous women.'

HOMEWARD BOUND

Molly, Daisy and Gracie's 1,600 km
walk home following
a rabbit-proof fence in Western Australia

"We followed that fence, that rabbit-proof fence, all the way home from the settlement to Jiggalong. Long way, alright. We stayed in the bush hiding there for a long time."

From Doris Pilkington's book, The Long Walk Home.

Rabbits are not indigenous to Australia. In 1859 English settler Thomas Austin released two dozen into the wild in Victoria, southeast Australia. 'The introduction of a few rabbits could do little harm and might provide a touch of home, in addition to a spot of hunting.' But Austin seemed to have forgotten what rabbits are good at and they were soon spreading across the continent like a plague.

Between 1901–7, the government constructed one of the most ambitious wildlife containment schemes the world has ever seen. The plan was simple: cordon off the entire western side of Australia so that the rabbits could not get into it. Three rabbit-proof fences crossed the country. They were one metre (3 ft) high and supported by wooden poles. No.1 Rabbit-Proof Fence ran for 1,833 km (1,139 miles) clear across the continent from Wallal Downs to Jerdacuttup. The total length of all three fences was 3,256 km (2,023 miles).

Bold though this act of segregation was, it was doomed to failure. Rabbits had already crossed west of the barrier and it was near-impossible to maintain such a structure in the harsh conditions of the Western Australian deserts, despite regular patrols by inspectors with bicycles, cars and even camels.

The fence also acts as a metaphor for another act of segregation imposed on the country by the government of the time.

The white settlers of Australia had many different attitudes to the Aboriginal population. To some they were simply an inferior race. Others believed they could be assimilated into white society and have their heritage 'bred out' of them. Some were tolerant and understanding and of course there were many mixed-race children. It was the most divisive issue in that period of Australian history.

From 1920–30 more than 100,000 mixed-race Aboriginal children were taken from their families.

Children were relocated to be educated for a useful life as a farmhand or domestic servant. The government built harsh remand homes where Dickensian conditions were the norm. The children, many as young as three, shared prison-like dormitories with barred windows. Thin blankets gave little protection against the chill nights and the food was basic. These grim educational centres, or 'native settlements', were often many hundreds of miles from the place the children called home. Any children caught escaping would have their heads shaved, be beaten with a strap and sent for a spell in solitary confinement. The food in the workhouse-like 'native settlements' was no better than gruel. The children had few clothes and no shoes.

Molly Craig, 14, her half-sister Daisy Kadibil, 11 and their cousin Gracie Fields, 8, arrived at the Moore River Settlement north of Perth in August 1931. They had been taken from their family in Jiggalong nearly 1,600 km (1,000 miles) away and they immediately decided to return home no matter what the consequences. Their plan was simple: they would follow the rabbit-proof fence.

The girls only had two simple dresses and two pairs of calico bloomers each. Their feet were shoeless. The only food they had was a little bread. Nevertheless, on only their second day in the settlement they hid in the dormitory and then, when no one was looking, they simply walked out into the bush. It held far fewer terrors for them than the settlement.

The fence itself was several days' walk away. Once they reached it they would then have several more weeks of trekking through dusty scrubland before they reached Jiggalong.

But the girls were confident that they could live off the land. Their biggest fear was getting caught by the inevitable search parties; all previous escapees had been found by Aboriginal trackers. To outfox them they would have to hide well and move fast: Molly set them a goal of covering 32 km (20 miles) a day.

They made good progress at first. They hid in a rabbit warren and managed to catch, cook and eat a couple of the creatures. The weather was wet, giving them water and removing their footprints. They met two Aboriginals who gave them food and matches.

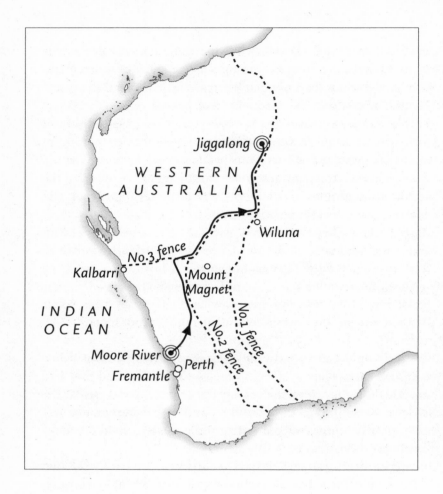

Often, when they came upon a farmhouse they simply walked up to the door and asked for help. Despite the news of their escape being widely publicised, none of the white farmers turned them in. Some gave them food and warmer clothes.

The police were on their trail, now genuinely concerned for the girls' welfare as well as eager to return them to Moore River.

But by the third week in September the strain of life in the bush was beginning to show. Gracie, the youngest, was exhausted and the other two often had to carry her. Her legs had been slashed by thorny underbrush and become infected. After hearing from an Aboriginal woman they met that her mother had moved to nearby Wiluna, she crept aboard a train to travel there.

Molly and Daisy kept walking towards Jiggalong. They could now move faster without their younger cousin to support, but it was still brutally hard going. The rains had gone, as summer crept up on them. Every day it got hotter yet every day they were determined to cover more ground to get home quicker.

At last, in early October, the two dusty, bedraggled girls walked into Jiggalong. They had trekked for more than 1,600 km (1,000 miles) through some of the most unforgiving terrain on Earth. They were still wanted by the authorities.

But now they were home.

The families of both girls swiftly moved house to stop the authorities taking their girls again. But, perhaps aware of what a powerful tale the girls had to tell, the government called off the chase a few weeks later.

However, although the girls' escape is a triumphant display of endurance and indomitable human spirit, their journey did not bring total happiness. They were still in a land where the law discriminated against them.

Gracie's mother was not in Wiluna and she was sent back to Moore River. She became a domestic servant and died in 1983.

Molly also became a domestic servant, marrying and having two daughters. But in 1940, after she was taken to Perth with appendicitis, she was sent back to Moore River by a direct government order. Amazingly, she once again walked out of the settlement and trekked back to Jiggalong. Unfortunately, she could only take one of her daughters with her; her 3-year-old girl, Doris remained in the settlement where she was brought up. Doris later wrote the book *Rabbit-Proof Fence* about her mother's first journey, which was made into a film in 2002.

Daisy's story had the happiest outcome. She stayed in the Jiggalong area for the rest of her life, where she became a housekeeper, married and had four daughters.

FINDING PETRA
JOHANN BURCKHARDT'S DISCOVERY OF THE FABLED CITY

"I was without protection in the midst of a desert where no traveller had ever before been seen; and a close examination of these works of the infidels, as they are called, would have excited suspicions that I was a magician in search of treasures."

Johann Burckhardt

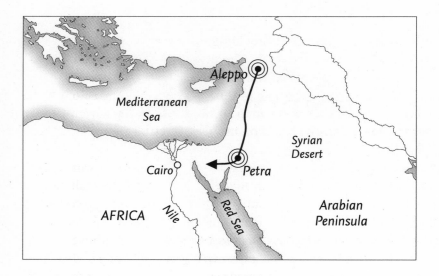

The Nabataeans were an ancient people who made their home in what is present-day Jordan. Their existence was first recorded in the fourth century BC. The Roman conquest of the Middle East diminished their influence, and by AD 106 the Nabataean culture was diluted and absorbed as other desert tribes rose to prominence. They did, however, leave a remarkable reminder of their civilisation in its pomp – a desert metropolis carved into the rock, which has beguiled travellers since those ancient times – the city of Petra.

The city was a wonder. Hidden among towering cliff faces in the Arabian desert, the Nabataeans harnessed every drop of rain water and created a man-made oasis using a system of dams and conduits. Petra became a hub for trade in the Middle East. It was also incredibly beautiful. A succession of intricate frontages, carved into the sandstone cliffs, opened into religious buildings, meeting halls, trading buildings and elaborate tombs.

The city of Petra died with the Nabataean civilization. A violent earthquake in the fourth century AD prompted most of the remaining residents to flee and for the next 1,400 years Petra was little more than a ghost city providing shelter for passing Bedouin tribesmen and their livestock. The buildings lived on, however, waiting to be 'discovered' again.

Petra is today considered one of the world's great archaeological treasures. Its rebirth was down to an ambitious young adventurer and a traveller's tale he heard on his way to Egypt.

In 1809, Johann Ludwig Burckhardt – a Swiss national working for the London-based African Association – landed in Malta en route to Cairo. Burckhardt had been commissioned to go to the Niger River and assess its viability as a trade route. He was to land in Cairo and head west across the Sahara to Timbuktu. At Malta, Burckhardt heard that a German explorer called Dr Ulrich Seetzen had gone missing, presumed murdered, after heading off from Cairo into the Arabian desert. It was rumoured he was searching for a long-lost city hidden in the hills. A city known as Petra. Burckhardt's interest was piqued. The story was also a timely reminder of the perils of travelling in the region; Seetzen was poisoned by his guides after falling foul of a local sheikh.

At the city of Aleppo in Syria, Burckhardt acquired lodgings and adopted a new identity. He made contact with John Barker, the British Consul in the city, but for the duration of his travels he would be known as Sheikh Ibrahim Ibn Abdallah. Burckhardt spent three years in Aleppo learning the ways of Islam, studying maps of the desert to the south and immersing himself in the customs of the region. He undertook some small-scale exploration, noting ancient hieroglyphs at ruined sites near Aleppo, but he saw the two-year hiatus in his travels chiefly as an investment in his future safety. A convincing disguise could be the difference between his expedition's success or failure — perhaps even between life or death.

There was only one truly effective way for Burckhardt to test the credibility of his Arab persona. He undertook three brief sojourns in Lebanon, Syria and Palestine in the company of nomadic merchants. It would be charitable to describe his fortunes on these journeys as mixed. He was attacked and robbed of his possessions while studying Bedouin tribespeople near Damascus. Barker, the British Consul, was to record that during a journey to the Euphrates River, Burkhardt was robbed, beaten and stripped and had to 'struggle with an Arab lady who took a fancy to the only garment which the delicacy or compassion of the men had left him'.

Despite these setbacks, Burckhardt was confident that his new identity would pass muster. 'I have completed the perusal of several of the best Arabic authors in prose as well as poetry,' he wrote in a letter to the African Association. 'I have read over the Koran twice and have got by heart several of its chapters and many of its sentences.'

In the spring of 1812, Johann Burckhardt left Aleppo for the last time and headed south. He was just 26-years-old. For much of the way, he followed in the path set by the unfortunate Dr Seetzen, even staying in the same lodgings during one stopover in TransJordan. In Kerak, near the Dead Sea, he endured the now familiar but still unpleasant experience of being robbed again. The Sheikh of Kerak agreed to provide Burkhardt with protection, only to renege on the arrangement and take most of his money. A guide provided by the sheikh then promptly made off with the meagre funds Burkhardt had left.

Now penniless but undeterred, Burkhardt found a Bedouin traveller and convinced the man to act as his guide to Cairo. Having been robbed yet again, the young Burkhardt would have been forgiven for heading to the Egyptian city with the utmost haste. Instead he chose a less straightforward route. Bedouin tales of spectacular ruins among the mountains nearby, and the story of Seetzen's search for the lost city, were enough to convince Burkhardt to take a detour into the wilderness. By now the Bedouin guide was suspecting that Burkhardt may not be the

Syrian merchant he claimed to be, but he agreed to lead on to the ruins.

> *A watch and compass were the only articles I regretted to have lost; as to cash, I had not a single farthing in my pocket.*

The pair crossed a sandy desert valley and entered the mouth of a steep-sided dry gorge. For half an hour they walked westwards, the walls of the gorge closing in on them all the time. Then the cliffs parted and Burkhardt was presented with the most spectacular site:

'On the side of the perpendicular rock, directly opposite to the issue of the main valley, an excavated mausoleum came in view, the situation and beauty of which are calculated to make an extraordinary impression upon the traveller, after having traversed for nearly half an hour such a gloomy and almost subterraneous passage as I have described. It is one of the most elegant remains of antiquity existing in Syria; its state of preservation resembles that of a building recently finished, and on closer examination I found it to be a work of immense labour.'

It was Petra.

Exploring the site would not be easy. By now Burkhardt's Bedouin companion was more than suspicious. As they entered the ancient city he said: 'I see clearly that you are an infidel who has some particular business among the ruins of the city ... But depend on it that we shall not suffer you to take out a single coin of all the treasures hidden therein for they are in our territory and belong to us.'

These words made it clear Burkhardt would be unwise to tarry too long in the ruins. He took such measurements, sketches and notes as he could over the course of the day but by the next morning they departed and resumed the journey south to Cairo.

Burkhardt went on to achieve much more during his exploration in north Africa and Arabia. He travelled more than 2,400 km (1,500 miles) down the Nile into the Sudan and, posing as a beggar, he spent several weeks in the 'closed' holy cities of Mecca and Medina. In 1813, he rediscovered another astonishing ancient monument when he found the sand-swallowed ruins of the Great Temple of Ramesses II at Abu Simbel. But he never was to fulfil his original ambition of travelling to the Niger River. Desperate with thirst while traversing the Sinai Desert in Egypt, Burkhardt drank water from a well of 'putrid, yellow-green colour ... our stomachs could not retain it'. He contracted dysentery and died in Cairo on 15 October 1817.

TRAIL OF TEARS
THE FORCED MIGRATION OF THE NATIVE AMERICAN TRIBES

*"In the whole scene there was an air of ruin and
destruction, something which betrayed a final
and irrevocable adieu; one couldn't watch without
feeling one's heart wrung. The Indians
were tranquil, but sombre and taciturn. There
was one who could speak English and of whom
I asked why the Chactas [sic] were leaving their
country. 'To be free,' he answered, could never
get any other reason out of him. We ... watch
the expulsion ... of one of the most celebrated
and ancient American peoples."*

*Alexis de Tocqueville, French philosopher, who witnessed the
Choctaw removals while in Memphis, Tennessee*

Just as there are momentous expeditions of triumph and bravery, so too are there travels that change history for tragic reasons. In the 1830s, there were a series of forced mass migrations of Native American peoples that reshaped the face of a continent at the cost of thousands of lives and incalculable anguish. Families, tribes – whole nations –were forced to leave their homelands and set out for a far off country that they had never seen and which was utterly alien to them. This would have been trial enough but a tragically large proportion of them would never even reach this far-from-promised land. They would die from hunger, disease, exhaustion or sheer cold on the long trek that would become known as the 'Trail of Tears'. In just one tribe, the Cherokees, more than 4,000 of 15,000 travellers died.

The young United States was growing fast in the early nineteenth century. The Louisiana Purchase in 1803 had more than doubled the size of the country. White settlers who had previously only occupied the original thirteen states in the east of the continent began to move in larger numbers to the south and west. The invention of the cotton gin in 1793 had revolutionized the country's cotton industry and settlers sought land to raise cotton, which flourished in southern climes. There was a problem — the native peoples who considered this land their home. These people were the Indian 'nations' — the Cherokee, Chicasaw, Choctaw, Creek, and Seminole peoples. Soon the settlers were pressurizing the federal government to remove the native peoples and annex their territory so that the land could be opened up. To build one nation, the government would destroy five.

In 1823, the Supreme Court decided that the United States' 'right of discovery' trumped the Indians' 'right of occupancy'. It ruled that Indians could only occupy lands within the United States, not hold title to those lands. The Cherokee, Chicasaw and Creeks knew that this threatened their home territories and they reined in their land sales to the government.

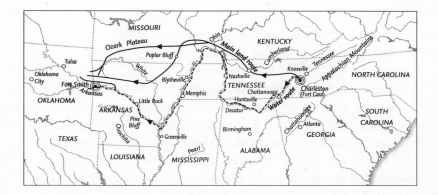

The Cherokee tried to fight fire with fire and turned to the law. They produced a written constitution in 1827 and declared themselves to be a sovereign nation. The Supreme Court ultimately ruled in their favour but the state of Georgia and President Andrew Jackson refused to recognize the ruling. The Cherokee were still tenants living on state land.

President Jackson hurried the 'Indian Removal Act' through both houses of Congress in 1830. Indian removal had long been a personal mission for Jackson. He had commanded the army forces that defeated Creek Indians in 1814, a battle that cost the Creeks 89,000 square kilometres (22 million acres) of land. Jackson's troops invaded Spanish Florida in 1818, winning even more territory. In the ten years to 1824, Jackson was the architect of nine treaties signed with southern tribes, which promised them new lands in the west in exchange for their eastern and southern areas. The president claimed the process was for the natives' own good; it would save them from being harassed by whites and would provide them with autonomy. But this was, in practice, an excuse for a sustained and savage campaign of theft, persecution and fraud.

The Act gave a President power to negotiate treaties that swapped Indian lands east of the Mississippi for lands to the west. The removal would be peaceful and voluntary. Natives wishing to remain in the east would become citizens of their state and could therefore expect to enjoy government protection.

In September 1830, the Choctaws became the first Nation to sign a treaty with the government. From the outset it did not go as promised. Those who stayed received no protection as 'state citizens' of Mississippi; white settlers used every trick in the book to cheat them out of their property and seize their lands. Almost all the disillusioned Choctaws ended up heading west. Choctaw representatives complained that, '[we] have had our habitations torn down and burned, our fences destroyed, cattle turned into our fields and we ourselves have been scourged, manacled, fettered and otherwise personally abused, until by such treatment some of our best men have died.' Around 17,000 Choctaw moved west, but as many as 6,000 died on the Trail of Tears. The Choctaw removal was used as the model for all future relocations.

The Chickasaws signed in 1832 — they thought relocation was inevitable and negotiated for western land and protection until they moved. But the settlers scented blood and were relentless in their persecution; the government refused to fulfil its promise. The Chickasaws ended up being forced to rent lands from the Choctaws' new western territory.

At the same time, the Creeks had opened some of their land to the government in return for secured ownership of the rest. Again, the government did not protect them and much Creek territory was seized by speculators. The Creeks were forced to travel west in 1836.

In 1833, Cherokee representatives signed a treaty with the government agreeing to leave their lands. But the signatories were not the true leaders of the Cherokee — the treaty was a sham and over 15,000 Cherokees signed a petition in protest. The Supreme Court ignored them; the treaty was ratified in 1836. The Cherokee had two years to migrate or face forcible removal. The illegitimate treaty caused great anger and resentment and when the deadline passed only 2,000 of 18,000 Cherokee had gone west. True to its word, the US Government dispatched 7,000 troops to force the removal.

The Cherokees were herded into stockades at bayonet point without even being able to collect their belongings. This left their homes wide open to looting by white settlers. The dangers of the trail started before a single step had been taken. The camps were overcrowded, unsanitary and inadequately supplied. Disease ripped through the fragile populations, killing hundreds before they had set out. In November, the Cherokee were divided into groups of 1,000 individuals for the journey west. The winter weather was abysmal, with heavy rain, snow and sub-zero temperatures. Over the coming months, over 4,000 Cherokee died of hunger, cold and disease on the 1,930 km (1,200 mile) march to what is now Oklahoma.

More than 46,000 Native Americans had been forced to leave their homelands by 1837. These lands covered an area larger than Portugal – 100,000 square kilometres (25 million acres) – which was now open for white settlers. Many settlers would create cotton plantations that would utilize slavery on a massive scale, creating an economy and culture that contained the seeds of the American Civil War.

We as Choctaws rather chose to suffer and be free, than live under the degrading influence of laws, which our voice could not be heard in their formation.

George W. Harkins, attorney & Choctaw chief

AROUND THE WORLD ON A BIKE

ANNIE LONDONDERRY'S 'CYCLE' AROUND THE WORLD

"What Annie accomplished with her bicycle in 1894–95 was a tour de force of moxie, self-promotion and athleticism. Though she was a skilled raconteur and gifted self-promoter with a penchant for embellishment and tall tales, she was also, as the evidence, shows, an accomplished cyclist who covered thousands of miles by bicycle during her journey."

From Around The World On Two Wheels:
Annie Londonderry's Extraordinary Ride *by Peter Zheutlin*

Annie Londonderry's stated aim was to become the first woman to circumnavigate the globe by bicycle. She began her adventure outside the Massachusetts State House on 25 June 1894. A crowd of more than 500 people gathered round to wish her farewell. Her route would take her across the continental United States, the Pacific Ocean, through Asia and Europe, across the Atlantic then back to Boston. She planned to complete the journey in no more than 15 months, thus winning a $10,000 wager staked by two Boston businessmen. The bold venture attracted the interest of press from across the country. But as Annie Londonderry set off, there were several things the well-wishers and journalists did not know.

Annie Londonderry was actually a 24-year-old Latvian immigrant from a poor neighbourhood in Boston's West End. She had a husband and three children: Mollie (aged five), Libbie (three) and Simon (two). Her real name was Annie Kopchovsky (she changed her name before departure at the behest of her sponsor, *Londonderry Lithia Spring Water*) and she was a novice cyclist, having only taken a couple of riding lessons before setting off on her globe-trotting trip.

Even the most sympathetic interpretation of her journey would acknowledge that the circumnavigation owed as much to the contribution of various ocean-going liners as it did to Londonderry's bicycle. But her voyage captured the people's imagination and was seen as a powerful example of female empowerment at a time when the women's rights movement was starting to mobilize in Europe and America.

Londonderry showed little aptitude for cycling – although her form on a bicycle did improve as she racked up the miles – but her greatest gift was an ability to drum up publicity for her expedition. She spoke eloquently (and often) in preparation for her journey, and, although the substance to some of her claims was sometimes questionable, the verve with which she spoke provided the press with great copy.

The true nature of the $10,000 wager, for instance, was cloaked in mystery. Londonderry told one newspaper that she was settling a bet between two upper-class clubmen of Boston, one of whom had offered $20,000 to his friend's $10,000 that no woman could travel round the world, earn $5,000 as she went, and return to Boston within 15 months. It was never made clear why Annie Kopchovsky would have been put forward to settle such a wager, or if in truth such a bet ever existed in the first place, but she seized the opportunity with both hands.

Before leaving she dropped the kind of soundbite which made her much appreciated by journalists. 'I am to go around the Earth in fifteen months,' she said, 'returning with five thousand dollars, and starting only with the clothes on my back. I cannot accept anything gratuitously from anyone.' Then, with a dramatic flourish, she turned out her pockets as confirmation of her penniless state. She also touched on one reason why she was prepared to break with the social conventions of the time and leave her family on a solo pursuit. 'I didn't want to spend my life at home with a baby under my apron every year,' she said.

She planned to earn money by selling sponsorship on the bike and her clothing, supplemented by newspaper columns and speaking engagements at various stopping points on the way. The concept of selling sponsorship space on an outfit and bicycle is completely commonplace today but in the late nineteenth century it was an innovative idea.

So in the summer of 1894, Annie Londonderry said goodbye to her family and friends and headed west towards Chicago. She was only 24-years-old. Her progress was slow but steady, hindered by two main problems; her bicycle and her attire. The bike was a *Columbia* model which weighed fully 20 kg (44 lb), around two-fifths of Londonderry's own bodyweight. Her clothing, including the corset which was viewed as mandatory for a respectable woman, was restrictive and she endured the persistent threat of her long skirt getting caught in the wheel spokes.

On reaching Chicago, Londonderry was able to switch to a *Sterling* gentleman's cycle which weighed a mere 9 kg (20 lb). The man's bike would not accommodate her in a skirt, however, and she switched to bloomers, considered scandalous in some quarters but far more practical. In time, Londonderry also ditched the corset, too. Much later on her journey, Annie Londonderry was to expand on this challenge to the social mores of the time.

> *I am a journalist and a 'new woman,' if that term means that I believe I can do anything that any man can do.*

The Omaha World Herald reported: 'Miss Londonderry expressed the opinion that the advent of the bicycle will create a reform in female dress that will be beneficial. She believes that in the near future all women, whether of high or low degree, will bestride the wheel except possibly the narrow-minded, long-skirted, lean and lank element.'

At Chicago, Annie Londonderry made a bold decision. She abandoned plans to head west and cycled back to New York, from where she caught a cruise ship to France.

Her progress to date had been sedate, but the expedition's reached a higher level of intensity once Annie Londonderry's expedition hit France. She ran into problems with French Customs at the port of Le Havre and, by her own account, lost a great deal of the money she had earned to date though the exact circumstances of this loss were unclear. Her fortunes were to take a change for the good in Paris. There she was given lodgings by a selling agent for *Sterling* cycles, who also helped to organize lectures, press interviews and public appearances in the French capital. Interest in the mission grew, and Londonderry drew crowds and attention as she made her way south. On reaching the port of Marseille she was something of a celebrity, giving more lectures and interviews, and a crowd several-hundred strong waved her off when she boarded the liner *Sydney* for Egypt.

Over the next few months, Annie Londonderry made port in Egypt, Ceylon (now Sri Lanka), Singapore, Hong Kong, Shanghai and Kobe in Japan. Her opportunities to cycle at some of these stops was somewhat limited. In the Ceylonese capital of Colombo, for instance, she reported taking a '30-mile spin' round the city with members of the local cycling club.

In every stop, however, Londonderry showed her talent for spinning a yarn and attracting interest in her expedition. The narrative she built was of a young, penniless woman who was seeking out and overcoming the most incredible challenges as she journeyed round the world with a bike.

By March 1895, Londonderry had made it back to the United States and was ready to set off from San Francisco on the last leg of her circumnavigation. She cycled through California, Arizona, New Mexico, Texas and Denver, giving interviews and acquiring sponsors as she went.

The tales she told of her overseas exploits, such as hunting with European aristocrats in India and suffering a gunshot wound in Japan, were difficult to verify but compelling to read.

On the empty expanses of the American prairies, the opportunities for publicizing her venture became fewer (and therefore less lucrative), so Londonderry travelled by train across Nebraska before getting back on her bike for one final push. A bad fall meant she arrived in Chicago with her arm in a cast, but by now there was no stopping Annie Londonderry. She pushed on east and closed the circle of her round the world trip by arriving in Boston on 24 September 1895.

Some critics scoffed about the scale of her achievements and particularly the amount of cycling which had taken place, but Londonderry brushed off the brickbats. She was to write several elaborate, and possibly somewhat fanciful, accounts of her expedition for the *New York World* newspaper before fading from public life. She died in New York in 1947.

UNLOCKING THE ISLAMIC WORLD
THE TRAVELS OF IBN BATTUTA

"I set out alone . . . Swayed by an overmastering impulse within me, and a long-cherished desire to visit those glorious sanctuaries [Mecca and Medina], I resolved to quit all my friends and tear myself away from my home."

The start of Ibn Battuta's Travels

Ibn Battuta was the greatest traveller of the medieval age. In nearly thirty years, he visited most of the known Muslim world, from Marrakesh in the west to Quanzhou (Zayton) on the Chinese coast in the east, and from Crimea in the north to Kilwa, now in Tanzania, in the south. He recorded his journeys in his account *Rihla (Travels)*. It is estimated that he travelled over 120,000 km (75,000 miles).

He was born in Tangier, Morocco, in 1304 into a family of legal scholars, a tradition he was initially trained in. However, as a young man, he wanted to make the *Hajj* to Mecca and Medina. It was expected that the journey, which started in 1325, would take around eighteen months. However, he was not to return to Morocco for another twenty-four years, and he made two further trips, one to Granada and one to Timbuktu, thereafter.

Unlike his near contemporary, Marco Polo, his travels were not driven by trade but by the wish to discover more about the world and to meet scholars and teachers. He also expressed a desire never to travel on the same road twice (though an approach not entirely applied consistently, for he made the *Hajj* to Mecca at least seven times). His route did not follow a particular path but appeared driven by opportunity, expediency, and a lack of patience, most spectacularly, when, frustrated at a small delay in catching a boat from the Red Sea to India, he made a two-year journey by land.

His journey from Tangier initially took him along the coast of North Africa to Cairo. At Constantine, as a scholar, the governor of the city provided him with new clothes and gave him money, the first of many such donations on his journey. He joined a pilgrimage caravan heading for Cairo — during the journey he married for the first of many times. Cairo was the first major Islamic city that he visited, and it somewhat overwhelmed him: 'boundless in multitude of buildings, peerless in beauty and splendour, the meeting-place of comer and goer, the halting-place of feeble and mighty'.

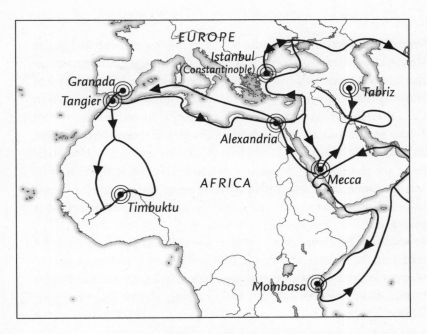

Map continued from above at same scale

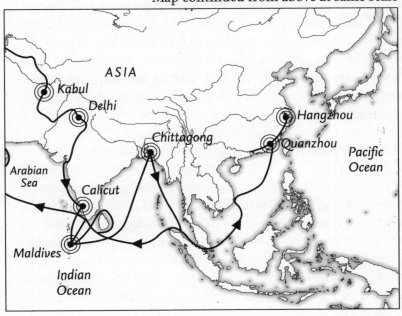

From Cairo he travelled up the Nile, hoping to cross the Red Sea as the quickest route to Mecca. But he found a civil war under way on the Red Sea coast and had to travel back down the Nile, the first of innumerable changes of plan in his years of travelling. He crossed the Sinai desert and travelled to Jerusalem, where he visited the Dome of the Rock, the spot where Muhammad ascended to heaven, as well as the Church of the Holy Sepulchre and other Christian sites. He travelled on to Damascus and marvelled at the Umayyad Mosque: 'the most magnificent mosque in the world, the finest in construction and noblest in beauty, grace and perfection; it is matchless and unequalled.'

From there he travelled to Medina and Mecca. He described the traditions of the practice of the *Hajj* and the architecture of Mecca at great length. Unlike most pilgrims to Mecca, he did not return home, but travelled east instead, visiting Basra, Baghdad and Persia.

After reaching Tabriz, he returned to Mecca and then sailed down the Red Sea to Yemen. When he visited its capital, Taxis, he tartly observed: 'Its people are overbearing, insolent, and rude, as is generally the case in towns where kings have their seats.' He then headed down the East African coast, visiting Djibouti, Mogadishu, Mombasa, and Kilwa. He despaired at the filth of some ports and was impressed by others, particularly Kilwa, and its beneficent Arab Sultan; it was a prosperous city that traded in gold and slaves and where wealthy merchants ate off Chinese porcelain and wore silk garments.

After another visit to Mecca, he decided to seek his fortune as a Muslim scholar at the court of the Sultan of Delhi. Impatient at the wait for a boat to India, he took an extraordinarily long detour through Turkey, across the Black Sea and through Central Asia to Afghanistan and then India. On the way, he visited Constantinople (now Istanbul) as part of an official caravan of Uzbek Khan and was treated as an honoured guest of the Christian ruler, particularly as he had visited the holy shrines of Jerusalem: 'I was astonished at their good opinion of one who, though not of their religion, had entered these places.'

Once he reached India, he was overwhelmed by its exoticism — the food, spices, fruits, luxurious clothes, exuberance of Hindu culture, and extravagance of their Muslim rulers. He was lavishly rewarded by the Sultan and then given the task of leading an embassy to China, taking with him a tribute that included thoroughbred horses and dancing girls. These gifts were lost in a storm off Calicut, and Ibn Battuta, afraid of the response of the Sultan, fled to the Maldives, where his judicial skills were welcomed. However, within two years he was on the move, visiting Sri Lanka, Bengal, Assam, Sumatra and finally making it to China, arriving at Quanzhou (Zayton), in southern China.

His accounts of China are limited and it is unlikely that he travelled to Beijing (though it is described in the *Travels*). He did not particularly enjoy his stay, 'China, for all its magnificence, did not please me . . . When I left my lodging I saw many offensive things which distressed me so much that I stayed at home and went out only when it was necessary.' He did comment upon the use of paper money and also mentioned the Great Wall of China (unlike Marco Polo).

The *Travels* records little of his journey back to Morocco. On the way, he escaped from the Black Death in Damascus and Aleppo in 1348, and in 1349 was back in Fez. During the next four years he made trips to Andalusia, where he was particularly impressed by Granada, 'its environs have not their equal in any country in the world', and to the ancient Saharan kingdom of Mali, about which he was less enthusiastic.

When he returned to Morocco, the Sultan insisted that he should record his travels, and so he dictated an account of his journeys to Ibn Juzayy, who completed the work in 1355. The resulting text, known as *Rilha (Travels)*, provides an account of his extraordinary journeys. It also includes text taken from other sources, such as some of the detailed description of Mecca and Beijing. It is all presented in a fairly matter-of-fact style, though he does recoil from practices that offended his traditional Muslim beliefs — in Basra, he complained to the authorities over a sermon that was full of grammatical errors, while in the Saharan city of Mali he railed against the fact that servants and slave girls went around naked.

Nothing is known about Ibn Battuta's later life, and he died in 1369 at the age of 65.

WALK THE AMAZON
ED STAFFORD: AMAZON ODYSSEY

"One of the boldest jungle journeys ever undertaken."
Bear Grylls

"Totally, completely and utterly mad."
Michael Palin

The Amazon measures 6,400 km (4,000 miles) from its source high in the Andes to the point where it flows into the Atlantic Ocean.

The river snakes and surges its way through some of the planet's most inhospitable terrain. In 2008, a former soldier called Ed Stafford embarked on one of the great expeditions of modern times, traversing the South American continent from west to east. During this marathon hike he became the first person to walk the length of the Amazon river from start to finish — an incredible triumph of endurance.

Stafford's prime motivations were twofold. He wanted to raise money for charity, particularly for environmental causes and cancer research after his father, Jeremy, was diagnosed with the condition. He also, by his own admission, wanted to make his mark in the manner of the great explorers of old. Hiking the length of the world's greatest waterway was one the few remaining challenges which humankind had not yet met.

'I had never been to the Amazon, my jungle experience had mostly come from Central America with some short trips to Borneo, but the Amazon undoubtedly had a mystique all of its own,' Stafford wrote in his account of the journey. 'Surely the trees would be much bigger, the wildlife had to be much richer and more diverse and the people would be that bit wilder and cut off from the outside world. It gave me butterflies to think of spending time in the Amazon. Not knowing the geography of the area in any detail, my dreams were restricted to what I did know. There was a ruddy great river that virtually crossed the whole continent from west to east, and . . . that was about it.'

Stafford was no novice. He had served in the British Army for four years, reaching the rank of captain, had travelled widely in Afghanistan, Borneo, Guatemala and Guyana and had led tourist groups through the rainforests of Belize. Even so, he was given little chance of success on his South American venture. He would not be alone, however. Luke Collyer, a 37-year-old outdoor activities instructor also from Britain, was to be his travelling partner.
Starting off from the Peruvian coastal town of Canama, they would cross the Peruvian Desert before ascending into the thin air of the Andes, locating the source of the Amazon and following the river east to the Atlantic Ocean. The route encompassed heavily forested areas where no human had ever set foot before. It was a daunting prospect for two men who had scant experience of the lands they would be travelling through. It would be a twenty-first century expedition. Both Stafford and Collyer took digital devices which would allow them to blog their progress to an expedition website. They would be followed for some sections of the trip by a television film crew.

Collyer's expedition was to end early. Very early. After just ninety days of walking, he flew home to Britain due to a breakdown in relations between the two men. They had barely reached the Amazon basin at the time. Stafford immediately advertised on his website for a replacement: 'Must have GSOH [good sense of humour], no fear of snakes or gun-toting guerrillas, have three months to spare, an interest in the environment and an ability to walk long distances without asking "are we nearly there yet?"'

This jocular response belied the serious problems posed by Collyer's departure. The loss of his travelling partner was a profound blow to Stafford's ambitions. The journey was a fraught endeavour for two people and quite probably impossible for a lone traveller. Finding someone who was willing to cope with the privations and dangers of a prolonged walk in the wilderness was one thing; finding someone who shared the necessary qualities of willpower, bushcraft and physical endurance was quite another.

> ❛ *Electric eels don't kill you outright. They stun you as you're walking through water and you drown.* ❜

It was here that Stafford experienced some good fortune. Gadiel Sánchez Rivera, a Peruvian forestry worker known as 'Cho', agreed to partner Stafford for a few days through a particularly notorious stretch of territory.

'I started walking with Ed at first because I felt a responsibility to try and help this crazy man through a very dangerous area with drugs traffickers and hostile tribes,' said Rivera. 'But as the days went on I really enjoyed the simple life and Ed and I became good friends. It was not long before I knew that I wanted to complete the whole trip and walk with Ed right to the finish.'

The two men were to reach the Atlantic together, but it was no simple walk in the woods. Heavy flooding forced the men from their planned trail and through cartel-run territory on the Columbia/Brazil border. This added thousands of kilometres to their route.

They had to deal with chronic hunger. Originally, Stafford hoped to avoid hunting animals by foraging for food among the jungle vegetation. Once in starvation-mode, however, he realized that survival depended on hunting and eating the Amazonian wildlife. The men's diet included turtle, ocelot and piranha fish. It was enough to sustain them — just.

Perhaps the most hair-raising encounter came with gun-toting tribesmen near the border between Peru and Brazil. Stafford's support team had radioed ahead to the tribe, explaining that they would be travelling downriver through their territory. The reply had been unequivocal — any white man who tried to travel through our country will be killed.

Stafford and Rivera tried to make their passage through the territory without attracting attention. But on a quiet riverbank at the end of a gruelling day, Stafford and Rivera watched, exhausted, as a flotilla of canoes approached them carrying Ashaninkan tribesmen armed with bow-and-arrows, shotguns and machetes. Stafford feared for his life but they were able to assuage the Ashaninkans by offering to employ the chief and his brother as their guides through the rest of the tribal lands.

The two men reached the Atlantic Ocean near Maruda on 9 August 2010. Stafford had been walking for 860 days and had covered more than 9,500 km (5,900 miles) on foot.

Stafford's achievement had been very much grounded in the technology of the twenty-first century – he used a satellite navigation device for most of the journey and posted updates to his expedition website throughout the trip – but in spirit it echoed back to the exploits of earlier generations. People such as Kingsley and Burckhardt who had been driven by a desire to break new ground. It was perhaps best summed up by another great modern explorer, Sir Ranulph Fiennes, who described Stafford's Amazon expedition as: '. . . in the top league of expeditions past and present'.

The final word should go Stafford himself. 'The cynics have been silenced,' he said upon reaching the Atlantic, 'it is possible to walk the Amazon — we've just done it.'

NATURAL BORN EXPLORER
Naomi Uemura and his solo winter ascent of Denali

"In all the splendour of solitude... it is a test of myself, and one thing I loathe is to have to test myself in front of other people."

Naomi Uemura

High on the vast white wall was a single bright red spot. Pilot Lowell Thomas Jr. knew the spot was Naomi Uemura, even though he was too far out to see the Japanese climber's face. There were no other solo climbers on the huge mountain. There had never been a solo climber there on the mountain at this time of year. Only Uemura. Thomas banked his small plane and as the aircraft came in closer, Uemura waved to the pilot and his cheerful voice crackled over the cockpit radio. He was going well, he was just 600 m (1,968 ft) from the top and he expected to summit in two hours. Just in time to drop down to shelter in a snow cave before the long winter night fell. Then the clouds billowed and swirled and Uemura was gone from sight. That was the last moment anyone saw the greatest individual adventurer of his time.

Eleven days before, on 1 February 1984, Uemura shouldered his pack and stepped out from base camp on the colossal Kahiltna Glacier. The task ahead of him was formidable — solo climb Denali, the tallest peak in North America, in the depths of winter. (Denali was known as Mount McKinley from 1917 to 2015 after

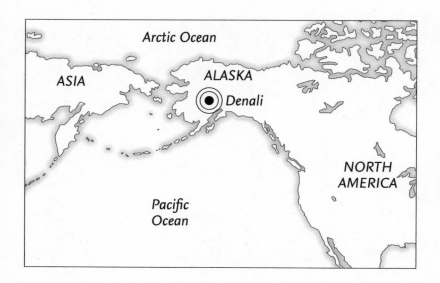

which it officially reassumed its traditional tribal name.) Standing 6,190 m (20,310 ft) high, it is a big-shouldered brute with five mighty glaciers cascading off its slopes. The glaciers are riddled with plunging crevasses, often hidden by snow drifts, which are difficult to cross without the support of a team. Uemura would have no one to rope himself to in the ice fields and on the rocky ascents.

Denali is also known for being a fiercely cold mountain. Even in July, the temperature can drop to –30.5°C (–22.9°F) with windchills as low as –50.7°C (–59.2°F). It is quite astonishingly cold in winter. Temperatures as low as –60°C (–76°F) are regularly recorded and –73°C (–100°F) has been noted more than once. A wind chill of –83.4°C (–118.1°F) has been registered at 5,700 m (18,733 ft). Another of Denali's most fearsome statistics is that its measurement of 5,500 m (18,000 ft) from base to peak is the largest of any mountain in the world. Mount Everest's maximum base-to-peak height is 4,700 m (15,300 ft). This means that climbers usually take at least two weeks, sometimes as many as four, to ascend Denali. In that bitter cold, this lengthy climb becomes one of the most formidable mountain expeditions on the planet. It was no surprise that Denali had never been climbed solo in winter before.

Most people would have been warned off such a dangerous expedition. But most people are not like Naomi Uemura. He was more than highly experienced; he was a legend in his own lifetime, an iconoclastic explorer who had repeatedly achieved things that others said could not be done — usually on his own. He was the first to raft down the Amazon solo. He shot an enraged polar bear on his way to becoming the first person to reach the North Pole solo. He was the first Japanese national to climb Mount Everest. He walked the length of Japan and in 1976 set the world long-distance dog-sled record of 12,000 km (7,500 miles), from Greenland to Alaska, on his own. His solo climbs included Mount Kilimanjaro, Aconcagua (the highest point in the Western Hemisphere), Mont Blanc and the Matterhorn. He had already become the first person to climb Denali solo in 1970; that was in summer but, nonetheless, he knew the mountain and had taken great pains to prepare for an ascent.

To save himself from plunging into a crevasse, Uemura had invented what he called a 'self-rescue' device — bamboo poles strapped to his shoulders. If he fell into a crevasse, they would catch on the edges and suspend him above the icy depths. He could then climb out.

Uemura cut right back on equipment so that he could move as fast as possible. Sleeping in snow caves meant he would not need to carry a tent. By eating only raw caribou meat (a protein-rich food he had discovered on his North Pole trip), he cut back on fuel. In the end, he took only 18 kg (40 lb) of gear.

The first two days passed relatively smoothly. The only incident was when Uemura fell into a crevasse — but in a good way because the fall proved that his rescue poles worked. At 2,900 m (9,500 ft), once he was past the most dangerous crevasse fields, Uemura discarded the poles so that he could go faster.

On day three, Uemura reached the appropriately named Windy Corner. Towering rock formations and extreme winds make this a dangerous place to spend time but Uemura ran into trouble here. The buffeting, biting gusts were so cold that he could not feel his face. Worse, he was having problems with his crampons. Several times he almost lost his footing; had he slipped he would have been blown clean off the mountain. He cleared the area eventually but for the next ten days Uemura would be in a constant fight to the death with the fearsome elements.

On 6 February, the temperature dropped, hitting -40°C (-40°F). The wind was also rising and Uemura was forced to seek shelter. He could only manage to dig a shallow hole which barely protected him from the wind. Pinned there by the tempest, he dropped both his pack and ice axe. He managed to venture out and collect them but when he could not find his snow pit on his return, the thought that he might die on this mountain first flashed through his mind.

At 4,300 m (14,000 ft), Uemura dug a deep snow cave for shelter and to stash gear to lighten his load for the summit push. He also left his diary there. One entry reads: 'My face skin got peeled off because of the frostbite ... The weather is very mean to me.' By now his sleeping bag had got wet and had then frozen, hindering its ability to keep him warm.

The snow conditions from 4,600 m to 4,950 m were incredibly dangerous — fragile, crusty snow on top of hard ice on a very steep slope. Given his malfunctioning crampons, every step must have been a dance with death.

Denali was sapping Uemura's seemingly superhuman strength. Near the summit, the winds picked up considerably and the temperature fell further to –46°C (–50°F). He had estimated the final summit push would take two hours. It actually took five. But he did it. Naomi Uemura became the first person to climb Denali in winter on 12 February — his forty-third birthday. The next day he radioed to say that he was back down at 5,500 m (18,000 ft) and would be at base camp in two days. There was a storm forecast however, Uemura being Uemura, no one at base camp thought there was anything to worry about yet.

But he did not appear in two days. Then the weather got even worse. Uemura was most likely trying to wait it out in one of his snow caves but he would be running low on food and fuel to melt snow for water. The weather would have to clear soon if a rescue was to be attempted. It did not. Four days passed. Six. Seven. The weather finally cleared on 20 February and spotters had perfect views. Uemura did not appear. He was never seen again.

Rescuers later found his equipment, his diary and other personal items in his snow cave. But his body has never been found. Until it is, no one will know for sure what happened to Naomi Uemura. Perhaps a crampon spike caught on the crusty snow and he tripped. Maybe high winds whipped him away. The most likely explanation is that the exhausted climber fell somewhere on the steep ice slope, with his body tumbling into a crevasse or being buried by snow.

❛ I wish I could sleep in a warm sleeping bag. No matter what happens I am going to climb McKinley. ❜

Naomi Uemura's last diary entry

He achieved his goal but paid the ultimate price. For his bravery, his ambition, his numerous astounding adventures and his humble, down-to-earth personality, Uemura is a revered hero in Japan.

MARATHON MAN
Amputee, Terry Fox's incredible run across Canada

"People thought I was going through hell. Maybe I was partly, but still I was doing what I wanted and a dream was coming true and that, above everything else, made it all worthwhile to me."

Terry Fox

Sports injuries often happen at the unluckiest times. Just as Terry Fox had secured his place on the junior varsity basketball team, the pounding on the court flared up a niggle in his knee. A ligament, probably. Happens all the time in basketball. And he was not going to give up his place now. See the season out. Go to the doctor then, get the knee strapped up and stick to golf over the summer.

But it was not a niggle, it was a malignant tumour. Four days after visiting his doctor, Terry's whole right leg was amputated. He was eighteen.

For the next sixteen months of his life, Terry Fox was in hospital enduring rigorous chemotherapy treatment. As well as the trauma of what was happening to him, the people he saw there – their suffering and their hope in the face of that suffering – changed him profoundly. He was angered by how little money was being spent on research to help the people he saw. The young man with one leg wanted to do something to help.

An article about an amputee who had run the New York Marathon sparked something deep within him. He envisioned a challenge – a mission – that was both beautifully simple and impossibly ambitious. He would run across Canada.

Terry was determined to the bone. Just three weeks after his leg was amputated he was walking around with an artificial limb. Soon after, he was playing golf. He then told his family he wanted to run a marathon –initially hiding from them the true scope of his plans – and embarked on an extraordinary 15-month training regime. From short, agonizing runs, he gradually built up his endurance until he could do 30 km (18 miles) a day. His gait looked awkward and painful — and it was. After stepping on his artificial leg he had to do a step and an extra hop on his good leg to give the springs in his artificial leg time to reset. This bruised his bones, caused myriad blisters and rubbed his stump raw. But after twenty minutes of running, Terry said, he got used to the pain and could settle into a rhythm and keep on going.

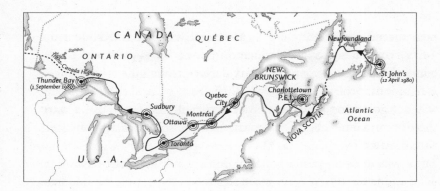

Terry trained for 101 days straight in the lead up to Christmas 1979. He would have run on Christmas Day too, but his mother pleaded with him to take a rest. By April 1980, he could wait no longer.

This would be one of the most extreme physical challenges every attempted: a run of 8,000 km (5,000 miles) from the Atlantic to the Pacific Ocean. Every single day, for 213 days, Terry would run a marathon distance of 42 km (26 miles). He would increase the public's awareness of cancer research, and raise $24 million — $1 for each of Canada's 24 million people. On 12 April, Terry Fox symbolically stepped his artificial right leg into the Atlantic Ocean near St John's, Newfoundland and started running towards the Pacific, where he also intended to take a paddle.

But the first stage of the journey was a rude awakening. Gale force winds, torrential rain and a snowstorm all hit him in first few days. And few people had heard of him; there was no support at the roadside. He was running alone.

He enjoyed an emotional and financial fillip at Port aux Basques, Newfoundland, where the town's 10,000 residents gave him $10,000. But he was still struggling as he ran through Quebec. The enormous physical strain of what he was doing erupted emotionally. He and his support-driver, Doug Alward, argued a lot. He had to constantly watch out for inconsiderate motorists, who forced him off the road. By Montreal, which marked one third of the way, he had raised $200,000 in donations — respectable by any ordinary measure but far below Fox's ambitions.

Then, something truly amazing happened. Suddenly, like a wave crashing on a beach, the story of what this young man was doing splashed all over Canada. There were people everywhere, lining the roads and cheering, pouring out encouragement, donations, love and tears. When Terry reached a town, the school would close its gates. The children tumbled out to cheer him on. To run with him. To talk to him.

Fox's incredible determination caught the eye of Isadore Sharp, founder of the Four Seasons hotel chain. Sharp had lost his own son to cancer; he donated $10,000 and challenged 999 other businesses to do the same.

On July 11, Fox was amazed to see 10,000 people turn out to meet him in Toronto. On that single day, the Cancer Society collected $100,000 in donations.

Terry made speeches and was feted by the media. In Ottawa, he met Prime Minister Pierre Trudeau and performed a ceremonial football kickoff in front of 16,000 fans. The crowd gave him a standing ovation. Fox saw how deeply moved Canadians were by his efforts and it spurred him on even further.

By the start of June, temperatures were topping 40°C (100°F). Despite the sweltering heat, Terry was still completing 42 km (26 miles) every day. On 7 June, he managed his best ever distance — 48 km (30 miles). He refused to take a day off, even on his twenty-second birthday.

But his body was suffering from the punishing schedule. Terry endured the pain of shin splints and his left knee became badly swollen. He developed cysts on his stump and frequently had to sit down to ride out dizzy spells. Still, he kept going.

❛ I'm not a dreamer, and I'm not saying this will initiate
any kind of definitive answer or cure to cancer, but I believe
in miracles. I have to. ❜

By August, he was so exhausted he found it hard to start running in the mornings. On 1 September, as he was approaching the city of Thunder Bay, a sudden coughing fit brought Terry to his knees. The crowds cheered their support and he managed another few miles before the pain in his chest stopped him cold. He asked to go to hospital. They found the cancer had returned and reached his lungs. That was Terry's last day on the road. He had run 5,342 km (3,339 miles) in 143 days.

Terry Fox died on 28 June 1981, aged twenty-two. He had not run all the way to Vancouver but it did not matter. He had inspired millions of souls in Canada and around the world. Today he is one of Canada's most respected heroes. There are seven statues, nine fitness trails, thirty-two streets and fourteen schools dedicated to him.

Every year since his death, the Terry Fox Run has been held to continue his money-raising mission. Millions of runners in more than sixty countries have helped make it the world's largest one-day fundraiser for cancer research. Terry wanted to raise C$24 million. To date, his run has raised more than C$650 million. He was unstoppable after all.

❛ It occurs very rarely in the life of a nation that the
courageous spirit of one person unites all people in the
celebration of his life and in the mourning of his death ...
We do not think of him as one who was defeated by misfortune
but as one who inspired us with the example of the triumph of
the human spirit over adversity. ❜

Pierre Trudeau, former Prime Minister of Canada

20,000 LEAGUES UNDER THE SEA

CHALLENGER DEEP: DESCENT
TO THE LOWEST POINT ON EARTH

"People ask me if was frightened. If I'd been frightened, I didn't belong in that business. It's just like a test pilot of a new airplane. You're on your game."

Don Walsh

Before 1875, no one knew how truly deep the oceans were. But on 23 March in that year, in the Pacific Ocean near Guam, the crew of the research vessel *HMS Challenger* made a historic discovery. While making a routine depth sounding, the crew of scientists gasped as the line they were paying out just kept on going and going. To their amazement, it finally touched bottom at 4,475 fathoms (8,184 metres) down. In their disbelief they made a second sounding. The depth was correct. They had discovered what is now known in their honour as the Challenger Deep, a precipitous notch in the floor of what is already a very deep ocean chasm, the Mariana Trench. It would be eighty-five more years before anyone actually visited this dark unknown — the deepest part of the world's oceans.

Modern soundings have shown that the Challenger Deep actually drops even deeper than that first sounding indicated — to 10,994 metres (36,070 ft). Mount Everest is 8,848 m (29,029 ft) tall, which means that if you dropped the world's highest mountain into the deepest part of the ocean, it would sink from sight and lie a full 2,000 m (6,562 ft) under the surface.
These depths are incredibly hostile. As well as the sheer distance to be travelled away from any form of support, there are waves, unseen currents and huge undersea cliffs to be negotiated. But the main danger is the colossal increase in pressure. At the bottom of the Challenger Deep, the pressure is 1.25 metric tons per cm^2 (110 MPa; 16,000 lb per square inch) — this is 1,000 times the standard atmospheric pressure at sea level.
No submarine can go so deep — its hull would be crushed. However, in 1948, the Swiss inventor and explorer Auguste Piccard had invented the bathyscaphe, a submersible that was capable of descending to unheard of depths. Piccard had previously twice broken the world altitude record in a balloon and it was ballooning principles that he followed when designing his underwater craft. The bathyscaphe has a large tank that is not for the crew but for 85,000 litres (22,000 US gal) of gasoline. Gasoline is less dense

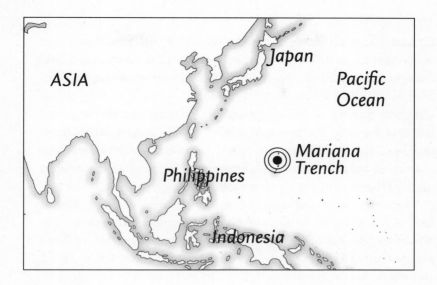

than water and virtually incompressible, so it stays buoyant even at extreme depths. This meant that the walls of its tank could be relatively lightly built and, unlike a submarine, not pressurized. The bathyscaphe functions like an inverted underwater balloon. Iron ballast allows it to descend; this is discarded at the bottom and the buoyant gasoline brings it back up. The crew work in a tiny pressured sphere attached below the gasoline tank.

Piccard spent years working with his son Jacques to perfect his design. In 1958, they demonstrated their third bathyscaphe, *Trieste*, to officials from the US Navy, who were impressed enough to buy it for $250,000. Jacques Piccard agreed to stay on board for a series of record breaking research dives that were codenamed Project *Nekton*.

Piccard's co-pilot in the descents would be Don Walsh, a submarine officer who volunteered for the programme. Walsh knew that Project *Nekton* was a deep diving programme but did not know just how deep. His first reaction when he heard the goal was, 'What? Why didn't you tell me this before I volunteered?'

The pressurized sphere that contained the crew had steel walls 12.7 cm (5.0 inches) thick. It had an independent oxygen supply and life support system powered by onboard batteries. Don Walsh noted that the crew's working space was about that of a household refrigerator and, at the depths, about the same temperature.

On 23 January 1960, *Trieste* uncoupled from her vessel and began her free fall into the abyss. The first hiccup came just 60–90 m (200–300 ft) down when they hit a thermocline, an area where the water sharply became more dense. The crew were bounced around their cabin with a heavy jolt.

From there, the drop proceeded smoothly until, at 9,000 metres (30,000 ft) down, there was a heart-stopping crack that shook the whole vessel. One of the Plexiglas window panes on the entrance had sustained a clear fracture. They were so very close to their goal, but would the window hold? Was the metalwork compromised? Would the sphere rupture and the colossal water pressure crush them? The crews' only solace was that, if their habitat did fail, death would be instantaneous. Piccard and Walsh judged that the crack was not on a pressure boundary and so did not endanger them. They continued the drop.

Finally, 4 hours and 47 minutes after they had cast off, they hit the bottom of Earth's ultimate deep, seven miles below the waves. To their astonishment, Piccard and Walsh observed several sea creatures just before they hit absolute bottom, including a 30-cm (12-inch) long flatfish that resembled a flounder. Unfortunately, when they bumped onto the ocean floor they saw it consisted of 'diatomaceous ooze' that promptly ballooned up around them in a milky cloud. This settled only slowly, and after twenty minutes they realized they would have to return to the surface without a photograph of their destination. They released their ballast and floated back up in 3 hours and 15 minutes.

The expedition was such a success that Walsh thought that another human would certainly voyage to the bottom within two years. In fact, the next person to touch down in the Challenger Deep was film director James Cameron in 2012, fifty-two years

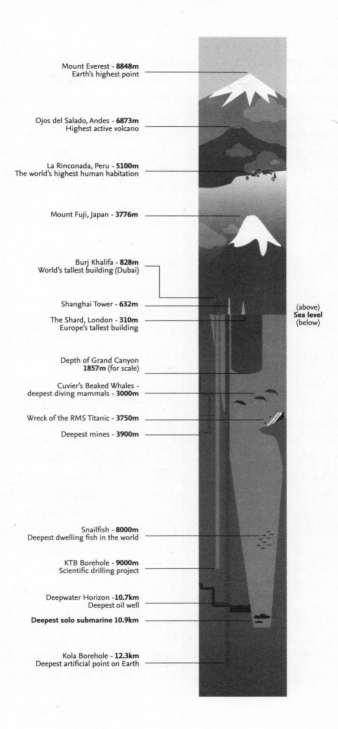

Mount Everest - **8848m**
Earth's highest point

Ojos del Salado, Andes - **6873m**
Highest active volcano

La Rinconada, Peru - **5100m**
The world's highest human habitation

Mount Fuji, Japan - **3776m**

Burj Khalifa - **828m**
World's tallest building (Dubai)

Shanghai Tower - **632m**

The Shard, London - **310m**
Europe's tallest building

(above)
Sea level
(below)

Depth of Grand Canyon
1857m (for scale)

Cuvier's Beaked Whales -
deepest diving mammals - **3000m**

Wreck of the RMS Titanic - **3750m**

Deepest mines - **3900m**

Snailfish - **8000m**
Deepest dwelling fish in the world

KTB Borehole - **9000m**
Scientific drilling project

Deepwater Horizon - **10.7km**
Deepest oil well

Deepest solo submarine 10.9km

Kola Borehole - **12.3km**
Deepest artificial point on Earth

after the first descent. The greatest depths of our oceans remain relatively unexplored.

Jacques' son, Bertrand, continued the family tradition of adventuring, piloting *Solar Impulse* 2 in its round-the-world flight (see page 211).

THE TRIALS
OF THE WAGER
GEORGE ANSON'S VOYAGE OF PRIDE AND GREED

"Thus was this expedition finished, when it had lasted 3 years and 9 months after having, by its event, strongly evinced this important truth: That thought prudence, intrepidity and perseverance united are not exempted from the blows of adverse fortune, in a long series of transactions they usually rise superior to its power and in the end rarely fail of proving successful."

George Anson, *from* Voyage Around the World 1751

It was 1739 and Great Britain was envious of the riches that Spain was milking from her New World empire: silver from Peru and Mexico, luxury goods from Manila, sugar, tobacco, dyes and spices from the Caribbean.

Britain had the sea power but not the trade agreements; action would have to be taken. Unfortunately for the 1,900 crew and troops enlisted for Commodore George Anson's venture, it would be a scheme of action undone by greed and poor planning that would lead to death, misery, murder and disaster.

Anson's mission was ambitious to say the least. He was to lead six warships through the fearsome waters of Cape Horn and up the west coast of South America where he was to capture Callao in Peru (the port that served Lima) and if possible take Lima as well. He was to then capture Panama, seizing any rich galleons that he could and lead a revolt of the Peruvians against Spanish colonial power.

He had a squadron of six warships: the *Centurion* (400 crew), *Gloucester* (300 crew), *Severn* (300 crew), *Pearl* (250 crew), *Wager* (120 crew), *Tryal* (70 crew). Two other vessels, the *Anna* and *Industry*, would carry supplies.

To achieve his goals Anson would also have the modest resource of 500 additional troops. But no regular troops were available so the 500 were to be drawn from the invalids of the Chelsea Hospital — men too sick, wounded or old for active duty. When these soldiers heard about the details of the proposed voyage, those able to run away promptly did. Only 259 came aboard, many on stretchers, and the numbers were made up with fresh recruits from the marines, most of who had yet to fire a gun.

The squadron left England on 18 September 1740 and immediately encountered delays, finally reaching Madeira on 25 October. It took three days at sea to transfer over the supplies and the *Industry* turned back on 20 November.

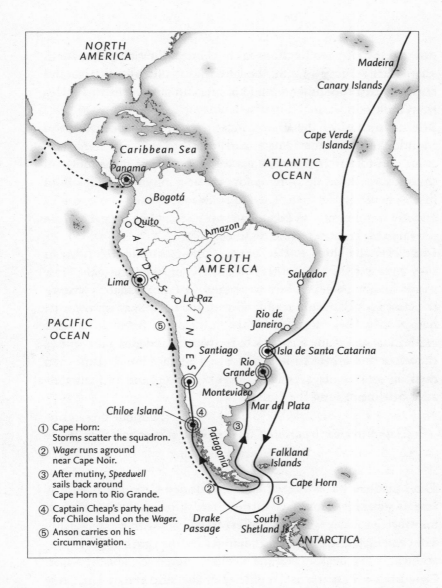

NORTH
AMERICA

Madeira

Canary Islands

Cape Verde
Islands

Caribbean Sea

ATLANTIC
OCEAN

Panama

Bogotá

Quito

Amazon

SOUTH
AMERICA

Salvador

Lima

La Paz

PACIFIC
OCEAN

⑤

Rio de
Janeiro

Isla de Santa Catarina

Santiago

Rio
Grande

Montevideo

Mar del Plata

Chiloe Island

④

Patagonia

① Cape Horn:
Storms scatter the squadron.

② Wager runs aground
near Cape Noir.

③ After mutiny, Speedwell
sails back around
Cape Horn to Rio Grande.

④ Captain Cheap's party head
for Chiloe Island on the Wager.

⑤ Anson carries on his
circumnavigation.

③

Falkland
Islands

Cape Horn

②

①

Drake
Passage

South
Shetland Is.

ANTARCTICA

The ships were overcrowded and typhus thrived in the hot, humid and unsanitary conditions. The men also came down with dysentery.

The squadron reached Isla de Santa Catarina off the coast of Brazil on 21 December and the sick were sent ashore. Anson then ordered the ships to be thoroughly cleaned. First the below-deck areas were scrubbed clean, then fires lit inside and the hatches closed so that the smoke would kill rats and other vermin. Finally, everything was washed down with vinegar.

The main mast of the *Tryal* needed repairs that took almost a month, far longer than Anson had hoped to stay. The men were stuck on shore all this time in makeshift tents and at the mercy of mosquitoes. It was not long before malaria joined the roll-call of diseases culling the men. The *Centurion* lost 28 men while in port and the number of sick taken back on board when they left on 18 January 1741 had risen from 80 to 96.

Soon after the ships started round Cape Horn on 7 March 1741 they were struck by another violent storm. Fighting gale force winds and huge seas while weakened by typhus and dysentery, the crew now also had to contend with the horrors of scurvy. One man who had been wounded at the Battle of the Boyne forty years earlier but had made a complete recovery found that his wounds reopened and a broken bone fractured again. Hundreds of men died of various diseases in the weeks during and immediately after battling around the Horn.

> ❛ *Life is not worth pursuing at the expense of such hardships.* ❜
>
> Phillip Saumarez, captain of the Tryal

The squadron was scattered after it rounded Cape Horn. All the vessels would go on to face further hardship, but the men aboard the *Wager* probably faced the stiffest trials.

The captain, David Cheap, had been sick during much of the voyage and was below decks when the storm scattered the squadron near Cape Noir. He then mistakenly sailed the ship into a large bay, which blocked their passage north. Struggling to turn the boat around with just twelve men fit for duty, a large wave smashed into the ship. Cheap tumbled down a ladder and dislocated his shoulder. The surgeon gave him opium and he retired below.

Instead of taking command, his lieutenant Baynes started drinking. The ship was dashed onto the rocks and discipline completely broke down as the crew helped themselves to liquor and arms.

Of the ship's original 300 crew and troops, 140 were now alive on the beach. Cheap tried to maintain control but the men were furious, blaming him for the loss of the ship and their current awful situation. They salvaged a little food from the wreck, but it was now winter and the men had little shelter against the driving winds and rain. Cheap only made things worse by shooting a drunken sailor and refusing to allow him any treatment. His victim lingered in agony for two weeks before dying, turning many of Cheap's remaining supporters against him.

They would all die eventually if they stayed where they were; their only hope was to take to sea again in the ship's boats which had not been damaged. The ship's carpenter set about lengthening the longboat and adding a deck so that most of the men would fit on board.

But there was a disagreement about where to go next, and a mutiny was brewing. Cheap insisted on heading to the rendezvous of Socorro Island, off the coast of Mexico, to find Anson. The gunner John Bulkeley thought their only viable option was to head 640 km (400 miles) south to the treacherous Strait of Magellan and sail north to Brazil. He convinced half the men to join him.

Cheap tried to win supporters for his plan with bribes of liquor, but when the modified longboat was ready on 9 October 1741, Bulkeley had him arrested on the charge of murder.

Four days later, the modified longboat, now-christened *Speedwell*, sailed south with fifty-nine men aboard under the command of Lieutenant Baynes. Following this was a cutter with twelve men, a barge with ten and another small boat with Cheap, a lieutenant and the surgeon.

About a dozen men who had fled the camp (to avoid Cheap's frequent punishments) were left behind on the island.

But more storms hit the boats, and the cutter was lost. The men on the barge decided to throw their lot in with Captain Cheap, so the mutineers sailed off on the *Speedwell* leaving them to their fate.

The *Speedwell* was the biggest boat, but this worked against the mutineers: it was too dangerous to land the vessel to look for food. Men had to risk their necks and swim through the icy water to do this job. They bickered over navigation, currents and weather, and it took a month to reach the Atlantic and many men died.

On 14 January 1742 the *Speedwell* entered Freshwater Bay, in what is today the resort city of Mar del Plata. Eight men swam ashore and found fresh water and seals. As they looked back out to sea they saw the boat leaving without them. Bulkeley claimed it was the wind; the men knew they had been abandoned to save rations. Eventually the *Speedwell* reached the Portuguese waters of the Rio Grande on 28 January. Only thirty men were still alive and they were little more than skeletons.

The eight men left at Freshwater Bay spent a month eating seal meat before they decided to make for Buenos Aires, 480 km (300 miles) further north. After a couple of failed attempts at this journey, two of the sailors murdered a pair of their fellows and ran off with the group's guns, flints and other supplies. The remaining four were later enslaved by Indians.

Meanwhile, Captain Cheap found that the deserters had returned to the camp, putting him in charge of a party of nineteen men. They tried rowing up the coast but lashing rain, brutal headwinds and huge waves made it very hard going. One boat was lost and a man drowned. It was impossible for everyone to fit in the remaining boat, so four marines were left ashore with muskets to fend for themselves. With one more death on the journey, there were now thirteen in the group.

A local Indian agreed to guide these men up the coast to Chiloe Island on payment of their boat on arrival. But three more men died en route and six of the seamen stole the boat never to be seen again. This left Cheap with three other officers and the Indian, who was finally persuaded to take them on by canoe in return for their only remaining possession, a musket.

They made it to Chiloe Island only to be taken prisoner by the Spanish. Eventually they were moved to the capital of Santiago where they were released on parole. They stayed there till late 1744 when three of them joined a French ship bound for Spain.

Whilst the men of the *Wager* were facing their ordeal, Anson continued with his journey, crossing the Pacific and taking many ships. One galleon was carrying 1,313,843 pieces of eight and 35,682 ounces of silver.

Of the 1,900 men who set out in the original squadron, only 188 made it back to England.

Anson became famous and was invited to meet the King. Huge crowds turned out to see the treasure he took as it was paraded through the streets of London.

He personally took three-eighths of the galleon's £91,000 (about £130 million today) prize money and earned £719 (about £100,000 today) as captain during the three year, nine month voyage. A seaman would have earned around £300 in prize money (about £440,000 today), equivalent to 20 years' wages.

Anson later became an Admiral.

COMPANY MAN

ABEL TASMAN: FIRST WHITE MAN TO SET FOOT ON AUSTRALIAN SOIL

*'In the afternoon, about 4 o'clock . . . we saw . . .
the first land we have met with in the South Sea . . .
very high . . .
and not known to any European nation.'*

*Abel Tasman's diary, 24 November 1642, on first sighting
what is now Tasmania*

The Dutch East India Company was one of the most powerful corporations the world has ever seen. It was created in 1602 to develop Dutch interests in Asia, and over the course of the seventeenth century it grew into an organization of incredible power and influence.

The Company (known as the Vereenigde Oost-Indische Compagnie, or VOC, in Dutch) had permission from the Government of the Netherlands to raise its own army, print its own money, create colonies and operate its own judicial system. Criminals could be executed by the decree of a Company official. Putting the colonial aspirations of an entire nation in the hands of a private business was a radical departure from the conventional approach to global expansion. It proved to be a success.

The VOC looked beyond the established practice of importing Asian commodities to Europe and vice-versa. Their traders set up supply chains between the various markets within Asia. They were among the first foreign traders to do business in Japan. Silk, spices, copper and gold, amongst a great many other commodities, were transported throughout the Asian continent and also to Europe. The money rolled in.

Where the VOC could not gain a foothold in a territory through diplomacy, they were not averse to using more forceful measures. In 1640, a Dutch East India Company fleet took the port of Galle, in what is now Sri Lanka, thus breaking Portugal's monopoly on the island's cinnamon trade. A year later they seized the strategically important port of Malacca on the Malaysian peninsula. The VOC's thirst for expansion was seemingly limitless.

So it was that in 1642, Abel Tasman, a Dutch sailor who had risen through the company ranks, was placed in command of an expedition to explore the 'Great South Land'. Dutch explorers had already charted much of Australia's north, west and south coast but the continent's eastern seaboard remained unknown. Tasman's mission was to discover the extent of this land and also,

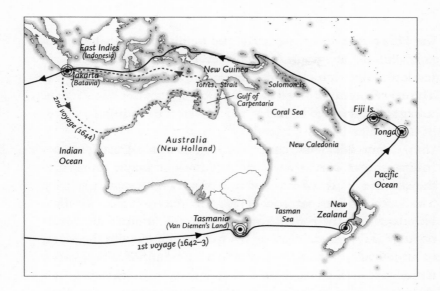

if possible, to investigate a route from the Great South Land to South America.

Tasman set sail from Batavia (present-day Jakarta) on 14 August 1642. The mission consisted of two ships, the *Heemskirk* and *Zee-Han*, and although their desired destination was to the southeast, they initially plotted a course south and west to the island of Mauritius. Tasman's strategy in heading for Mauritius was twofold. The Indian Ocean island boasted plentiful supplies of food and timber to allow his crew to stock for the expedition ahead, and the island's latitude would allow him to use the strong prevailing ocean winds to head east at increased pace. Having successfully negotiated the 5,500-km (3,400-mile) journey from Jakarta to Mauritius, and acquired the further provisions he thought necessary, Tasman began his expedition in earnest. He set a course to the south and east and re-crossed the Indian Ocean. Tasman made landfall on 24 November at a sweeping bay surrounded by undulating hills and thick forest. He named his discovery Van Diemen's Land, in honour of the governor-general of Batavia, and claimed the territory for The Netherlands. There was little pomp or ceremony: 'We did nothing more than set up a post,' Tasman later wrote, 'on which everyone cut his name, or his mark, and upon which I hoisted a flag.'

The expedition continued east until Tasman spotted the shore of 'a large land, uplifted high'. He had arrived at the northern shores of New Zealand's South Island.

Unlike Van Diemen's land, where the only sign of human habitation had been a few distant plumes of smoke rising into the sky, the South Island coastline was humming with activity. The Dutch sailors set anchor at Cape Farewell and within a few days had their first contact with the indigenous Maori population. Tasman described the first encounter with the Maori in his journal: 'Early in the morning a boat manned with thirteen natives approached to about a stone's cast from our ships; they called out several times but we did not understand them, their speech not bearing any resemblance to the vocabulary given us by the Honourable Governor-General and Councillors of India . . . As far as we could observe these people were of ordinary height; they had rough voices and strong bones, the colour of their skin being brown and yellow; they wore tufts of black hair right upon the top of their heads, tied fast in the manner of the Japanese at the back of their heads, but somewhat longer and thicker, and surmounted by a large, thick white feather . . . We repeatedly made signs for them to come on board of us, showing them white linen and some knives that formed part of our cargo. They did not come nearer, however, but at last paddled back to shore.'

> ❨ [A warrior] blew several times on an instrument . . . we then ordered our sailors . . . to play them some tunes in answer. ❩
>
> Abel Tasman, misunderstanding the Maori challenge

The next meeting between the Maori and the Dutch sailors was to end in disaster. A delegation of Maori approached the *Van Heem* and, through the fog of the language barrier, were invited to board the vessel. For reasons which remain unclear, a Maori canoe collided heavily with one of the *Van Heem's* supply boats. In the ensuing scuffle, three Dutch crewmen were killed by Maori wielding clubs and paddles. A fourth crewman later died of his injuries.

Tasman unsurprisingly decided to move on, 'since we could not hope to enter into friendly relations with these people, or to be able to get water or refreshments here'. Tasman named the spot Murderers Bay and sailed away. In fairness to the Maori, the encounter with Tasman's expedition must have been singularly unnerving. They had never before seen white men, or a tall ship, nor experienced musket fire or cannon shot. It would be 120 years, when Captain James Cook arrived in New Zealand, before their next encounter with European explorers.

Tasman did not get far before stormy weather forced him to take shelter off the coast of nearby D'Urville Island. The expedition celebrated Christmas in their anchorage before skirting the coast of New Zealand's North Island. They continued to be dogged by poor weather. At the northernmost tip of the North Island the expedition tried to make landfall again. On the first occasion they were deterred by the sight of '30 to 35 men' armed with clubs and spears on the shore. The next day they were prevented from landing by yet more storms. Tasman and his officers disconsolately agreed to move on. They sailed north into the Pacific and discovered Tonga and Fiji, without landing on either, before heading west and returning to Batavia in June 1643.

The hierarchy of the Dutch East India Company were unimpressed with the outcome of Tasman's expedition. His journey had gone some way to proving that a sea voyage to South America could be possible – one of the main objectives – but his failure to make landfall for all but the briefest of moments, or to return with any evidence of valuable resources, counted against him.

A year later, Tasman was back at sea at the head of a new expedition, charting the coasts of New Guinea and northern Australia. Again the fruits of his voyage were viewed as unproductive by the VOC and for the same reasons. The expedition produced no new trade routes and Tasman again proved reticent to make landfall and explore inland. The VOC decided that a more 'persistent explorer' should be found for future expeditions. Tasman was moved on to an administrative position with the company in Batavia. He died on 10 October 1659.

Tasman's achievements received little recognition during his lifetime. The lack of commercial return from his ventures was one factor; the VOC's commitment to keeping their exploration secret to avoid piquing the interest of their competitors was another. It was only after the achievements of much later seamen such as Captain Cook gained publicity that Tasman's efforts were reappraised. In 1854, nearly 200 years after Abel Tasman's death, Van Diemen's Land was renamed Tasmania in his honour. The Dutch East India Company was gone by then. A succession of wars with the British had seriously damaged the corporation's ability to trade and the world's first multinational company was wound up in 1799.

THE NORTHWEST PASSAGE

Sir John Franklin's search for a sea route to the Orient

"At 8 P.M. received on board ten of the chief officers of
the expedition under the command of Captain Sir John
Franklin, of the 'Terror' and 'Erebus'. Both ships' crews
are all well, and in remarkable spirits, expecting to
finish the operation in good time."

Captain Dannet of the whaler Prince of Wales, 15 July 1845,
the last sighting of Franklin and his expedition

Sir John Franklin led two ships, equipped with the advanced technology of the day, to complete the last 480 km (300 miles) of the Northwest Passage that were still undiscovered. The ships became trapped in the ice, however, and all the crew perished either in the ships or after they were abandoned. The first successful navigation of the Northwest Passage was by Roald Amundsen in 1906.

In the late sixteenth century, northern Europeans were looking for a route to China and the Spice Islands that was not controlled by Spain or Portugal. They hoped to find a northwest passage across the top of North America. This led to many fruitless European voyages. The first European sailor to enter the Arctic Archipelago was Martin Frobisher, who sailed into what is now Frobisher Bay, Baffin Island, in July 1576 and made contact with the local Inuit, and he led two further expeditions there in 1577 and 1578. In 1585, John Davis explored the Cumberland Peninsula on Baffin Island and Davis Strait, which bears his name. In 1610, Henry Hudson entered what is now Hudson Bay and other seamen followed, trying to find a western exit to the Bay (James Bay and Foxe Channel are named after two of them). In 1616, Robert Bylot and William Baffin sailed up the eastern coast of what is now Baffin Island (so-named in the nineteenth century) and mapped out Baffin Bay, calling the three outlets 'Sir Thomas Smith's Sound', 'Alderman Jones Sound' and 'Sir James Lancaster's Sound'. The latter was established as the entrance to the Northwest Passage in the nineteenth century.

After Bylot and Baffin, it was another 200 years before further European ships explored the Arctic Archipelago. After the end of the Napoleonic wars in 1815, the British Admiralty put some of its resources into finding the Northwest Passage and mapping the Arctic coast of Canada. In 1818, John Ross explored Lancaster Sound and the following year Edward Parry reached Melville Island, where he overwintered. John Franklin made two overland expeditions to the Arctic coast in the 1820s. Ross returned in 1829, this time on a privately sponsored expedition, and was trapped in the ice in the Gulf of Boothia, so named after his main sponsor, the gin distiller, Felix Booth. On that voyage, Ross's nephew, James Clark Ross discovered the magnetic north, then positioned on the western coast of the Boothia Peninsula. In 1845, Franklin was chosen to lead a further expedition to find the Northwest Passage.

Sir John Franklin was born at Spilsby in Lincolnshire in 1786 into a large family. Against his father's wishes, in 1800 he joined the Royal Navy. He was a crew member in Matthew Flinders' circumnavigation of Australia (1801–3) during which he survived six weeks stranded on a sandbank. His naval career for the rest of the Napoleonic wars was more conventional. From 1818, however, he became part of the Admiralty's plan to discover the Northwest Passage. His first voyage, in 1818, was sent northeast, but got no further than Spitzbergen. The following year, he was chosen to lead an overland expedition from Hudson Bay to the Canadian Arctic coast. The expedition was a disaster, dogged by continuing problems with supplies. It did reach the Arctic coast at the estuary of the Coppermine River, but little exploration of the coast was possible. On the return journey, eleven of his party of eighteen died from starvation and internal feuding, triggered by an accusation of cannibalism against one member of the party. The lack of supplies led to his reputation as being 'the man who ate his boots' in order to survive. Although the expedition achieved little, his popular account of the mission was well received. He returned in 1825, leading a much more successful trip, mapping a significant section of the Canadian Arctic coast, returning to London in 1827 a hero.

From 1837 to 1843, Franklin was Lieutenant Governor of Van Diemen's Land (now Tasmania), but his relatively liberal administration displeased some vested interests and the Colonial Office, and he returned under a cloud. He renewed his enthusiasm for finding the Northwest Passage, and he and others persuaded the Admiralty to fund another expedition, which it agreed to. He was appointed as commander (then aged nearly fifty-nine).

The expedition consisted of two vessels, HMS *Erebus* and HMS *Terror*, and a total crew of 128 people. The ships, of sturdy wooden construction, had already proved themselves in Arctic voyages, but were modified for the expedition, with their bows protected by steel, their keels extended, and steam engines to provide additional power for manoeuvring in ice, while a heating system was installed for the cabins. The ships were provisioned for a three-year voyage, including over 8,000 cans of tinned food, a recent technological advance and 4,200 litres (930 gallons) of lemon juice, to protect the crew against scurvy. In the expectation of a straightforward mission, officers dined using silver cutlery and drank out of cut-glasses. There was even a large library in each ship. However, the crews were not equipped for spending extended periods away from the ships.

The expedition left the Thames on 19 May 1845. By early July, they were at Whitefish Island, off Greenland, where final supplies were loaded on board from a supply vessel. In mid-July, they set sail for the Lancaster Channel, their first objective. Towards the end of July, they met two whalers near Baffin Island, the last sighting of the expedition.

It is known that they overwintered on Beechey Island. Three crew members died here (their tombs were discovered in 1850). It was not until the 1980s that the corpses were medically examined. All three had died of tuberculosis and it may be that other crew members had been weakened by the disease. The expedition only had a short summer period during which they could move through the ice. By September 1846, both ships were trapped in the ice off the northwestern tip of King William Island and to the west of Boothia Peninsula.

Concerns for the fate of the expedition only began to be raised in 1847, as it was expected that the ships would be away for around three years. Calls for a search were led by Franklin's wife, Lady Jane, and between 1847 and 1859 over thirty different voyages were made, including a few sponsored by Lady Jane. From these voyages, and from more recent research, an account of what happened can be put forward.

The ships overwintered in 1846 and the pack ice held the ship throughout 1847 (during which time Franklin died on the *Erebus*). In April 1848, after another winter in the ice, the crews abandoned their ships. One message, left at a stone cairn on King William Island, was found in 1859:

'April 25, 1848.—H.M. ships *Terror* and *Erebus* were deserted on April 22, five leagues NNW. of this, having been beset since September 1846. The officers and crews, consisting of 105 souls, under the command of Captain F.R.M. Crozier . . . Sir John Franklin died on June 11, 1847, and the total loss by death in the expedition has been, up to this date, nine officers and fifteen men. Start on to-morrow, 26th, for Back's Fish River [on the mainland of Canada.]'

None of the 105 men who left the ships survived. They had mounted a number of small boats on wooden runners, though hauling them put a great strain on weakened crew members. One boat with two skeletons was discovered a short distance from where they started. Further remains, both human and of artefacts, have been found along the coast of King William Island. Later an Inuit elder, Iggiararjuk recalled, 'They had once been many; now they were only few . . . They were not met with again, and no one knows where they went to.' In 1854, John Rae, working for the Hudson's Bay Company, bought expedition artefacts from some Inuit, including a silver dish engraved with Franklin's name, broken chronometers and some silver cutlery. He also reported that the Inuit had seen signs of cannibalism, a revelation deeply shocking to Victorian Britain. In 1859, the discovery of the message reproduced above, brought the period of intensive searching to an end.

Examination of the human remains found on King William Island in the 1980s established that they contained very high levels of lead and it is assumed by many that this came from the lead solder used in making the tinned food upon which the expedition relied. It has also been suggested that the supply of lemon juice fermented, so no longer protecting the crew from scurvy. Further analysis of the reasons will likely follow the examination of the wrecks of the *Erebus*, discovered in 2014 in shallow water in Wilmot and Crampton Bay, Adelaide Peninsula, close to where Inuit tradition said it sank, and the *Terror*, found in 2016 in Terror Bay on the southwest coast of King William Island, 50 km (31 miles) from the *Erebus*.

The many voyages sent to discover what happened greatly increased knowledge of the area. In 1853, the route of the Northwest Passage was established by Robert McClure, using sledges for part of the journey. Roald Amundsen made the first successful voyage through the Northwest Passage in 1903–6 in his 47-tonne wooden boat, the *Gjøa*. The scale and practicality of his voyage is in stark contrast to the technocratic Franklin adventure. He had a crew of six, and sixteen sled dogs when he reached Beechey Island in August 1903. He then overwintered in a protected bay in the southeast of King William Island, where he and his crew stayed until the summer of 1905, learning Inuit skills and undertaking scientific research. He left in August 1905 and, rather to his surprise, met a whaling ship coming in the opposite direction, which confirmed that he would make a journey to the end of the passage: 'The North West Passage was done. My boyhood dream— at that moment it was accomplished.' He completed his passage through the Arctic Archipelago on 17 August 1905 and reached the Pacific coast of Alaska in August 1906.

INTO THE EMPTY QUARTER

Wilfred Thesiger's travels in Arabia

"...a bitter, desiccated land that knows nothing of gentleness or ease ... a cruel land that can cast a spell which no temperate clime can match."

Wilfred Thesiger

The Englishman was starving to death on a sand dune. His Bedu travelling companions had left him three days ago in search of food and he had seen nothing of them since. His mind was filled with tortuous hallucinations of cars and lorries arriving to whisk him off to civilization and safety. It was at this moment of ultimate desperation that he made a vow to himself that very few men would ever consider making; he later wrote, 'I would rather be here starving as I was than sitting in a chair, replete with food, listening to the wireless and dependent on cars to take me through Arabia.'

The Rub 'al Khali – the Empty Quarter – is an ocean of sand larger than France, Belgium and the Netherlands combined. Outside the poles, there is probably no more savage and unforgiving landscape on Earth. The heat is scorching — the air temperature averages 47°C (117°F) and regularly tops 50°C (122°F), while the sand can reach 80°C (175°F). There is less than 3 cm (1.2 in.) of rain a year. In some places the sand dunes are more like mini-mountains, standing almost 300 m (1,000 ft) high and running for 160 km (100 miles). There are deadly quicksands that will swallow careless travellers whole.

This is not a land to live in but a danger zone to be crossed only in extreme circumstances. And yet, there are people of extraordinary endurance and resourcefulness, who have survived here for centuries. If you are so foolhardy as to attempt to cross its withering spaces, you need the complete trust and support of people who very rarely trust any strangers — the Bedu. Luckily the Englishman had just such friends and they saved him as he lay starving.

Wilfred Thesiger had a remarkable background that he developed into an even more remarkable life. Born in Abyssinia (in modern-day Ethiopia) to a diplomat father, he saw first-hand the people and the rituals of that country's imperial court; a noble, grand but violent world which he loved for its 'barbaric splendour'. He was

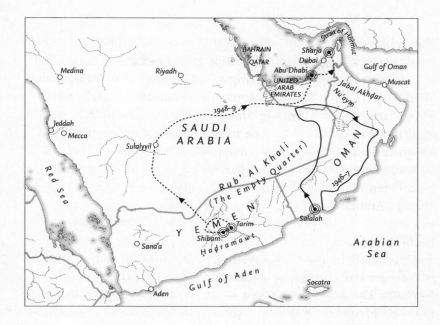

sent to England for his upper-class education at Eton College and Oxford University but his heart was never in those places even if his body was. As soon as he got the chance he went travelling, usually in as arduous a manner as possible. For Thesiger, the satisfaction of achieving a goal was directly in proportion to the hardship endured in attaining it — his motto was 'The harder the life, the finer the man.' He learned how to go without sleep by working on a fishing trawler in Icelandic waters and took the roughest passage to Istanbul.

He joined the Sudan Political Service after university and learnt to ride camels in the deserts of Darfur. He once rode 185 km (115 miles) in 24 hours to prove his mettle. In the swamplands of the Sudd he was employed to shoot troublesome lions. He bagged seventy. He also developed a respect for the desert peoples that would come to define his life. He fought to liberate Abyssinia with the Sudan Defence Force during the Second World War and was decorated for bravery. He also served in the SAS and went behind enemy lines in the Western Desert of north Africa.

When fighting ceased in 1945, Thesiger was determined to once again resume his self-directed expeditions in Arabia. The Sultan of Oman had expressly forbidden Thesiger from entering the Empty Quarter but he used a UN-funded study of locust breeding sites as an excuse to go exploring the ocean of sand. Entering was hard enough but if he wanted to get out alive Thesiger knew that he had to gain the trust of the local Bedu people. That was far from easy; the Bedu saw outsiders as Christian infidels who threatened their way of life. Thesiger wrote, 'To win respect [the stranger] must match their endurance, walking as far and riding as long, and bear heat, hunger, and cold with their uncomplaining indifference.'

Thesiger had just those qualities and he did make trusted Bedouin friends. In fact, Thesiger's expeditions were unique in that they were motivated not merely by a desire to explore a place, but to understand a whole way of life. He wrote: 'Yet those travels in the empty quarter would have been for me a meaningless penance but for the comradeship of my Bedu companions.' Thesiger always travelled as the native people did, on foot or mounted and in small groups. He despised cars and planes, among other inventions, although he did embrace photography, producing thousands of stunning images throughout his life.

The small group set off on October 1946 from Salalah, a town on the coast of Dhofar, in Oman. They headed north to Dhafara and Lira, crossing the 215 m (700 ft) high sand dunes of Uruq al Shaiba. Thesiger and his Bedu would criss-cross the Empty Quarter over the next four years on a remarkable expedition which covered 16,000 km (10,000 miles) on camel-back in one of the world's harshest and strangest environments. In this alien world, distances were measured in hours on camel-back. The men faced extreme privation, suffering from incessant hunger and thirsting for days at a time. A good ration was one pint of brackish water a day, mixed with camel milk and only drunk after sunset.

But the desert was in Thesiger's soul and he was at his happiest here. His efforts were rewarded with some remarkable achievements.

Thesiger was the first European to see the Liwa oasis and the quicksands at Umm al Samim. He made the first detailed maps of large parts of the Empty Quarter including the mountains of Oman. He described his travels in eloquent depth in his seminal 1959 book, *Arabian Sands.*

He was also perceptively aware that just as he was discovering this way of life, it was dying out. 'I know that amongst them in the desert, I have found a freedom of the spirit which may not survive their passing.' In 1948, while Thesiger was exploring the sands in the south of the Empty Quarter, a very different exploration was being made 2,000 m (6,500 ft) beneath the sands to the north. Geologists discovered the Ghawar oil field, the single largest oil field ever found. This extraordinary find of natural wealth would bring men, machines and modernization to the ancient peoples whom Thesiger so admired. Ironically, many of his maps aided the oil-hungry intruders who would change the life of this land that he loved, forever.

By 1949, news of the Christian infidel travelling through Rub' al Khali had reached Ibn Saud, the King of Saudi Arabia, who had him imprisoned. Thesiger was released, but by this time enraged tribesmen had put a bounty on his head. The Englishman made it out (more by luck than by judgement) but his great expedition in the Empty Quarter was over. When he reached Sharja on The Gulf, to depart for the final time, he was distraught at having to leave his beloved Bedu friends who '...were out of place among these soft townsmen... Lonely and apart I watched them drive in their camels and depart, back to the clean emptiness of the desert.'

Thesiger continued travelling throughout almost all of his life. He was knighted in 1995 and was an inspiration to later generations of travellers, in particular Sir Ranulph Fiennes. Wilfred Thesiger died in 2003 aged 93.

ACROSS SIBERIA
Cornelius Rost's escape from a Siberian Gulag

"After a time, Forell [Cornelius Rost] began to think of escape. His school knowledge of Russian geography stopped at the Urals."

from Joseph M. Bauer's book As Far As My Feet Will Carry Me

Some escapes seem so incredible that they defy belief. For years Cornelius Rost had to contend with people who doubted his tale. Could he really have escaped from the forced labour camp of a gulag and trekked 13,000 km (8,000 miles) through Stalinist Russia? If so, why had he changed his name in the book about his exploits to Clemens Forell?

The truth seems to be that Rost did indeed make this epic journey, and his name change adds credence to his tale: he took on one of the most powerful and brutal dictatorships in history and lived to tell the tale. It was natural that he would fear reprisals.

At the end of the Second World War, 20,000 defeated German soldiers were trapped in the Soviet Union, a country keen to get revenge for its millions of fallen men. Cornelius Rost was one of these unlucky soldiers.

Captured by the Russians in 1944, he was held like any other Prisoner Of War for a year. Then he was sentenced to twenty-five years' hard labour in a lead mine in a far, frozen corner of Siberia. In October 1945, he was among 3,000 prisoners who boarded cattle wagons in Moscow station for the journey to East Cape (Cape Dezhnev), just south of the Arctic Circle by the Bering Strait. The journey to the gulag lasted nearly a year. More than half the men who started it died — from exhaustion, malnutrition or dysentery. Many just froze to death.

Their destination was incredibly remote – so remote in fact that the journey took nearly a year, moving by cattle train, horse-drawn sledges and finally dog sledges. Only 1,236 men made it – less than half of those who started.

The prisoners lived in the lead mine itself, in caves lit by a single lamp. Guards forced them to work brutally hard for twelve hours every day. Bread, potatoes and water barley gruel was all they had to sustain their efforts.

Once a week, if they were lucky, they would see the sun for an hour. If the men did not die of exhaustion, they would certainly succumb to lead poisoning. Rost's sentence of twenty-five years was clearly nominal; he would be dead long before then.

It was an existence almost beyond endurance. Rost knew he would soon be emaciated and exhausted so despite being surrounded by hundreds of miles of frozen nothingness, he thought it would be better to at least try to escape.

He tried almost immediately. But after he went missing, guards cut the rations of his fellow prisoners to almost nothing. When they recaptured Rost eleven days later, they made him run between lines of the nearly starving men. His fellows beat Rost so badly he almost died. Three more years passed before Rost found another opportunity to break out.

The camp doctor was a fellow German who had been using his more privileged position to put together an escape plan. He had stashed a map, food, money, clothing, a pair of skis and, remarkably, a gun.

He then made a heart-breaking self-diagnosis: he had cancer. There was no way he would make it. He asked Rost to take his place, on the condition that he contact his wife in Germany when he made it to freedom. On 30 October 1949, the doctor distracted the guards long enough for Rost to slip out of the hospital. For the next three years he would be on the run in a savage landscape ruled by an even more brutal dictatorship.

His plan was simple: go west as far and as fast as he could. Pursuit was a certainty, but Rost believed that if he could put 320 km (200 miles) between himself and the gulag then the guards would probably give up trying to find him. From there he could head south into Manchuria.

Rost set himself a punishing daily target of at least 32 km (20 miles), although he often topped 48 km (30 miles) — an incredible achievement in the savage terrain of Siberia. The icy winds and frozen terrain stretched his endurance to the limit but the environment also protected him: there were very few people out here.

Nevertheless, he took specific care to avoid human contact. He did not dare light a fire, so the little food he had was solid with cold. A whole month passed before he met two nomadic reindeer herders. Rost was convinced they would either kill him or turn him in, but it seems the men felt they had more in common with the fugitive than they did with Moscow. They welcomed him into their camp, looking after him for nearly three months. That winter with the herdsmen was invaluable for learning practical skills.

Rost learned how to live in the Siberian wilds: how to fish and hunt; how to improvise a tent; the knack of lighting a fire from moss. He also learned the importance of help from others. But the very necessity of seeking such a trust would bring him danger as well as aid.

Rost spent two more months with another group of herdsmen. Then in June 1950 he encountered three fellow fugitives — Russians who had fled prison to eke out a living as hunters in the winter and gold prospectors in summer. He threw in his lot with them for a year, and adopted the Russian name Pyotr Jakubovitsch. The men worked as a team, panning for gold twelve hours a day from June till October. It was punishing work but by autumn they had gathered a small pile of gold dust, which they divided into even shares.

With the days shortening, the men stole six reindeer to drag their sledges and headed for the plains to hunt for fur. It was perhaps inevitable that greed and death would be close companions to men in such a situation, and they duly arrived to turn Rost's world upside down again.

One of Rost's colleagues, a man named Grigori, had a gold nugget that he had filched during his days as a prisoner working in a gold mine. His colleagues discovered the nugget and there was

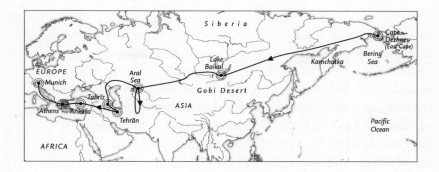

a deadly battle that left Rost alone with Grigori. The man had seemed mad to start with; now he was also highly paranoid. Five days later Grigori stole Rost's gold too and shoved him off a cliff, leaving him for dead. Rost very nearly died, but he was saved again by another group of sympathetic herdsmen. They tended to his wounds and helped him recuperate before sending him on his way with one of their huskies, which Rost named Willem.

It was summer 1951 and Rost had been out of the lead mine for twenty months. But he was still a long way from home: even the border with Manchuria lay 1,280 km (800 miles) away. But as he began to pass more signs of civilization, he knew he had to develop a cover story. He claimed to be a Latvian who had finished his eight-year sentence in a labour camp and been ordered to Chita, a city near Manchuria. This explained his limited Russian and his battered physical condition.

His tale passed muster with some woodcutters who had a cargo of timber to send to Chita. They offered Rost the job of escorting the shipment and even gave him a travel permit. Rather than getting off at Chita, Rost stayed on the train until the end of the line at Ulan Ude and his good fortune kept running: a drunk Chinese truck driver gave him a lift to the Manchurian border. Here his lucky streak came to a sad end. The border was fortified and impassable. A suspicious guard shot Willem and Rost once again had to take to his heels.

For the next few weeks he lived a precarious existence, hiding by day and sneaking onto trains at night, stealing food when he could. It was clear he would need a sympathetic ally if he were to make any significant progress across the vast Soviet Union. He met a forestry worker whose father was an Austrian captured by the Russians in 1914. This man instantly recognised Rost's German accent. But rather than hand him over to the authorities, he helped him plot out a route to the border with Iran, some 2,400 km (1,500 miles) away.

By early 1952, Rost had made it to Novo-Kazalinsk, east of the Aral Sea. He briefly lived with the members of a local underground movement who promised to smuggle him out of the country by heading north round the Caspian Sea and then passing into Iran through the Caucasus. But Rost scented a trap and he abandoned the group, striking out south on his own, the most direct route to Iran.

It was a bad decision. Rost spent the next five months trekking south to no avail. He lost a dangerous amount of weight, became utterly exhausted and in the end was forced to retrace his steps. In June he made it back to Novo-Kazalinsk and decided that this time he would trust the underground. He was passed from safe house to safe house on a northwest route towards Uralsk, then southwest to Urda. By November he had reached the Caucasus.

As he closed in on his goal, so the risks increased. He was travelling through more populous regions now, making his chance of being caught by the police much higher. Although he was thousands of miles from the gulag, this was still Stalinist Russia and if caught Rost would be arrested as a German spy and returned there. Even when his smuggling companions told him they had crossed the icy river that marked the border with Iran, Rost felt sure he would be caught.

But the unbelievable story had come true: he had made it out of the Soviet Union.

Three days later he was in the nearest town, Tabrīz. He walked into the police station and told them his story. It was so incredible they assumed he was a Soviet spy and arrested him. Rost was taken to Tehrān where he endured weeks of daily interrogation. He stuck to his story, but still the Iranians were convinced he was a spy.

Rost's uncle had moved to neighbouring Turkey before the war. Rost begged that his captors bring this man to Tehrān to identify him as a German. The Iranians agreed and a week later, Rost's uncle stepped into his cell. It looked like fate had played a final cruel trick on Rost: he was so exhausted and emaciated from his years on the run that his uncle did not recognise him. But he had brought a photograph album that had belonged to Rost's mother. Rost told him to look at a particular picture of his mother. On the back he claimed that he, in a different lifetime, had written his mother's birthday — the day he had presented her with the photo. The Iranian officers pulled out the photo and flipped it over. Written on the back was: '18 October 1939'. Rost was released and flew with his uncle to Ankara. He then flew via Athens and Rome to Munich.

He walked into his home city on 22 December 1952, nearly three years and 13,000 km (8,000 miles) after his journey started. It was one of the most amazing journeys of all time.

INDEX

CREDITS

Maps and images © HarperCollins Publishers unless noted.

CC 2.0 Creative Commons Attribution License 2.0 Generic

Cover illustrations © Julia Murray
  Front cover: Darwin and the Beagle
  Back cover: Race to the South Pole
  Front flap: Mary Kingsley
  Back flap: Amelia Earhart
p19 Gordon Home
p27 N/A
p65 *The Times*
p241 CC 2.0
p303 Chiltern Thrust Bore Ltd